RAGS·TO RICHES

·

ENTREPRENEURS OF·WELSH ORIGIN

by
Jonathan Morgan

*This book is dedicated to Lord Richard Livsey,
a good friend, mentor, fishing companion
and great Welsh patriot,
I thank him for all his encouragement.*

Old Bakehouse Publications

Abertillery

1

ISBN 978-1-905967-28-5

Published in the U.K. by
Old Bakehouse Publications
Church Street,
Abertillery, Gwent NP13 1EA
Telephone: 01495 212600 Fax: 01495 216222
Email: theoldbakeprint@btconnect.com
Website: www.oldbakehouseprint.co.uk

Made and printed in the UK
by J.R. Davies (Printers) Ltd.

British Library Cataloguing in Publication Data: a catalogue
record for this book is available from the British Library.

Contents

Introduction

The motive for writing this book on entrepreneurs of Welsh origin was a conversation that Jonathan Morgan had with a former High Sheriff of South Glamorgan, who suggested that such a book would be the thinnest in the world. There is a prevailing view in Wales that, although we produce brilliant lawyers, politicians, teachers and doctors, we are not an entrepreneurial race. The main reason for this we suspect, was partly because initially there was not a lot of capital in Wales; therefore we had a risk-averse culture. Secondly, it was perceived that many of those who developed the coalfields, such as the Halls, the Guests, the Crawshays and the Baileys were not of Welsh origin, although we would argue that at least half were, including Lord Merthyr, Lord Rhondda and, of course, David Davies.

Capital has been a problem and has not all that often, originated from inside Wales. Even in recent times, unlike Scotland, it has not developed many of its own financial institutions and money; hence control has come from outside. One of our entrepreneurs, Sir Julian Hodge has tried hard to rectify this situation. The aggression of the Anglo-Saxon culture has now for many generations been channelled into the build-up of wealth and the acquisition of money. This is something the hard-headed Anglo-Saxons here and in the United States really respect. Therefore, we deemed it necessary to trawl through some of the greatest names in enterprise to look for a Welsh connection. Either they would have a direct Welsh connection, or if they had not been brought up in Wales, they would have Welsh roots.

When we started looking around that great Mecca of finance, the City of London, we were surprised by the number of Welsh names: Lloyd's Insurance started in Edward Lloyd's café; Lloyds Bank started by the Quaker Lloyds of Dolobran; Williams and Glyns Bank; J.P. Morgan and Morgan Stanley, the two great American Welsh banks; and of course the Bevan family of Barclays. Today a farmer from our local village has started the investment bank called Evolution. His name is Richard Griffiths and it is interesting that he comes from the small village where David Morgan set out to found his great store in Cardiff. Other famous London names with Welsh connections are the John Lewis Partnership, incorporating Peter Jones, Dickens and Jones and Laura Ashley. The Vaughan Morgans of Glasbury founded the famous engineering firm of Morgan Crucible; one of the Vaughan Morgans was one of the eight Lord Mayors of London born in Wales. Our book is essentially an historical one; it does not aspire to be particularly scholarly, but more a read for young Welsh people, in particular those who might be inspired by such former notables, although we have left out Thomas Williams who dominated the copper market in the eighteenth-century and also many of the dairy kings who supplied London in the nineteenth-century. Also we have left out the slate barons of North Wales, such as the Douglas Pennants. However we believe we have put together an interesting collection ranging from Captain Sir Henry Morgan in the seventeenth-century, right up to recent times and modern entrepreneurs. All have interesting stories to be told about them. We regret not having enough information about some of the entrepreneurs we have left out and would have liked to include such as Archdeacon Morgan and Morgan cars, and the famous architect Inigo Jones. Generally our entrepreneurs were the most creative of people, who had an impact much further afield than Wales, whose horizons sometimes were too limited for them. There were also certain families outside my book who were very involved with specific towns, like the Alban Davies family in Aberaeron and the Mostyns in Llandudno.

The American-Welsh have been neglected in the wider world, although we have produced seven Presidents of Welsh extraction and Hilary Clinton, who has Welsh on both sides. J.P. Morgan's family were originally harness-makers in Glamorgan; although he did not make much of this himself, it does mean we had one of the robber barons.

Universities such as Yale, John Hopkins, Brown's of Rhode Island and Brynmawr all had Welsh roots. American history is plastered with Welsh names, including Thomas Jefferson who drew up the Declaration of Independence. A third of U.S. signatories were originally of Welsh stock. Perhaps the reason we don't hear so much about the Welsh connection is that they were more easily assimilated into American society than other minorities. The first wave of Welsh settlers tended to be of yeoman stock and had enough money to buy land. Future waves became the foremen and managers in steel and coal because of their expertise in these industries. There are, currently, about three million Welsh-Americans, many of them centred on Pennsylvania, with William Penn himself being a Quaker of Welsh stock.

Our first entrepreneur was a pirate, Captain Sir Henry Morgan, related to the Morgans of Tredegar House; a valiant fighter who acquired much booty and an estate in Jamaica. In becoming deputy-governor of that colony, he acquired a certain respectability in the eyes of the Crown for his exploits against the Spanish. Charles Lloyd of Dolobran was a Quaker in the reign of Charles II and started the Lloyds family on its path to riches. Elihu Yale, whose family will always be associated with the famous American university, hailed from Wrexham and made his money in the East India Company as did a number of businessmen from Breconshire. John Nash, the famous architect who designed Regent Street, had a Welsh mother and returned to work in Wales at one stage of his life. Robert Owen, that great philanthropist and man of ideas, came from Newtown in Powys, and in many ways could be considered the British father of socialism. David Davies, the greatest native-born coal owner who struck rich in the Rhondda, started another great philanthropic family, which included the Miss Davies's of Gregynog, who gave their wonderful collection of Impressionist paintings to the National Museum.

William Morris, who was not of Welsh birth but always acknowledged and revered his Welsh origins, (like David Davies and Robert Owen, an enlightened man) initiated and played a major part in the Arts and Crafts Movement. There is no doubt that one of the themes running through this book is the enlightenment of many of these entrepreneurs. J.P. Morgan, perhaps, was not so forthright in proclaiming his Welsh roots, but it is interesting that even the Pierponts came over to Powys with the Normans, but were one of the families that returned to France pretty quickly. Morgan became one of the great American entrepreneurs and his library in New York is a great memorial to his impeccable artistic tastes. Frank Lloyd Wright is another great Welsh-American, who called his famous home Taliesen after the Welsh poet. Probably his most well known structure is the Guggenheim Museum in New York. Lord Camrose was part of the Berry family from Merthyr Tydfil; their father was an estate agent and their grandfather worked on the railways in Pembrokeshire; the other two brothers became Lord Kemsley and Lord Buckland and the family came to have a major interest in the *Telegraph* newspaper.

Clough Williams Ellis was a tremendous character who despite lack of formal training became a very well-known architect, leaving Wales the wonderfully eccentric village of Portmeirion. He was a man of so many parts and his family carry on his legacy today in North Wales. John Spedan Lewis came originally from Somerset, but always acknowledged his Welsh roots. The company he set up still flourishes today, built on the enlightened ideas of employee partnership. Julian Hodge did so much for Wales but never really achieved his goal of giving it a sound independent financial base. He was a brilliant financier and did so much for charity, but was very disappointed that an independent Welsh bank never really took off. Laura Ashley was the darling of mid-Wales. She was a woman of her time and was a highly successful designer, with her husband Bernard directing the financial base of the company. One of the most interesting developments of the Welsh Industrial base has been the evolution of the breweries, which have been looked at with some specific reference to families that are still involved and were so from the start such as Brains. There is a chapter on the coal industry. Tyrone O'Sullivan represents the last great fight for Welsh coal and was a huge character in the fight to save the coal industry with his Tower Colliery. Lastly, some of the modern entrepreneurs that have made good are Sir Terry Mathews, Richard Griffiths, Peter and Stan Thomas, Sir Christopher Evans and Sir Roger Jones. Many of these new entrepreneurs have established highly original enterprises in Wales and show that there is still an entrepreneurial spirit which really emphasises that this book is not thin but could be a great deal thicker.

Foreword
by
Roger Williams MP

I have looked forward to the publication of this work with great anticipation. Welsh Entrepreneurs have been prominent driving forward the economic expansion and wealth creation of the Western World. Jonathan has drawn together an account of their achievements which shows just how important they were and how Wales' contribution has often been overlooked.

Now, as we face rebuilding our shattered economies, I hope that Jonathan's celebration of Welsh Entrepreneurial excellence will help to stimulate the young Welsh women and men to follow and exceed their examples set out in this important work. Only they will be able to drive forward the Welsh economy and maximise its contribution in the wider world.

Roger Williams

Acknowledgements

Peter Brooke for helping me to write the book, and for his meticulous attention to detail; Robert Macdonald for his entertaining illustrations; Roy Powell for his cover design; Alun Jones for reading the proofs; also the following for their generous subsidy: Lord Richard Livsey, Elizabeth Daniel of Brecon Beacons Holiday Cottages, Ann Mathias of Oriel Penyfan, Sir Roger Jones for all his help, Roger Williams MP, Dan Clayton-Jones, Paul and Kathryn Silk, Joyce Griffiths, Chris Thomas, David Jones, Leo McMahon, Kirsty Williams AM and Nicholas Berry.

Thanks also to the entrepreneurs I interviewed and to Frances Chaffey for all her hard work in typing up the copy.

Chapter One
Henry Morgan
c.1635-1688

Sir Henry Morgan

It does not seem at all extraordinary to me to include a former pirate in the book, for after all, pirates are the pure example of entrepreneurs and to start the book with Henry Morgan seems most appropriate

The great Welsh 'buccaneer' Henry Morgan acquired a very lurid reputation through the publication of *'The Buccaneers of America'* by A.O. (Alexander Oliver, though early English translations call him John) Exquemelin, a Dutch sailor who was with him at the rape of Panamá. Exquemelin's book was published in English in 1684. Morgan was upset by it and eventually was awarded damages, apparently the first case of money being awarded for a literary libel. But it seems that what upset him most was not the accounts of torture and pillage, distressing as these are, but the account Exquemelin gives of his origins. Exquemelin claimed that he had run away from home and joined a ship going to Barbados as an indentured servant. Other versions said he had been kidnapped in Bristol, or that he had been sold by his parents.

As a result of Morgan's challenge, one of the English publishers of Exquemelin's book added in explanation:

'John Exquemelin hath mistaken the origin of Sir Henry Morgan, for he was a Gentleman's Son of good Quality, in the County of Monmouth, and was never a Servant unto anybody in his life, unless unto his Majesty, the late King of England.'

Most historians now think he was the eldest son of the Robert Morgan of Llanrhymney, near Cardiff, a yeoman farmer related to the Morgans of Tredegar, in which case he would have been quite well connected. One of his uncles would have been Edward Morgan, who was to become Deputy Governor of Jamaica. Henry married his daughter, Mary Elizabeth.

The circumstances of Morgan's arrival in Jamaica are also debated. The idea most commonly accepted is that he arrived with the army sent by Oliver Cromwell in pursuit of what was called the 'Western Design', an attempt to strengthen the English position in the West Indies, indeed perhaps to prepare the way for a full English takeover of Spanish possessions in the area. The plan was to begin with the seizure of the Spanish island of Hispaniola (present day Haiti and Santo Domingo).

The attempt on Hispaniola in April 1655 was, in the event, a disaster. The invasion turned into a humiliating rout, with perhaps six-hundred soldiers killed at the hands of a couple of hundred Spanish, many of them black slaves.

The English then turned their attention to Jamaica. It was taken with ease, but the occupation quickly fell into chaos. The American, Major Robert Sedgwick who arrived soon afterward wrote back to London. *'Should I give you a character of the dispositions and qualifications of our army in general (some few particulars excepted), I profess my heart would grieve to write, as it doth to think of them. I believe they are not to be paralleled in the whole world; a people so lazy and idle, as it cannot enter into the heart of any Englishman that such blood should run in the veins of any born in England - so unworthy, slothful, and basely secure; and have, out of a strange kind of spirit, desired rather to die than live ...'*

This helps to explain the importance of the privateers and buccaneers in the early history of Jamaica.

Buccaneering methods were used from the start by Vice-Admiral Goodson, who had remained behind with twelve ships after the departure of the English fleet. In October 1655 he launched a raid on the town of Santa Marta de la

Victoria, near Cartagena on the mainland in what is now Colombia - it was then part of the Audiencia of Santa Fe. The population fled with their possessions. Goodson pursued them for twelve miles, then plundered and burnt their houses. Some weeks later, his lieutenant, Captain Nuberry, returned and found that some of the people had begun to rebuild, so he burnt them a second time.

The Santa Marta attack was followed by a very similar raid in April 1656 on Rio de la Hacha. Thereafter, through 1657 and 1658, Goodson concentrated his efforts on an effort to seize the Spanish treasure fleet but eventually it slipped through his hands and, apparently in spite, the English then destroyed the town of Tolú, also in Santa Fe and, yet again, Santa Marta, destroying everything for miles around.

But the real triumph came in 1659, when Captain Christopher Myngs arrived with what the historian Clarence Haring calls *'the richest prize that ever entered Jamaica.'* They had attacked the towns of Cumana, Puerto Cabello and Coro, all on the coast of Venezuela. At Coro they followed the fleeing inhabitants into the woods where they found twenty-two chests of treasure, each containing 400 lbs of silver intended for the King of Spain. Together with plates, jewels and cocoa, the whole came to something between £20,000 and £30,000, a huge sum for the age.

With the restoration of the monarchy in England in 1660 it looked for a moment as if this policy of brigandage might have to change. A new governor, Lord Windsor, arrived with instructions *'to endeavour to obtain and preserve a good correspondence and free commerce with the plantations belonging to the King of Spain.'* To this end, however, he was empowered to use force. He arrived accompanied by Christopher Myngs, with a forty-six gun frigate, *The Centurion*. The following month Myngs sailed out with some 1,300 men and eleven ships to raid the nearest Spanish port, Santiago, after Havana the most important port in Cuba. As one historian comments: *'the soldiery, poor and destitute of the necessary means of settling, joyfully embraced the opportunity of pillage.'* The fortress was razed to the ground and Myngs returned to a hero's welcome.

The following January 1663, Myngs set out again this time to San Francisco de Campeche in the Gulf of Mexico, near Yucatan. He was badly wounded during this raid and the command was briefly taken by the buccaneer Edward Mansfield, or Mansveldt. As a result of his wounds Myngs returned to England in July with *The Centurion*. He would be active in the Anglo-Dutch war in 1664, promoted to Vice-Admiral and knighted for his involvement in the battle of Lowestoft in June 1665.

In January 1664, Thomas Modyford, a well-known planter in Barbados was appointed as governor of Jamaica. As England was involved in a war with the Dutch, an expedition was organised with a very ambitious programme of capturing the Dutch properties of St. Eustatia, Saba and Curaçao and then, on the return journey, the French stations at Tortuga and Hispaniola. It was led by Modyford's deputy, Col. Edward Morgan. They took St. Eustatia and Saba with embarrassing ease - the Dutch put up no resistance - but Morgan, an old man, died in the heat. This expedition of privateers led by an army officer with targets specified by the council was on the same pattern as the exploits of Captain Myngs but it hardly had Myngs's charismatic leadership. It broke up in disputes over the division of the spoil (some 900 Negroes with livestock and cotton) and returned to Jamaica with a clear sense of failure.

It was at this point, on 20th August 1665, that a group of privateers led by a Captain Fackman, or Jackman, arrived in Jamaica. Fackman was accompanied by a Captain Morris and a Captain Morgan and it is generally assumed that these were the Welshmen, John Morris and Henry Morgan.

They arrived with a tale of derring-do starting with an ascent up the river Tabasco in the Campeche province guided by Indians to the (largely Indian populated) town of Villa de Moos - Villahermosa - which they took and

Henry Morgan as a young man.

plundered. On their return to the mouth of the Tabasco they found that their ships had been seized by the Spanish. With 100 men they fought off 300 Spanish but failed to regain the ships. Using two barques and four canoes they crossed the Gulf of Honduras then traversed the Mosquito coast *'like a devouring flame, consuming all in their path'*, to quote one admiring account, until they reached Monkey Bay. They ascended the San Juan river in canoes for one-hundred miles to Lake Nicaragua and then, accompanied by 1,000 Indians, they took and plundered the city of Granada.

It was all stirring stuff and arrived at a quite propitious moment. Modyford had abandoned the policy of trying to organise the privateers under the command of army officers and turned instead for leaders to the buccaneers themselves. A reunion was held at Bluefields Bay in Jamaica which elected Edward Mansfield as their head for an expedition supposedly against the Dutch at Curaçao. But it was really rather fanciful to expect that this pirate band, led by a Dutchman, would be interested in attacking the Dutch when there were so many very much easier Spanish targets to attack.

The expedition, predictably, never came anywhere near Curaçao. It started by raiding Santo Spirito in Cuba then went on to Boca del Toro, on the borderline between Panamá and Costa Rica. Then they launched another raid on Granada, the victim of Fackman's exploits the previous year, and harried Costa Rica, *'burning plantations, breaking the images in the churches, hamstringing cows and mules, cutting down the fruit trees and in general destroying everything they found'*, to quote Haring.

On his way back, Mansfield, probably trying to think of something that could be construed as a service to the King of England, attacked Santa Catalina, a small island strategically positioned in the middle of the ocean off the Nicaraguan (or 'Mosquito') coast. This had been 'Providence Island', originally occupied by the English Providence Island Company, which had been active in persuading Cromwell to adopt the Western Design. It could be represented as a matter of reclaiming British territory and after Mansfield returned to Jamaica in June 1666, Modyford sent an army officer, Major Samuel Smith, to strengthen it while in England Modyford's brother, Sir James Modyford was appointed governor. But in August, in a rare display of energy, the Spanish took it back again. The treatment of the prisoners they took was to provide some colour of justification for the subsequent depredations of Henry Morgan.

Morgan may have participated with Mansfield in the seizure of Providence. Exquemelin gives him a leading role but he also states, inaccurately, that Modyford did not support the venture. Exquemelin only arrived in the region in 1666 and only met up with Morgan a couple of years later so his account is based on hearsay. The really salient characteristic of Morgan's career up to 1668, is its obscurity - an obscurity that persists through the latter part of 1666, from the time of Mansfield's return in June, assuming Morgan had been part of his operation, through the whole of 1667, to early in 1668. It was not a period in which nothing was happening. Early in 1666, the French entered into alliance with the Dutch and there was intense fighting between French and English, with some Dutch involvement, through the Antilles. But during this period, when the English interest in the West Indies really was under attack from formidable enemies, Henry Morgan seems to have been inactive. It may have been then that he married Edward Morgan's recently orphaned daughter, Mary Elizabeth, and began his alternative career as a planter.

Modyford was now clearly committed to the view that the well-being of Jamaica required a permanent state of war. From this perspective the peace with Spain that was concluded in Madrid in May 1667 was bad news. It was publicly announced in Jamaica and at about the same time Modyford gave a commission to Henry Morgan - the moment when he first appears unequivocally as a leading figure on the stage - 'to draw together the English privateers and take prisoners of the Spanish nation, whereby he might inform of [sic] the intention of that enemy to invade Jamaica.'

Morgan sailed off early in 1668. He sailed to Cuba, demanded provisions and used the predictable refusal as an excuse to go inland, wasting and pillaging everywhere he went. He went to Puerto de Principe where, naturally he learned that the Spanish were indeed planning an invasion of Jamaica and of course that musters were being summoned at towns on the mainland, which naturally meant he would have to go there. So far, so banal. It was his choice of target that distinguished him from the ordinary run of buccaneers. He chose to go to Portobello.

Portobello was a town on the coast of Panamá which derived its importance from the great treasure fleets that sailed from America to Spain; the source of the treasure was the mines on the Pacific side, the west coast of the country. The isthmus of Panamá was the shortest route from the west to the east. The produce of the mines was brought to Panamá on the west coast, then transported to Portobello on the east coast to be loaded onto the ships to face the long dangerous journey to Europe. But these sailings of the treasure fleet had become more and more infrequent. They were now held only once every two years. At that moment Panamá and Portobello were like something out of a fairy tale with a vast temporary population surrounded by the signs of unimaginable wealth. Otherwise they were both rather depressing places situated in an area notorious for disease. Peter Earle describes Portobello as 'a stinking, half-empty fever hole' which, however, because of its importance at the times of the fleet was, or at least was reputed to be, well fortified.

Exquemelin gives a very dramatic account of the actual seizure of Portobello but it should probably be read in the light of Peter Earle's version based on research in the Spanish archives. He says that Morgan put soldiers and officers into a single room then blew it up with gunpowder, but this does not appear in Earle's account. Exquemelin has the governor in one of the two forts overlooking the port putting up a desperate fight until eventually Morgan used religious men and women to set the siege ladders, forcing the defenders to fire on them - the Spanish account has a little group of citizens including friars and nuns being used as human shields while the English approached the main door with axes and fire. The Spanish accounts do not repeat Exquemelin's accounts of torture but Earle does not think that is a reason for disbelieving them.

Morgan threatened to torch the city unless a ransom was paid. He initially demanded 350,000 pesos in silver but eventually settled for 100,000. It was this, not what he found in Portobello, that enabled him to count the expedition a financial success. He was in Portobello for fifteen days *'in which space of time'*, Exquemelin says, *'they had lost many of their men, both by the unhealthiness of the country and the extravagant debauch they had committed.'* They brought the fever back with them to Jamaica and Modyford's wife, among others, died of it.

The rape of Portobello was, however, immensely popular among a British public demoralised by ten years of fire, plague and defeat at the hands of the Dutch, and uneasy at the peace with Spain, the hereditary enemy, at the change of mood since the more glorious days of the Commonwealth and suspicious of the possibility of papist influence in court. It looked like a glorious English victory and the court was not above taking advantage of it. They assumed a high tone, insisting that the peace treaty did not cover the West Indies where the Spanish refused to recognise English possessions and had only recently invaded Providence Island and had the clear intention, as proved by the depositions obtained by Morgan, to invade Jamaica.

In October 1668, Morgan was off again to the Isla Vaca, off the coast of Hispaniola, to gather a new band of privateers for a further adventure which, if it was to be more spectacular than Portobello, had to be either Panamá or Cartagena, capital of the Audiencia of Santa Fe. These were the towns that the audience back in England would have heard of. His possibilities were enhanced enormously when, shortly afterwards, he was joined by a thirty-four gun frigate, the *Oxford*, a gift from the Lord High Admiral, the Duke of York, to Modyford.

With such means at their disposal, Morgan and his cronies fixed on Cartagena as their target but as they were celebrating the coming adventure, an accidental spark, apparently, in the powder room, blew the ship up. Morgan himself had been feasting on the deck. All those on the opposite side of the table from him were killed. Those on his side of the table were thrown into the sea and had to be fished out. This naturally rather dampened the spirits of the assembly Morgan had brought together and the group broke up. Morgan was left with a small flotilla of undecked ships reduced to eight, with five-hundred men, about half the original number.

Under these circumstances, the best he could do was to repeat the exploit performed two years earlier by the French privateer, Jean-David Nau, *'L'Ollonais'*, and attack Maracaibo in the Gulf of Venezuela. Maracaibo was situated in a huge salt water lake which was connected to the Gulf by a narrow pass. Morgan found that since the visit of *L'Ollonais*, a fort had been built at the pass. By good fortune, however, it was seriously undermanned, with only eight men and a castellan who, after a brief spirited defence, lost their nerve and crept away. Exquemelin tells us they left a long slow fuse running to the powder magazine but Morgan spotted it and stamped it out in the nick of time.

Morgan made a good haul of slaves, jewels, silk, pieces of eight and prisoners to be ransomed but it was still just an ordinary pirate raid without the element of glory that seems to have been so important to him. That, however, was about to change.

By the mid-1660s privateering attacks on the Spanish colonies were so widespread that the authorities in Spain had finally sent a small fleet of five well-armed, rapid ships to deal with it. It sailed in July 1667 and was actually in Havana at the very moment when Morgan was raiding Puerto de Principe and sailing to

The battle between Henry Morgan and Don Alonzo at Maracaibo.

Portobello. In July 1668, after the raid on Portobello, orders were received recalling two of the ships. The Vice-Admiral of the three ships that were left, Don Alonzo de Campas, had learned of the intended raid on Cartagena and finally discovered that Morgan's ships were bottled up in what was more or less the perfect trap of Lake Maracaibo. All he had to do was to invest the bottle neck leading to the Gulf and wait for them to come out.

It was here that Morgan, or at least Morgan's team, revealed something resembling genius. What they did was to prepare a 'fire ship' - a ship primed to explode. But it was decked out as a flagship. It was equipped with logs disguised as canons and as men. It came on ahead, looking as if it was Morgan's own ship, daringly headed straight for De Campos's main ship, the *Magdelena*. Once the two ships were in contact the small team piloting the fire ship escaped and it blew up, taking the *Magdelena* with it. The second of the Spanish ships, the *San Luis*, seeing that the situation of the *Magdelena* was hopeless, was beached in an effort to gain the fort, while the third, the smallest, the *Nuestra Senora de Soledad*, got its sails in a muddle and was seized as a prize by the pirates. The victory over the 'Armada de Barlovento' was complete.

That still left the port, which still commanded the bottleneck and now had a garrison to man its guns. Morgan attempted to storm it but was repeatedly repulsed, losing many of his men. Eventually he got out through an old

Pirate Wars.

but spectacularly successful ruse. In sight of the fort, he landed successive boatloads of buccaneers in a nearby mangrove swamp. He was obviously preparing a land assault; as a result, De Campos moved his guns so that they were facing landward. But in fact, the buccaneers landed in the swamp had returned to their ships concealed in the apparently empty canoes that had brought them out. In the night, the ships slipped their anchor and drifted past the fort. They were seen but by the time the guns had been brought back again, they were through and safe. The privateers sailed back in triumph, arriving in Port Royal on the 27th May, 1669, headed by Morgan's new flagship, *Nuestra Senora de Soledad*. An expedition which had started in disaster had ended in glory with the destruction of the only defensive sea force the Spanish had in the area.

In the meantime, in reaction to the humiliation at Portobello, the Queen Regent in Spain had sent instructions that the Spanish authorities could do to the English what the English authorities had been doing to the Spanish. Private individuals could *'proceed against the English in the Indies with every sort of hostility...'*. On the receipt of this letter, the governor of Cartagena, in October 1699, publicly announced war with Jamaica and a number of incidents occurred which indicated to the Jamaicans that the Spanish were adopting a more aggressive approach. These climaxed in the activities of the Portuguese corsair, Manoel Rivero Pardal who made a couple of landings in the sparsely populated parts of Jamaica and burned some houses. This was a flea bite but the Jamaicans, so used to operating with impunity, did not know what it might mean for the future.

As a result of all this, Morgan was given a commission to assemble a force *'and if necessary attack any place inland that he suspected was being used for war.'* Among those who joined him was John Morris, fresh from the triumph of having killed Pardal and seized his ship. Another ship that had worked with Pardal, *La Gallardina*, was also seized. The Spanish captain of *La Gallardina* was hanged by Morgan for declining to give evidence that an invasion was being prepared at Cartagena and Panamá, but two of the crew duly agreed. As Morgan's surgeon, Richard Browne, put it: *'Some through torments, confesse what wee please. Other more ingenious and stoute will not be drawne to speake or subscribe what they know not, who are then cutt in pieces, shott or hanged.'*

Morgan now had the pretext he needed for what was to be the great achievement of his life, the rape of Panamá, and he had the largest assembly of privateers yet seen in the West Indies. Morgan planned to attack Panamá along the river Chagre, which was protected by a fort, San Lorenzo. He sent three ships ahead under the command of Lt. Col. Joseph Bradley, to reduce the fort before the main body of the privateers would follow.

At Lake Maracaibo we have seen that Morgan initially encountered a well-built fort manned by a pathetically small garrison. At San Lorenzo, Bradley encountered a badly built fort manned by a garrison that was both strong - equal in numbers to Bradley's force - and well led. But the fort was built of wood and straw, and the privateers succeeded, probably to their own amazement, in setting it alight. Bradley died as a result of the attack together with over a hundred of his men. Morgan arrived some days later in his flagship, *The Satisfaction*, which, together with the four ships following, sailed straight on to a reef and broke up. Peter Earle wonders if the seamanship of the buccaneers was always all it was cracked up to be.

What follows - the march to Panamá on the west side of the isthmus, was a monument to dogged determination and courage in facing the unknown. The trek across the isthmus was hellish. Morgan had expected the jungle to be full of game and had wanted his men to travel light so, once the boats had been abandoned, they were not carrying food. In fact the jungle yielded nothing they could recognise as being edible and the Spaniards were retreating before them destroying any possible source of provisions as they went. After four days without food, the pirate army was a disorganised rabble which could probably have been routed easily. But, alas for the Spanish, no sooner did they leave the jungle than they encountered a plain full of cattle.

Panamá lay before them - an open city without fortifications. The 'army' standing between the pirates and Panamá, though numerous, was made up of the more courageous citizens together with a large number of black slaves and Indians. Now that the pirates were fed and rested this was all simply feeble, the more so because the Spanish had neglected to defend a small hill on their right flank. Once the English had seized that, the victory was won.

It was followed by a scene from hell as the citizenry, crazed with fear, set fire to the town. Historians have questioned if this was the work of the English or the Spanish but the Spanish accounts leave no room for doubt. It was not at all in the interests of the English to find themselves presiding over a heap of charred timber in the middle of a disease-ridden swamp. There was the usual job to be done rounding up the citizens and torturing them to get hold of their valuables, but the biggest prizes had disappeared on three ships which had been loaded and got away before the city fell.

On 24th February, after an occupation that had lasted four weeks, they left. Inevitably, Morgan's army broke up. Some were shipwrecked on the central American coast. Long's History of Jamaica tells us that *'In 1671, when the fleet commanded by Sir Henry Morgan returned from that coast, his crews brought with them the malignant fever of Portobello, and the greater part of them died of it; the contagion spread to those on shore where it produced a terrible mortality.'* From the point of view of Morgan's political intentions - if we can guess what they were - we may wonder if the venture really succeeded. Although piracy in the region was to have a great future and Jamaica remained at the centre of it, Panamá marked the end of the policy of piracy sponsored as a matter of government policy.

A decision to replace Sir Thomas Modyford had already been made in December 1670, before the news of the rape of Panamá had arrived. His successor was Thomas Lynch, knighted for the occasion. Lynch was himself a Jamaica planter. He had left Jamaica in 1665, after Modyford had removed him from the council and from his office of chief justice, probably about the time Modyford was committing himself to a policy of encouraging the privateers.

He now returned with clear instructions to suppress privateering and encourage agriculture and also had the delicate task of arresting Modyford and Morgan, the two most popular men on the island, whose policies had brought in so much easily obtained wealth. Modyford was kept for some months imprisoned on a ship before being sent to London where he was put in the Tower of London. He was still there in 1674, though he was back in Jamaica by 1676. Morgan was not arrested until 1672, perhaps because he was ill, presumably with the fever he had brought back with him from Panamá. When he did go to London, however, he was lionised, everyone wanting to bask in the glory of the conqueror of Panamá and enjoy the excitement of

associating with such a dashing rogue. His main problem was that being lionised in such circles was an expensive business and he was quickly running through his means, but Morgan was making connections which would be useful to him, including two future governors of Jamaica - the Earl of Carlisle and the Duke of Albemarle, son of General Monck, the Cromwellian leader who had been largely responsible for the restoration of Charles II.

Morgan was tried in 1673, defending himself on the absurd grounds that his attack on Panamá had been a war to end war, necessary to prevent a Spanish aggression. Soon after being acquitted he was knighted and appointed to return to Jamaica as lieutenant-governor together with Carlisle as governor.

In the event, however, Carlisle was unable to go and in 1675 Morgan and Carlisle's replacement, John Vaughan, departed in two separate ships. Morgan's ship, to Vaughan's annoyance raced ahead. It was blown on to the Isla Vaca, losing much of its stores, but Morgan still reached Jamaica before Vaughan. It is not clear why Morgan was so anxious to arrive first. The loss of the stores - which included a great deal of military equipment - on the island that had been and still was the great meeting place of the privateers arouses feelings of suspicion.

Vaughan continued Lynch's policy of trying to suppress the privateers but soon found that he had a deadly enemy in Morgan. The two men were temperamentally unsuited to each other, despite their common Welsh origins. Vaughan was a highly cultured member of the aristocracy. He was member of Parliament for the borough of Carmarthen and the Vaughan estates were counted as among the largest in Wales. Eventually, however, worn down by the confrontation with Morgan and with the island's assembly, he left in March 1678. Carlisle arrived in July and in the interim Morgan ruled as lieutenant-governor.

Carlisle had come to Jamaica with instructions to introduce a new form of government, similar to the Irish 'Poyning's Law', which concentrated legislative power in the hands of the government in England. The result was a ferocious contest with the assembly which may have been a continuation of earlier disputes with Vaughan except that Morgan was now aligned with Carlisle and was passing himself off as a Tory and a King's man.

In May 1680, Carlisle left to argue his case in London. Morgan was left in charge and seemed full of drive and energy. He had two new forts built - Fort

Rupert and Fort Carlisle, and strengthened the already existing Fort James. He may have been inspired by a new aggressiveness among the Spaniards, and by an edict from the King of France forbidding all privateering against the Spanish and withdrawing all existing commissions. The last thing Jamaica wanted was an alliance between France and Spain.

In London, the new constitutional arrangement was withdrawn, and Lynch replaced Carlisle as governor. He seems to have returned with a determination to root out Morgan and his friends once and for all. He died in 1684 but the exclusion of the Morgan faction continued under his friend and close colleague, Hender Molesworth. Morgan seems to have fallen into ever greater depths of alcoholism. He did, however, have one last moment of recognition when his old drinking companion from his days in London, Christopher Monck, second Duke of Albemarle, was appointed governor in November 1687. Albemarle had asked permission from the King to re-appoint Morgan to the Council but he only received it in July 1688. Morgan died in August, at the age of fifty-three. Albemarle himself died a couple of months later, of jaundice and dropsy.

They died on the eve of the 'Glorious Revolution', which brought the Dutch, William of Orange to the throne of England. The result really did turn the world of Henry Morgan upside down. For the next twenty years, England would be an ally of Holland and Spain against France. Instead of the straw man enemy, Spain, Jamaica found itself at war with France. In these circumstances the Jamaican planters were to have some small taste of the medicine Morgan and his predecessors had been giving the Spanish in America, relentlessly and with an amazing conviction of their own righteousness, for the previous thirty years.

Bibliography
Terry Breverton: 'Admiral Sir Henry Morgan - The greatest buccaneer of them all', Pontypridd, Glyndwr Publishing, 2005

Rev George Wilson Bridges: 'The Annals of Jamaica', vol i, London, John Murry, 1828

Peter Earle: 'The Sack of Panama - Captain Morgan and the Battle for the Caribbean', New York, Thomas Dunne Books, 2007 (first published in 1981)

'The Pirate Wars', London, Methuen, 2004

Bryan Edwards: 'The History, Civil and Commercial of the British Colonies in the West Indies', Dublin, Luke White, 1793

Alexander O. Exquemelin: 'The Buccaneers of America, translated from the Dutch by Alexis Brown', New York, Dover Publications, 2000

C.H. Haring: 'The Buccaneers in the West Indies in the Seventeenth Century', London, Methuen and Co, 1910

Interesting Tracts relating to the Island of Jamaica, consisting of curious state papers, councils of war, letters, petitions, narratives, St Iago de la Vega, 1800

Thomas Southey: 'Chronological History of the West Indies', vol ii, London 1827

Chapter Two
Elihu Yale
1649-1721
and the Five Welshmen from Breconshire including John Lloyd
and the De Winton family
East India Company and Yale University

In the late sixteenth-century, Elihu's great-grandfather, Dr. David Yale, who came from Plas Yn Ial, Clwyd, who was appointed Vicar General to George Lloyd, the Bishop of Chester. He bought an estate, Einon's Grove, near Wrexham. His son, Thomas, married the Bishop's daughter, Anne and they had four children. Thomas died in 1619 and his young widow married a wealthy merchant, Theophilus Eaton, himself a widower with two children.

Anne arrived in London with her children, including her sixteen year-old son David, in 1630, and they lived in the house of Sir Richard Saltonstall who had left for America. Some seventy years later, Saltonstall's great grandson, Gurdon, was governor of Connecticut when the college at New Haven was named after Elihu Yale.

Theophilus Eaton and his family, including his own children by his first marriage and Anne's children by her first marriage, left London to go to North America in 1637, on board the ship *Hector,* together with Davenport. They were reacting to the radical reforms introduced in the Church of England under Charles I and the Archbishop of Canterbury, William Laud, who insisted on a ritual-based church in which all the King's subjects were expected to take Communion. Laud's reforms were soon to be one of the causes of the English Civil War. Eaton eventually settled in New Haven, where he and his old vicar in London, John Davenport, set up a new colony. The constitution, drawn up by Eaton, limited the rights of citizenship to those who could provide convincing proof that they had experienced saving grace. Eaton's brother, Samuel, disagreed with this policy and so did his stepson, David Yale. They left New Haven and returned to Boston in 1641. Some two years later David married and in 1649 his son, Elihu was born.

In the meantime, in New Haven, the life of Anne Eaton was deeply unhappy. She quarrelled both with the church and with her family and eventually, in 1645, she was ex-communicated *'wherein God showed a wonderful presence to the satisfaction of all that were present.'*

David Yale and his family left Boston in 1651-52 to return to England. Anne Eaton joined them a few years later, after the death of her husband, Theophilus, the governor. Although Elihu Yale was only three years-old at the end of this first

Elihu Yale.

25

period in his life - the only time he ever spent in America - we will see that it has its importance in the history of the University that bears his name.

Elihu Yale began his career with the East India Company as a clerk in the company's offices in Leadenhall Street in London. He was twenty-one years-old. In October 1671, he was chosen as one of twenty young men to go to India as a 'writer'. After a six month voyage he landed in Fort Saint George in June 1672.

Trade in the East Indies had to be established in competition, often amounting to open warfare, with the Portuguese and the Dutch. The company also needed to negotiate rights and privileges with local rulers, both in India and to the East, initially in the area that is now Indonesia, which was the major producer of spices, a trade largely controlled by the Dutch. In India, the dominant power was the Muslim Mughal Empire, with its capital in Delhi. The English initially established a presence, against Dutch opposition, in Surat, a port in the Mughal territory, on the West Coast of India. They had also established themselves at an early stage in the seventeenth-century in Bantam, in a Muslim kingdom in what is now Java. Cloth bought in India would be traded against the very desirable pepper bought in Bantam.

Fort Saint George, where Elihu Yale arrived in 1672, was on the East Coast of India called the Coromandel coast, and was part of the Muslim kingdom of Golconda. Fort St. George was situated beside two villages, Madraspatnam (hence the English name 'Madras') and Chennapatnam (hence the modern Indian name, Chennai). Golconda was known for its diamond mines.

The East India Company was still far from being the great power it was to become. It was still dependent on the good will of the Indian powers, subject to terms decided by them. Under Charles II and James II, however, the idea was becoming established that, wherever it was present, the company should be able to exercise the rights of a sovereign power. This more aggressive approach, with the example of the Dutch East India Company in mind, was particularly associated with Sir Josiah Child, the dominant figure in the London-based directorate during Yale's period. One nineteenth-century historian of the company, J. Talboys Wheeler, describes Child as *'the first man in England who seems to have formed a just conception of what ought to be the relations between the English and the Natives in this country.'*

Robert Grant, in his *'Sketch of the History of the East India Company'*, gives a brief description of how the company functioned. He explains that the company's employees were given a very wide latitude to engage in trade on their own behalf, and indeed that *'the emoluments of the service would, from the scale given, appear most pitiful, unless we suppose that they were meant to be filled out by opportunities of private trade.'*

The Governor of Madras when Yale arrived was Sir William Langhorne and his second in command, or 'book-keeper', was Joseph Hynmers, whose wife Catherine would later marry Yale. Minutes of the Council were kept by an apprentice, John Nicks, who, together with his wife, would later be a close associate in Yale's commercial affairs. Yale, despite his junior status, was entrusted with missions in 1674 to negotiate the establishment of a station in the principality of Jinjee and in 1675 to accompany a representative of the company, Major William Puckle, on a tour of inspection of the company's properties in

Bengal. A report by Puckle into irregularities in Madras resulted in Langhorne's dismissal for, among other things, receiving money for favours from one of the leading Indian traders, Kasi Viranna.

Early in 1680, Joseph Hynmers died, and in November of the same year, Yale married his widow, Catherine. He refers to her in his will rather mysteriously as *'my wicked wife'* but the marriage brought him a small fortune which he used mainly to set up in business trading precious stones. Catherine Hynmers was herself a native Indian and probably had a fortune of her own, independent of Hynmers. In 1682, with William Gyfford as governor, he joined the council at Fort Saint George with the rank of 'mint master'. He had been in India for ten years. Towards the end of the year he set out on an important mission to establish a new agency at Cuddalore, in the land of the Mahrattas, a Hindu people originating in the Western Ghat mountains, who, in the mid-seventeenth century were engaged in an extraordinary adventure of war against the dominant Muslim kingdoms - both the Mughals to the North and to the East, where they had suppressed the Muslim kingdom of Bijapur. This gave them control over Jinjee and over the port of Cuddalore, South of Madras. Yale was charged with negotiating the use of this or other similar ports.

Yale wrote a report of his journey and of the negotiations with the Mahrattas which has been preserved, though in very poor condition. There is a detailed account in Hiram Bingham's biography of Yale. Near Cuddalore, Yale saw a Dutch factory called Tegnapatam. *'Within less than half-a-mile Sanbojee (Sambhaji, Shivaji's son and successor) has an indifferent large fort, well fortified, which undoubtedly is a troublesome and dangerous neighbour to them.'* In 1690, as governor of Madras, Yale arranged the purchase of this fort from the Mahrattas through his brother Thomas. He renamed it Fort Saint David.

Yale finally became governor, or 'President', of the Madras factory in 1687. By this time he was a very wealthy man. The records of the council mention several occasions when they had to borrow money from him and Bingham reckons that he owned at least four ships. The main source of this wealth seems to have been his involvement in the precious stones trade made possible through his marriage with Catherine Hynmers.

Yale's period as governor was very fraught and turbulent. It was a period of intense war and conflict within India, within England, and among the European powers. Fort Saint George was threatened successively by the Mahrattas, the Mughals and the French. It was also a period of conflict between the company and the population of Madras and between Yale himself and a number of members of the governing council; and it was a turbulent period in his own personal life.

In India, the rise of the Mahrattas prompted the Great Mughal, Aurungzebe, to sweep southwards in a vast campaign of conquest. At the same time the company at Child's instigation organised an invasion of Bengal because of perceived mistreatment of the English at the Mughal's hands. The attempt went disastrously wrong and the English agencies in Surat and Bombay in the West and Houghly in the East were seized by Aurungzebe at the very moment when he was also suppressing the Kingdom of Golconda, where Madras was situated. Fortunately for the English, though, Aurungzebe considered their trade too profitable to be suppressed and in the end the quarrel was settled.

Meanwhile, the Company as a whole was sinking deeper into debt and its problems were compounded by the loss of the crucially important station at Bantam to the Dutch. In these circumstances, the Directors had been pressing Yale's predecessor, William Gyfford, to impose a tax on the residents of Madras to help pay the costs of the garrison in Fort Saint George.

The area controlled by the British had been divided between the fort, called 'White Town', which was essentially the company and the garrison, and the area outside the fort with its native population, called 'Black Town'. The 'Black Town' (based largely on the two Indian villages - Chennapatnam and Madraspatnam) had grown enormously in size, attracting merchants and craftsmen with the prospect of selling to the Europeans. As well as its Indian population, 'Black Town' also attracted Portuguese, Jewish (largely Portuguese in origin) and Armenian traders.

The attempt to impose a tax provoked determined opposition in the town - conflict that continued throughout the 1680s in which strikes by local workers and shopkeepers were met by threats to pull down houses and execute ringleaders. The conflict was intensified by conditions of famine and disease and by instructions coming from London calling for ever harsher measures.

Yale's presidency also coincided with the 'Glorious Revolution' in England, 1688-89, when the Roman Catholic King, James II, was replaced by his daughter, Mary, and her husband, William, Prince of Orange, Stadtholder and military commander of the Netherlands. The transition seems to have been accepted with equanimity, despite the huge investment that the directors in London had made in the form of bribes to James' court. The change did, however, have important consequences. Under the Stuarts, England had been aligned with France in opposition to the rest of Europe - the papacy, the Holy Roman Empire and, most significantly for the English in India, the Dutch. Now they were aligned with their old enemies the Dutch in opposition to the French, who were becoming much more active in the East Indian trade. Since 1673 they had had a station at Pondicherry, between Madras and Cuddalore, in what was now Mahrattas territory. In August 1690 there was a sea battle outside Madras between a French fleet and the newly allied English and Dutch.

One might have thought that these external threats would create a feeling of solidarity among the company's servants in Madras but in fact the council was driven by a number of very vicious and personal disputes. Among them was a dispute over Yale's defensive measures - that he built a temporary fortification round the Black Town which other members of the council thought was a waste of money; and also his purchase of the Fort at Tegnapatam, near Cuddalore. The purchase, in 1690, was negotiated with the local representatives of the Mahrattas by Yale's brother, Thomas, whom Yale also wanted to be appointed as its first governor. Thomas Yale's trading activities on his brother's behalf were also regarded with suspicion and there seems to have been a feeling that Yale was carving out a personal fiefdom for himself at the company's expense.

Yale's personal life was also a cause for scandal. He had one son and three daughters by Catherine Hynmers. The son died, aged three, in 1688 and soon afterwards Catherine departed with her daughters to London. At that point, Yale took up with another wealthy widow, the Portuguese Jewess, Hieronima de Paiva, whose husband, Jacques (Jaime) de Paiva (Pavia), originally from Amsterdam, had acquired mines in Golconda and played an important part in the establishment of the Jewish community in Madras. He died in 1687.

Hieronima de Paiva moved in with Yale not long after Catherine Hynmers' departure and in July 1690 she bore him a son. Like his relationship with the widow of Joseph Hynmers, the relationship with the widow of Jacques de Paiva was very profitable. Yale and Hieronima were joined later in the 1690s by Katherine Nicks, wife of John Nicks, who had been imprisoned by the company for commercial activities, some of which had been conducted on Yale's behalf. Katherine Nicks continued to act as Yale's agent in India after his return to England.

Yale was dismissed as governor in October 1692 and replaced by Francis Higginson. Higginson came from Connecticut and was, as it happens, related to the American Yales by marriage. Much of the rest of Yale's time in India was spent defending himself against numerous charges that he had abused the trust of the company to build his huge personal fortune (in a letter written in January 1691, Yale said that he had accumulated 500,000 'pagodas' - the Indian coinage of the time - which his biographer, Hiram Bingham translates as $5,000,000 in the values of 1937). Yale, however, was vindicated after an appeal to the Privy Council made by Thomas and two of his other associates in 1695. The Company's reply to this appeal complained that Yale had *amassed a great estate injuriously, and committed such unprecedented crimes and abuses that the whole Council of the Fort protested against, and separated from him, and wrote two letters... Soon after which, all who subscribed the said letters dyed, except Mr. Fraser, not without suspicion of being poisoned.'*

Higginson was replaced in 1697 by Thomas Pitt, an old friend and business associate of Yale's, nicknamed 'Diamond Pitt'. He was the grandfather of the Prime Minister, William Pitt, 'the elder'. Under Thomas Pitt, Yale was able to leave India in style, bringing with him five-tons of valuable merchandise. It seems, according to an article published in *The Hindu*, 24.04.2000, that he was accompanied by Hieronima but that she died on the journey, thus avoiding the embarrassment of an encounter with Catherine Hynmers in England.

At this point our story reverts to New Haven and Connecticut, and the process by which Elihu Yale gave his name to the university.

The Puritans in New England had decided to establish a college in Cambridge, just across the Charles River from Boston. It was called *Harvard* after Rev. John Harvard, who may have come over on the same boat in 1637 as the Eatons and the Yales. He had died soon afterwards leaving his library and half his estate to the new college, which was established for *'the education of the English and Indian youth of this country in knowledge and godliness'* by an Act of Parliament passed under the Commonwealth in 1650.

In 1681-82, the Acting President of Harvard was Increase Mather, leader of the opposition to the attempts by Charles II and especially James II to impose the episcopal system of church government on the colony. In 1688 Mather eluded capture at the hands of James II's energetic governor of New England, Sir Edmund Andros, and escaped to England, where he argued the colony's case with little success while James was still King. After the Revolution he secured a new charter for the colony but from his own point of view it was unsatisfactory. The rights of citizenship were made dependent on property not, as previously, on approval by the clergy.

While Increase Mather was still in England, the people of Massachussets were celebrating their freedom from James' tyranny by indulging in the great Salem witchcraft hysteria, the subject of Arthur Miller's play *The Crucible*. 200 people were accused, 150 imprisoned, 19 hanged and one pressed to death. The trials were instigated by Increase Mather's son, Cotton Mather, who celebrated the whole affair in his book *The Wonders of the Invisible World*. Increase resumed command of Harvard College on his return and he and Cotton worked closely together as joint ministers of the church in Boston.

Through the 1690s, the Mathers encountered a growing movement among the New England community opposed to the practice of confining Communion to 'visible saints' who could give proof of the signs of salvation in their hearts. One of the strongholds of the new movement was Harvard College.

In 1701, after a long controversy with the council, Increase Mather was ousted from the presidency. The pretext was his refusal to leave his congregation in Boston and settle permanently in Cambridge but since his successor did not live permanently in Cambridge either it was obvious that this was not the real reason. It was in this context that a meeting was held in 1700 to form a new college in Connecticut - initially at Saybrook. One of the leading promoters of the new college was Rev. James Pierpont, minister of the church in New Haven, a successor to the Rev. John Davenport who, over fifty years previously, had excommunicated Elihu Yale's grandmother, Anne Eaton. The name 'Pierpont' will appear again in this book when we come to consider another of our entrepreneurs of Welsh origin, John Pierpont Morgan. Rev. James Pierpont was a close friend of Cotton Mather.

Meanwhile, in Wales, Elihu's brother Thomas died. He had inherited part of the Yale estate near Wrexham and in his will, published shortly before Elihu left India, he left it to *'the heir male, lawfully begotten of my brother Elihu Yale.'* This excluded both Elihu himself and Charles Yale, Yale's son by Hieronima de Paiva (Charles was to die in Cape Town, South Africa, in 1712). Yale's nearest legitimate male heir was David Yale, son of his cousin, John Yale, in New Haven, Connecticut. In 1710, Yale was in contact with Jeremy Dummer, agent for the Massachussets Bay Colony in London, to help him find David Yale and in May 1711, Dummer wrote to Pierpont saying:

'Here is Mr. Yale, formerly Governor of Fort George in the Indies, who has got a prodigious estate, and now by Mr. Dixwell sends for a relation of his from Connecticut to make him his heir, having no son. He told me lately, that he intended to bestow a charity upon some college in Oxford, under certain restrictions which he mentioned. But I think he should much rather do it to your college, seeing he is a New England and I think a Connecticut man. If therefore when his kinsman comes over, you will write him a proper letter on that subject, I will take care to press it home.'

Yale sent two packets of books to the college, in 1712 and 1713. In 1716 the decision was made to move the college from Saybrook to New Haven. Building work began in September 1717 and in January 1718, Cotton Mather wrote to Yale suggesting that he might like to make a substantial contribution and that, if he did, the college could be named after him. In the light of the history we have just been reading the letter is a masterpiece of obfuscation.

Original building 1718-1782.

The Mathers were supporting the Connecticut College in opposition to Harvard because, as they saw it, Harvard had been taken over by a faction who were advocating loose terms of communion and encouraging their students to read outside the framework of what they interpreted as Calvinist orthodoxy. But Mather, wanting to extract money from a man he would have known was an episcopalian, presents the Connecticut venture as a model of non-sectarianism and touches lightly on the theological differences there might be between himself and Yale as matters of little importance:

'The people for whom we bespeak your favors are such sound, generous Christians and Protestants, that their not observing some disputable right (which no act of Parliament has imposed on these plantations), ought by no means to exclude them from the respects of all that are indeed such, and from the good will which we all owe to the rest of the reformed churches, all of which have their little varieties.'

He continues: *'Sir, though you have your felicities in your family, which I pray God continue and multiply, yet certainly, if what is forming at New Haven might wear the name of YALE COLLEGE, it would be better than a name of sons and daughters. And your munificence might easily obtain for you such a commemoration and perpetuation of your valuable name, which would indeed be much better than an Egyptian pyramid.'*

(Mather could hardly have known that Yale's three year-old son, David, was buried under a pyramid shaped monument in Madras ...)

As Hiram Bingham points out, however, Yale may have been motivated by something other than mere personal vanity: *'Little as he (Mather) suspected it, this may have given Elihu a vision of restoring all the New England churches to the Anglican persuasion.'*

Only a few months previous to receiving Mather's letter, Yale had been proposed as a member of the very exclusive 'Society for the Propagation of the Gospel in Foreign Parts.' Despite its neutral sounding name this society was mainly devoted to supporting the episcopalian interest in areas of North America where 'the Gospel', in its militant congregationalist form, was already well-established. The Subscription Rolls of the Society's projects for Bishops in America and establishing a building of its own in London, were in the hands of the Archbishop of Canterbury, the Archbishop of York, the Bishop of London *'and Elihu Yale, Esq.'*

On 11th June 1718, Yale sent two trunks of textiles to be sold for the college, a collection of 417 books and a portrait of George I. The total sum came to £1162.00,

Old Brick Row, Yale 1807.

the biggest donation made to the college in its first 120 years. In February 1721, he sent another gift of goods that raised £562. In 1722, the rector of Yale College, the well-respected Rev. Timothy Cutler, together with one of the tutors Daniel Brown, and Samuel Johnson a minister at West Haven who had been a distinguished student at the college and only recently a tutor, announced that they no longer considered their non-episcopal orders to be valid. After a public debate on the matter, the three resigned their positions and went to England to be ordained as Anglican priests. Brown died shortly afterwards but Cutler and Johnson returned. Johnson was responsible for the first episcopal church to be built in Connecticut, Stratford, ready for service on Christmas Day, 1723.

It may be fanciful to think Yale really *'had a vision of restoring all the New England churches to the Anglican persuasion'* by supporting a college that had been set up by supporters of the more extreme wing of New England puritanism, but Cutler, Brown and Johnson had been influenced by the preaching of Rev. George Pigot, who had been sent to Stratford as a missionary by the Society for the Propagation of the Gospel and also, according to Bingham, by the substantial Anglican library that was interwoven together with the books on historical, geographical, medical, commercial and legal matters in the packets sent by Yale. David Hoeveler in his book *Creating the American Mind* confirms the influence of this material on Johnson and adds that after a further donation of books from Johnson's friend, the philosopher and bishop George Berkeley:

'In Connecticut new Anglican churches appeared. Samuel Johnson, upon his return from England in 1723, had become the colony's only Anglican minister. Twenty years later Connecticut had twenty Anglican ministers and the Church of England could claim over two thousand communicants. And all of its ministers had graduated from Yale!' (p.63)

Perhaps it would be possible to write an account of the early history of Yale University under the title Mrs. Eaton's Revenge.

We may assume that Yale would have been happy with the defection of Cutler and his friends had he known about it, but he died the previous year, in 1721. On returning to England he divided his time between London and Wrexham, in Wales. He had a special gallery constructed for himself and his family across the arc of the chancel in the church at Wrexham, behind the pulpit, facing the congregation. In 1710-11, he bought a house in London, in Queen Square, near Ormond Street, whence his nickname, 'The Nabob of Queen Square.' He was surrounded by his immense wealth, including several

Woolsey Hall, Yale 1905.

thousand paintings. After his death, it took forty days and six sales to dispose of it. He is buried in the churchyard at Wrexham. There is a replica of the remarkable mediaeval vertical Gothic tower of Wrexham church on the Yale College campus. However, in 2007 a portrait of Yale in the college was removed from public view because it showed him attended by a black slave wearing a neck iron.

Five Men from Breconshire

In the second half of the eighteenth-century when the East India Company became a major player on the sub-continent with its own army, five Welshmen from Breconshire were involved with its evolution. When Walter Wilkins went to India the company was still small with a few trading posts around which small towns had grown. When David Price died the company ran almost two-thirds of India. The Welsh were not many in the company; for instance only 4% of the sea captains were Welsh. These men were all between 17 and 19 when they went to India; they hoped to make lots of money; some were aware of how much Yale had made. They all achieved this; three achieved national reputations in scholarship, politics and banking. The directors of the East India Company regularly stated that their aim was to trade peacefully and profitably. During the time the five Brecon men served, the Company was changed from one of four European nations with trading stations in India into the ruler of 100 million Indians.

Walter and Jeffreys Wilkins were two of the children of John Wilkins and Sybill Jeffreys; Walter was educated at Christ College Brecon, Winchester and Reeves Academy in Bishopsgate Street London, in 1758. Jeffreys followed a similar pattern. In the second half of the eighteenth-century after the famous victory at Plassey, appointments in the Company were highly coveted and it was thanks to Charles Pratt, Attorney General and a relation of the Wilkins family that both were proposed and able to get on the lowest rung of Writer Jeffreys; in 1765 commenced his career as a writer in Bengal. The following year he was promoted to the position of assistant at the Treasury at Fort William. From there he moved to Patna where he was promoted to Factor. Here there were considerable opportunities for the Company's servants to make money. Of all the goods the Company purchased, saltpetre used in the making of gunpowder and opium were the most profitable. Patna was the centre of trade for these commodities. In February 1771 Jeffreys, who was then twenty-three requested the permission of the Bengal Board to resign on health grounds. He returned to Brecon with some wealth. He never returned to India.

By 1772 Walter was a senior merchant and a member of the Governing Board and Secret Committee of Bengal under the governorship of Warren Hastings. He was not that for long and returned to Wales as a very wealthy man at the age of 32, a year before, his father had bought on his behalf the Maesllwch estate at Glasbury-on-Wye. When he got back, he became involved with the economy of the area by entering into a partnership with Jeffreys Wilkins and Walter Jeffreys and William Williams to establish the joint stock bank of Wilkins and Company. The bank became one of the most successful in Wales and invested in coal, railways and canals. In 1802 Jeffreys bought 900 acres of land from Viscount Ashbrook in Llanfrynach, and Maesderwen was built in 1811. Walter took a great interest in public life; he was high sheriff of Breconshire in 1778 and in 1796, was elected M.P for Radnorshire and, as a reforming Whig, opposed the post-Waterloo repressive measures of the administration. He held the seat until his death in 1828. The Wilkins family changed their name to De Winton.

John Lloyd was the eldest son and the second child of the ten children of Rees and Elizabeth Lloyd of Dinas, Llanwrtyd. John whose first language was probably Welsh was educated by two vicars, the last being a noted mathematician the Reverend Davies of St. Harmon's, Rhayader. At the time John left school at sixteen, his father was experiencing financial difficulties, so although it was realised that the East India Company was so lucrative there was no way John could have joined as a Writer. A connection was made however with Thomas Evans a relation of one of his teachers, who had been, for a number of years, a surgeon on various Indiamen. John became the surgeon's servant. These ships differed from other merchant ships. In many ways they were like naval vessels. They were armed with twenty-four to twenty-eight 18 lb. guns and during the wars of the second half of the eighteenth-century; they were involved in many naval engagements. Between 1766 and 1796 John Lloyd completed 10 voyages to the East during which he was involved in battles, wounded, shipwrecked and imprisoned in Mysore for almost two years. Most of the time he sailed to India but he also had three trips to China. His progress through the ranks was not smooth and rapid. This was because of the one year spent on a non-Indiaman in the Mediterranean, his shipwreck in 1774 after which he worked on 'country ships' in the Indian Ocean for two years and his imprisonment following the capture of the *Fotritude* by a French Frigate near Madras. On 15th October 1790, aged 41 he was approved as Commander of the Manship, having used the sea for 25 years. During his first eleven years at sea his total earnings were £200. However by 1777 he was able to clear his father's debts and had raised about £1,500, much of which came from the country trade, which proved most lucrative. In November 1787, having returned to Breconshire after his imprisonment, he married Elizabeth Williams, the wealthy daughter of a former Brecon mercer who owned some property. In June 1795 towards the end of his last voyage, he was involved in the capture of seven Dutch Indiamen near St. Helena. The argument about the prize money continued until a meeting of the Privy Council chaired by George III in November 1797 resolved the issue. The prize money for John Lloyd was paid at the Horn Tavern, Doctor's Commons, London and Lloyd received £5,000. He retired in 1796 with assets in excess of £2 million in today's values. Within a few years he had bought the Abercynrig estate Brecon of 745 acres for which he paid £13,460. John believed in investing his money in business enterprises; he was one of the original two-hundred proprietors of the Brecknock and Abergavenny Canal Navigation Company. In 1797 he invested in the Brecknock Boat Company. This was concerned with the working and selling of coal and limestone, some of which was quarried on the Abercynrig estate. A year before he died he was one of the five lessees of the first section of the tram road between Brecon and Hay, a deputy-lieutenant, justice of the peace and high sheriff; also mayor of Brecon and an Alderman. He died in Brecon on the 19th February 1818.

Frederick Jones was born at Trefonnen, Cefnllys near Llandrindod Wells; he came back to live in Brecon after service in the East India Company. The youngest of nine surviving children of Thomas and Hannah Jones. He was a brother to the eminent painter Thomas Jones although he was not like his brother educated at Christ College, Brecon but firstly at the Methodist Kingswood School at Bath and later at Carmarthen Grammar School. A good Latin and Greek scholar and a fluent French speaker, he did go up to Oxford for a short time but as his brother knew Walter Wilkins he was sponsored by the latter to join the East India Company. Arriving in India in February 1778 and was posted to Bombay as a lieutenant fire worker on the Battalion of Artillery. His salary was about £12 a month; he had to provide out of this his quarter's food clothes and five servants. During the next six years he was involved in three campaigns against the Marathas, in the first near Poona one-third of the force he was with was killed; during his next campaign 4,000 out of the 6,000 company troops were killed so he was lucky to survive. In April 1783 the army he was with commanded by General Matthews, was defeated by Tipu Sultan, but Jones had been posted just before to the siege of Cannore, he was promoted to Captain in May 1786. In July 1787 Jones applied to return home; he never returned to India but returned to Brecon where he wrote extensively about his experiences in India. He had built up a modest fortune in India and was considered a man of substance in Brecon where he bought a house for 600 guineas in the Struet, probably County House. His tailor and doctor were among the most expensive in London and he had an interesting social life. Frederick remained a friend of Walter Wilkins and helped in the election of 1802 by organising a ride of 150 voters from Rhayader to Presteigne to vote for Walter. He kept a diary for 50 years, which was a fascinating account of the local social scene. Frederick died on 26th of January 1834 and was buried in what is now the cathedral, where there is a memorial to him in the South Transept.

David Price was the eldest son of five children; he was born in Merthyr Cynog where his father had been curate since 1758. After his father died he was offered a free place at Christ College, Brecon where the headmaster, the Rev. David Griffith had been his father's former rector. After performing well at Classics, David was awarded a scholarship to Jesus College, Cambridge. Even on his way to the university he spent extravagantly and despite coaxing money out of his relatives, he eventually found himself down and out. He saw an advertisement while he was at the 'Green Man and Still', an Inn in Oxford Street inviting all spirited young men to enlist in the East India Company; he thus volunteered as a private soldier. Whilst waiting to board the ship to India he was horrified by the atmosphere that prevailed at the port, of debauchery and vice. Luckily he was rescued by the same surgeon Thomas Evans, a relation who had also rescued John Lloyd. The latter arranged for Price to be accepted as an officer cadet. When Price arrived in India he was attached to an infantry regiment and soon in an action off Ceylon won some valuable prize money which he soon lost in the boredom of the rainy season on gambling at cards and horses. Initially, he had some luck on the battlefield, two musket balls just missing him but in 1791 during the siege of Darwr he was wounded and lost a leg. He was now posted to various staff officer jobs and he began to study Persian extensively. Thus he was appointed Persian translator to General James Stuart. David was then promoted captain and in 1795 he achieved the important position of Judge Advocate of the Bombay army. In 1799 he had secured such a reputation for integrity that he was appointed one of the seven prize agents during the campaign to capture Seringpatam, Tipu Sultan's, capital. The official booty amounted to a huge sum of which Price's share as prize agent was about £400,000. David was promoted to major in 1804 and then went home on leave, staying the winter and spring with friends in London and finally reached Brecon in June 1806 after an absence of twenty-nine years. He married in April 1807, the daughter of a kinswoman and moved to Watton House where he lived for the rest of his life. After six months he resigned his commission. Price held many public positions including Bailiff of Brecon, magistrate and deputy-lieutenant of the County. He spent much of his time devoted to oriental studies and wrote a series of books concerned with Islamic and Indian culture and history; he was also recognized as one of the leading oriental scholars of his day. A renowned translator of Persian, in 1830 he received the Gold medal of the Oriental Translation Committee. When he died on 16th December 1835, he was held in such standing that all the local gentry balls were cancelled. To some however he was the *'jolly old Major'* who in social events was *'drunk as usual'*. He left seventy-three rare manuscripts to the Royal Asiatic Society and the sons of Walter Wilkins were left £6,000.

The East India Company had made great strides in some ways between the time Walter Wilkins joined it and David Price left it. It was latterly the ruler of most of India with many of its servants held in the highest esteem. However, by 1807 it owed £26 million and its operations in India were a financial liability. If it had not been for the lucrative opium trade to China and the tea trade from China to Europe it could well have gone bust. In India the attitudes of the British went through great change; they did not interfere or integrate with the native culture, but more and more the races became mixed and many of these Eurasians held high positions in the company; many took to Indian ways of dress. It also became customary for the military and commercial servants of the company, at all levels, to have a bibi, who was sometimes a mistress and sometimes a wife. The second wife of Sir William Jones chairman of the Company was an Indian, however the more the British defeated well-equipped Indian armies the more they came to regard them as racially inferior. The tide changed and in 1791 an edict excluded not only Indians but also those of mixed parentage from the more senior positions in both the commercial and military service. After the Indian mutiny in which racial tensions reached their zenith, an Act was passed in 1858 in which all the Company's assets were vested in the British Crown and Victoria became Empress of India.

Bibliography

Mordechai Arbell: *'The Portuguese Jewish community of Madras, India, in the seventeenth century'*, www.sefarad.org

Leonard Bacon: *'Historical Discourses on the completion of 200 yrs from the beginning of the first church in New Haven'*, New Haven 1839

Hiram Bingham: *'Elihu Yale: the American nabob of Queen Square'*, New York, Dodd, Mead & Co, 1939

Robert Grant: *'A Sketch of the History of the East India Company'*, London 1813

David Hoeveler: *'Creating the American Mind'*, Rowman and Littlefield, 2007

E. Brooks Holifield: *'Theology in America: Christian Thought from the Age of the Puritans to the Civil War'*, New Haven and London, Yale University Press, 2003

Josiah Quincy: *'The History of Harvard University'*, Vol 1, Cambridge, Mass., 1840

J.Talboys Wheeler: *'Madras in the Olden Time, being a History of the Presidency from the first foundation to the governorship of Thomas Pitt, grandfather of the Earl of Chatham, 1689-1702'*, Madras, 1861

'Breconshire Men of the East India Company' by Ken Jones, Brecknock Museum

Chapter Three
The Lloyds of Lloyds Bank

The Lloyds of Lloyds Bank have a family tree, which claims descent on the male side from Aleth, who in the eleventh-century was king of Dyfed a part of the country which now includes Cardigan, Carmarthen and Pembroke. The number six in descent was Celynin who acquired Llwydiarth in 1300 and the family owned Dolobran from that time to 1780. Llewellyn Einion, grandson of Celynin had three sons and to David fell Dolobran. After him came Ifan Teg whose son and heir Owen about the year 1476 assumed the name of Lloyd. This he took from the estate named Llwydiarth in Montgomeryshire the seat of his grandfather. His grandson David was born in 1523; he was a commissioner of the peace; his great-grandson John Lloyd of Dolobran was a well-known antiquary and also a county J.P. Interested in tracing his family's roots. John Lloyd made his home at Coedcowrid; he was a prosperous landowner who had twenty-four tenants. His son the first Charles Lloyd was born in 1613 and married one of the Stanley's, who were the family of the Earls of Derby. He added many timber buildings to Dolobran and although much of this has disappeared, it looked quite grand after he had finished.

Here we are particularly interested in Charles Lloyd II of Dolobran born in 1637. Charles went to Oxford in 1655 and was educated with his brothers John and Thomas at Jesus College Oxford, the first purely Protestant college at that university.

Arms of Charles Lloyd of Dolobran.

His father died after Charles had been at Oxford for two years and he had to come back to run Dolobran. He married Elizabeth Lort from Stackpole, whose family had large estates in Pembrokeshire. The Lorts were an old Norman family, Sampson, Elizabeth's father being named after a Norman saint, this is how the name entered the family of Lloyd. Charles was subject to spiritual sufferings as an intelligent and sensitive man and there lived near Welshpool a man, who had been converted by the famous Quaker George Fox to the latter's beliefs. This man Richard Davies, one day arranged for a religious meeting to be held at Dolobran at the house of Hugh David one of Charles Lloyd's tenants. After several meetings, some at his own house, in November 1662 Charles became a Quaker, within a fortnight he was in Welshpool jail having been summoned before Lord Herbert of Cherbury and having refused to take the Oaths of Allegiance and Supremacy. One of the ways the Quakers were persecuted was when they refused to take the oath of Allegiance and Supremacy;

they were sent to jail often without trial. Elizabeth took the brave decision to share her husband's lot in prison. Charles Lloyd was imprisoned for another 9 years until 1672, and the family were hit by further impositions although some concessions in the prison conditions were allowed.

In May 1662 despite the Kings promise on his return to allow liberty of conscience for his subjects, Parliament passed the Quaker Act, which made it an offence either to decline an oath or for more than five persons to assemble for a Non-Anglican worship. Hundreds of Friends died in prisons all over the country. Elizabeth had six children; the second was Sampson, who became very significant in the Lloyds story. The Declaration of Indulgence by Charles II in 1672 was marked by the release of Quakers including Charles Lloyd; they then returned to Dolobran. By 1683 only three of the children remained alive, Charles, Sampson and the much younger Elizabeth. Thomas Lloyd, Charles's elder brother, meanwhile emigrated to America and became Deputy Governor of Pennsylvania and was a friend of William Penn. Elizabeth, the older Charles's wife died aged fifty-one in 1685. Charles soon married again to Anne Lawrence, a dissenter. At the same time, Sampson aged twenty-two also married Elizabeth Good from Leominster. However, he lost his wife in 1692 when he was only twenty-eight. Young Charles meanwhile had married a Crowley from the busy town of Stourbridge near Birmingham. In November 1698 Charles Lloyd the elder, died in Birmingham.

Meanwhile, young Charles back in Dolobran took the lease of a local iron forge, for which he paid rent to Powis Castle. Charles's sister Elizabeth had married a Pemberton, a well-to-do corn merchant in Birmingham. Sampson meanwhile had just gone to Birmingham to take up a similar occupation, giving up farming. He like Charles was married to one of Ambrose Crowley's daughters.

Charles Lloyd was full of energy, even at the age of fifty in 1712. Between 1717 and 1719 he gives up the forge he rented and build his own forge in the Dolobran estate and gains an iron furnace at Bersham near Wrexham.

Charles Lloyd lost so much money at his furnace at Bersham that he went broke. Charles junior was also involved and both lost their credibility with the Quakers. Charles senior lived to eighty-five and died on 21st January 1748; he had taken too many business risks and had been a failure in that field, although many described him as a humble and devout personality.

Charles Lloyd's brother Sampson had farmed for twelve years in Herefordshire before moving to Birmingham. His first marriage was to Elizabeth Good of a Leominster family. He farmed Lea Farm which still stands on the rising ground to the east of Kimbolton village, the farm belonged to the Goods. He and his wife had four daughters but she was to die of smallpox in June 1692 and he became a widower at twenty-eight. In December 1695 he married Mary Cowley thirteen years younger than himself. Sampson and Mary Lloyd moved to Birmingham with their five children in 1698. There is much speculation why he moved and we don't know the full truth of it yet. Mary would be near her own people who were in iron as were other relations; the Pembertons. Sibbel Good, his mother-in-law, might have been difficult on the farm; also part of her inheritance had come his way. In 1710 Sampson and Mary moved to a roomy, newly built terrace house in Edgbaston Street. It had plenty of ground, stables and outbuildings. There were a number of second generation Quakers in

Birmingham and the Sampson Lloyds became a useful addition to their community, as were Sampson's brother-in-law John Pemberton and Mary Lloyd's father Ambrose who was to become Sampson's associate and friend. Crowley was greatly established in the early English iron industry. He was later to be a Sheriff of the City of London and Knighted. Sampson's association with Crowley was to be an enormous boon to him in his trade as an ironmonger and he benefited from it for many years.

The Lloyds had many contacts with the second city of the land Bristol and it was to be there that Sampson Lloyd II was apprenticed to Thomas Sharp of the Brasswarehouse in 1717.

Sampson Lloyd senior died on 3rd January 1725 aged sixty, leaving eleven children still living; his estate was £10,000.

In 1710 after Sampson Lloyd I's demise, the ironmonger's business was in the hands of Sampson Lloyd II and his brother, the senior partner Charles, who were both in their twenties. Charles was already married to Sarah, daughter of Benjamin Charles, an ironmonger of an established Quaker family. Sampson in 1727 married Sarah Parker whose father was also a Quaker and an ironmonger. Jane Parkes his sister had married Thomas Pemberton, who was connected to the Lloyds. In 1728 the two Lloyd brothers started to branch out by purchasing the corn mill in the middle of Birmingham called the Town Mill. It was quite miraculous that Charles Lloyd was granted the lease for ninety-nine years as many others had had their eye on this mill. It might have been providential that the previous lessee was a Quaker. They soon began to convert it to a shotting mill for the shotting of iron for rods. Meanwhile Sampson's wife Sarah had a windfall as a result of the death of the father Richard Parker. However Sarah herself soon died leaving Sampson Lloyd having been married just a year and a half, a widower at thirty. In two years he had married again to Rachel, daughter of Nehemiah Champion I, a merchant of the City of Bristol.

Sampson Lloyd II.

The story of the Lloyds for three generations was the story of nailing; the demand for nails was perpetual. They were essentially nailers as they were rod-ironmongers, bolstered by shotting and a number of production based activities. It was their rods from which the nails were made.

As a merchant Sampson preferred his business and trade to be free, and did not much mind where he obtained his profit

As regards the qualities of the two brothers and partners, Sampson was enterprising and energetic but cautious, Charles busy and steady but rather casual. Charles died in April 1741 not leaving a will, although his widow Sarah was content for Sampson to run the mill.

At the time of Charles's death Sampson was forty-one and had been married to his second wife for a little under ten years. After two marriages and thirteen years of marriage, Sampson had only two children. Quite soon after his brother's death Sampson invested in a country estate. It became known by the family as 'The Farm' Owens Farm of fifty-six acres with its Tudor farmhouse was about two miles out of Birmingham. The price Samson paid on 29th April 1742 was £1,290. He was forever a cautious opportunist and soon also in partnership with John Willetts, started the construction of a steel furnace near Tetbury.

Through his Bristol connection he took an interest in a new enterprise in the town, the Warmley Company, which was set up to engage in the production of metals such as brass, zinc and copper. The market in these metals at the time were profiting from the Seven Years War. The company was for some time profitable and only later did it fail. Meantime Sampson had also taken on a forge for making his own bar iron on the Trent at Burton.

Sampson II's son, Sampson III was a bit of a mystery until in 1755 he completely changed his ways due only to some religious experience. The business was still expanding; the father and son partnership took on a second forge located near Powick, about three miles to the South of Worcester. The Sampsons were now in charge of four works, which were being run through managers. A rolling and shutting mill was added at Powick.

The time after the Seven Years War was exciting and explosive in terms of industry and commerce. The Lloyds themselves began to expand into banking. Birmingham needed a more streamlined service for the discounting of bills and rudimentary banking was needed for credit and services. The issue of bank notes would help the circulation of business and in 1765 Birmingham's first bank was set up, the firm of Taylors and Lloyds, a partnership of four men two from each family.

The Taylors in particular were a very prosperous family and there is no doubt as manufacturers they obtained some of their materials from Lloyds the metal merchant. John Taylor was an Unitarian who had started life in Birmingham as a cabinet maker, but was soon in partnership with John Pemberton (brother-in-law of Sampson Lloyd[1]) as a maker of buttons, he also became known for his snuff boxes and became a substantial owner of property, this is why his name was placed first in the Bank's title. There is no doubt that after the Seven Years War the iron trade was at a low, therefore the Lloyds needed new avenues for their energy. Messrs. Taylors and Lloyds, bankers at Dale End, Birmingham opened their accounts in June 1765 and were paying interest on deposits from September 1765.

[1]*It is interesting that the two banks were formed at the start of the canal boom. In a time when roads were rudimentary and railways hardly heard of, canals were of fundamental importance. Birmingham was in the forefront of this enthusiasm for canals; from the Lloyds point of view it brought all their disperse works much closer together. The Lloyds and Taylor bank became the treasurers of the Birmingham canal. The London bank known as Messrs. Hanbury, Taylor, Lloyd and Bowman opened in 1770 with William Bowman as manager living on the premises. In 1779 they moved to 60 Lombard Street and there they stayed until their amalgamation in 1864 with Barnetts Hoares. Throughout this time the London House continued to act as London agent of the Birmingham House. The last Lloyd to be a partner in both was Sampson III who died in 1807. The amalgamation of Lloyd's Banking Company as the Birmingham company was called and Barnett, Hoares, Hanbury and Lloyd of London took place in 1884 and brought all the bankers together.*

Ten years later they had 277 customers on their books about 40 of these were Quakers, who were particularly valuable to the bank for their reliability. 72 of their clients were quite surprisingly ladies. The capital of £8,000 was saved by the two families on an even basis.

The bank at no 7 Dale End near Birmingham High Street was purchased by Sampson Lloyd III, who it is said took the main executive part in the bank, and John Taylor II, the younger Taylor who took a very energetic position and took part in establishing another bank in London. This was an unusual and in fact an exceptional moves for a regional bank.

The structure of the bank at no 14 Lombard Street was that it consisted of four partners Hanbury Taylor Lloyd and Bowman. Hanbury had been married to Mary Lloyd for some years. The Hanburys had originally come from Worcestershire, and were rich Quaker merchants, who had iron interests in South Wales where the Lloyds had just come across them.

It was during the 1770s that Sampson Lloyd III entered the most fruitful period of his life. He had helped establish two banks and helped to run the businesses associated with a network of family connections. Sampson and Rachel had seventeen children altogether and despite this and contrary to some images of the Quaker sect, he was a man who nearly always maintained a cheerful countenance.

While Sampson Lloyd III was doing so much in Birmingham his father nearing the ripe old age of seventy was busy making sure the younger members of the family were married off successfully. He had seven children, only one of which was not married out of which would come the family firm of Lloyds in the next generation. One of his daughters married David Barclay II who eventually in the next century gave the family name to Barclays Bank. When Sampson Lloyd II died the Birmingham interests passed into the hands of the three elder sons, the younger ones established in London, with Sampson, a partner in both banks as the bridge between the two. It is interesting that the family kept up their Quaker connection and worship throughout this time. Charles Lloyd for instance kept the accounts of the General Hospital in Birmingham.

John Lloyd one of the younger brothers became an established banker and was very much involved in the movement to abolish the slave trade mainly begun by the Society of Friends.

Going back to the Bank in Birmingham, it was Birmingham's only bank for about fifteen to twenty years and in the final quarter of the eighteenth-century it enjoyed a period of expansion. In the other businesses, the refining of iron with charcoal was giving place to the new coal process which was cheaper, and it was not long and by 1812 that the Lloyds closed all their mills including the one at Burton.

They were out of Powick by the end of 1801, Edgbaston closed in 1908 and Digbeth in 1804.

The bank in Birmingham stood the test of time in the war against France and did not fail as so many did. In 1815 the fifty-fifty relationship between the two families of Taylor and Lloyd were restored at the Bank.

Five of Sampson Lloyd II's sons became bankers Sampson and Samuel in Taylor and Lloyds at Birmingham, Henry in Hanbury, Taylor and Co. in London,

David with the Gurneys of Norwich and Alfred in a bank at Leamington, Richard the sixth son was a brewer in Coventry. Sampson Lloyd III died on 27th December 1807 aged seventy-nine, he was essentially a Quaker, a banker and a good businessman.

In the other main branch of the family Charles's son James became one of the mainstays of the bank and his eldest boy Charles was quite the wrong image for the family. He lived with Coleridge in Somerset lodged with Southey in Hampshire and suffered a number of breakdowns, brought out both verse and a two volume novel. He also became a friend of Charles Lamb.

Two other difficult characters in Charles the elder's family were Robert, a sensitive and intelligent man who took his brother Charles's side and formed a great friendship with Lamb. Priscilla, the first of the daughters became engaged to Christopher Wordsworth brother of William and an Anglican clergyman, much to her Quaker father Charles's chagrin.

Charles Lloyd was a natural scholar; he carried most of the New Testament around in his head, translated many of the great classical texts and had a good aptitude for languages. But it was not Charles the senior partner of the bank but Samuel who in the December 1825 run on the banks, arranged with great foresight money to be galloped from London to prevent any panic at the Lloyds bank. Charles eventually died on 16th January 1828 at the age of seventy-nine. He had sixty-two grandchildren at the time. His funeral was large reflecting the goodwill he had generated in his lifetime by the display of many good and sound qualities.

During the time of about forty years from Charles Lloyds death to the Banks great change in 1865 the Taylor Lloyd Bank carried on after from strength to strength, but with the odd downturn as well. After Francis Lloyd's resignation from the bank on trumped up charges of malpractice, George Lloyd became one of the main principals spending almost fifty years in the Banks service.

James killed himself in 1852, no Taylor offered to come in, and in April 1853 the name of the firm changed to Lloyds and Co. with firm partners James Lloyd senior, George Lloyd and their respective sons James junior and Sampson Samuel. George Lloyd died in 1857 and James senior being a sick man, George B. Lloyd and Thomas Lloyd came into the firm, both reasonable businesses. After the passing of the Companies Act of 1862 in which Parliament had approved the limitation of liability by shares, Lloyds decided to convert the partnership into a public limited company. The new company's business opened on 1st May 1865, one-hundred years since the bank of Taylors and Lloyds had been formed.

In 1869 Sampson Samuel Lloyd took over as chairman of the new company, a position he held for eighteen years. A few years later he repurchased the Dolobran estate, the purchase cost him £20,000. The quest to repurchase the original family estate was a long and varied one. In 1805 Sampson Lloyd II had gone into the whole question of its purchase price, seventy years later Charles Lloyd had been tempted but had not fallen for the temptation. When the estate was purchased again, it returned to a Lloyd again after ninety-eight years and was to remain with the family for nearly as long again.

By 1975 the estate was still in existence and the house externally had hardly been altered.

When the bank ceased to be a partnership, only one Lloyd among the partners was still a Quaker. They had transmuted from a Quaker family with some land in Wales through the whole business of iron working to banking in Birmingham. For the most part they had been practical sound businessmen, which gave them success. Upright and honest, these Welsh Quakers were an example to many throughout the centuries. These early private banks often grew out of other concerns such as manufacturing; Lloyds themselves came from metal traders; they determinedly went into banking seeing it as a opportunity, where there was a need and a shortage. They made this choice largely independently. Many of the banks assimilated into Lloyds were started as all sorts of different businesses. Grant and Burbey at Portsmouth, Wyatt Inge and Lant at Coventry were grocers, Walters Voss at Swansea was started by a draper. Some brewers became bankers such as Cobbs of Margate. The sign of the black horse is interesting. The use of the sign as a banker's emblem goes back to the very early years of Charles II when Samuel Stoakes, a goldsmith started banking transactions under that sign in London. John Bland took over from the Stokes. Until 1749 the business carried on under the Black Horse sign at 54 Lombard Street; it then moved to number 62 in 1772 when Samuel Hoare joined the firm; it became Bland Barnett and Hoare; this title remained with only one slight alteration until the amalgamation with Hanbury Lloyds and Co. This brought Lloyds and the Black Horse together.

Bibliography:
'The Quaker Lloyds in the Industrial Revolution' by Humphrey Lloyd 1975 London Hutchinson and co.
'Lloyds Bank in the History of English Banking' R.S. Sayers 1957 Oxford at the Clarendon Press
'The Lloyds of Birmingham' by Samuel Lloyd, Cornish Bros Birmingham

John Nash.

John Nash had obvious links to the Principality of Wales and it was there that he retreated to, when things initially went wrong for him. He steadily built up his work in that country until he was doing some rather exciting and innovative work. It was from there that his long march started back to respectability, London and fame.

The first mystery surrounding the architect Nash is the place of his birth. We know that he was certainly born in 1752, of a Welsh mother who is now buried in Carmarthen. Professor Price believed that Nash was born in Neath. It is likely that he was brought up in Lambeth and that his father was William Nash, a millwright who died, most probably when Nash - the youngest of three sons - was about eight years-old. At a very young age he entered the office of Robert Taylor the distinguished architect. Nash did not hold a high opinion of his master who, despite this was awarded a knighthood in 1782. He continued to work for Taylor for ten years, from 1767-1770, and no doubt he was greatly influenced by Taylor and Sir William Chambers who was rebuilding Somerset House, despite his low opinion of the former.

When his rich uncle died in Paris, Nash was left a legacy of £1,000, a considerable sum in those days. He moved to Bloomsbury, setting up a property company with a few houses in Bloomsbury Square, and proceeded to transform these houses both inside and out into a Stuccoed mansion. However the building was a financial disaster. Nash, in October 1783, was declared bankrupt and at the age of thirty had to begin all over again.

It is likely that at this point in his life he returned to his mother country, Wales, where his name is next heard of in partnership with a man named Saxon, a builder-carpenter of Carmarthen. Together they won the tender of 600 guineas for re-roofing and providing a new ceiling for St. Peter's Church, Carmarthen, after a fire. Several buildings in the town have been attributed to Nash: he is said to have built a public house near the church called The Six Bells and Jeremy's Hotel. He built a modest home for himself too, known as Green Gardens also, he was a man who saw no possible social barriers and his personality - uninhibited and witty - was appreciated by almost everyone he came into contact with. His wit and originality smoothed his path in society and made him welcome and amusing to many. Short and bullet-headed - in temperament he was pugnacious and thrusting and a twinkle of mischief was ever-present in his eyes. Mrs. Arbuthnot writing in her journal (1820-1832 edited by F.B. Amford and the Duke of Wellington 1950) said that he was '.... *a very clever, odd, amusing man, with a face like a monkey's but civil and good humoured to the greatest degree'.*

It was in 1792 that Nash finished work as the designer of Carmarthen Gaol, the first important work of his career. In 1793 he designed the rebuilt West front of St. David's Cathedral, one of his first known and crudest attempts at Gothic. The whole front was replaced in 1862 by Sir George Vilber Scott when the cathedral was restored. Nash, through the landowner John Vaughan, was then asked to improve and redesign the market place in Abergavenny. At this time he was also in contact with another useful Whig - J.G. Phillips of Cwmgwilli, a Whig member for the Borough of Carmarthen with whom he had much correspondence.

He returned to Wales after a sojourn in England at Stamford Court. His business was expanding and he employed a very successful French draughtsman called Auguste Charles de Rugun, a refugee from the revolution. Rugin shared Nash's love of amateur theatricals, the latter even performing in the 'School For Scandal' presented in 1796 at Carmarthen Theatre.

Meanwhile Nash had done many commissions for the gentry of West Wales. In particular he improved Thomas John's famous house at Hafod where the ideas of a picturesque style of the Romantic period of building was fast evolving. At this time Nash's first commission to design a complete country home came about. It was to be for Uvidale Price of Herefordshire, on the wild coast of Aberystwyth, a Stuccoed villa in Gothic style which has long since disappeared. Nash was kept busy - involving himself at the same time in building Ffynone, situated on a hill near Boncath, Pembrokeshire. The house is square in plan and originally presented four identical Palladian facades. Each facade was surmounted by a pediment. Broad timber eves formed a deep recess. Nash's typical interior layout is present, characterised by the

emphasis placed on a central hall, and included the first of several semi-circular staircases - this example at Ffynone being a forerunner. The main rooms were dispersed around Nash's central features - the hall, staircase and vestibule. The house was built of Painswick stone and cantilevered from the wall and the S-shaped iron balustrades were to become Nash's favourite design. He 'created' a number of other houses in Wales and throughout his career he kept up his Welsh connection.

By early March 1795 Nash had returned to London. In a few short years he was unrivalled in his field, although some would say he never really understood the Gothic style - this did not prevent him from creating in it though. His main asset was his personality, and his uninhibited behaviour stood him in good stead in London. Humphrey Repton decided his and Nash's talents were complimentary, and a partnership lasted until 1803. At that time the enthusiasm was for the castle Gothic style building. It was at Southgate Grove that they first collaborated where, here in 1797; Nash built his first large Christian mansion. A number of other Classical houses were constructed or altered after his success. Nash had always found it hard to concentrate on just one scheme at any one time, and here he was no different, spreading his expertise over many ongoing projects. He even built a number of houses in Ireland including the beautiful Killymoon.

The first we hear of Mrs. Nash is in her husband's letter of 1802 to Mrs. Stewart. Her name was Mary Ann Bradley, the daughter of an unsuccessful coal merchant, and had married Nash in December 1798. He was forty-six, his bride twenty-one years his junior and possibly his second wife. Another unanswered question is whether she was one of the Prince

Regent's mistresses. Whatever the case, Nash had - or recognised - no children of his own.

There is no doubt that the possibility of such a connection with the Prince Regent might have allowed Nash to live well above the means we might expect of someone of his profession.

In 1806, Nash was appointed architect to the Chief Commissioner of Woods and Forests. This gave him the great opportunity of planning Regents Park, whilst at about the same time the Crown Lands around Marylebone, which had been rented to the Treasury. Park Crescent was built in Regents Park in 1812 - perhaps Nash's greatest single stroke of urban architecture. The building of Park Crescent was not completed until 1820, and the remainder of the terraces were missing after 1812 until the last one, Gloucester Gate, was finished in 1827. Many other squares and terraces were constructed at this time by Nash or his associates around the Park. York Gate, Cornwall Terrace, Clarence Terrace, Sussex Place, Hanover Terrace. He was also one of the founders behind the construction of the Regents Canal and was very involved in the construction of Regents Street and Piccadilly. His buildings were a jumbled amalgamation of every sort of style. The work Nash did was exclusive and encompassed all aspects - the commissioners had an architect, planner, interior decorator, surveyor and estate agent all in one. His responsibilities were enormous, his rewards FEW and his critics on every side. Nash also designed the Haymarket Theatre and old King's Opera House, which was replaced by her Majesty's in 1893.

Nash went on to design and build the King's Cottage in Windsor Park, which became the Royal Lodge of today. Nash at this time was trying to maintain a dual role, the architect to the Commissions of the Crown Lands and personal architect to the Prince of Wales.

The Royal Pavilion at Brighton was constructed at the behest of the Prince who had become the centre of an alternative court at Brighton, and led a life of notorious licentiousness. Nash, thanks to the Prince's influence, was appointed Deputy Surveyor General. The banqueting room and the music room in the pavilion were of the ultimate sumptuousness and luxury and the building was very popular with royalty up to the reign of Queen Victoria who decided to remove most of the furnishings and furniture. The estate was finally bought by the Brighton Town Commissioners in 1850, for £53,000. It had cost over £500,000 to create. Today it has been restored to some of its former glory.

There is no doubt that Nash aspired to circulate as a society figure, and as such was lampooned unmercifully on all sides. His relationship with other architects such as Soane was full of friction, and he made an enemy of Repton.

Nash was seventy-three when he started the rebuilding and extension of Buckingham Palace. He organised the rebuilding of the Palace's wings, which were raised to the same height as the main block. The great rooms of state inside were reconstituted by Nash and they have never been equalled in grandeur. The King William IV died in 1837, the Treasury suspended Nash's commission - dismissing him from the Board of Works - and his patron was not there to defend him. Buckingham Palace was somewhat of a laughing stock.

In 1830 he suffered a stroke, which laid him up for eight months and from which he never fully recovered. By the spring of 1835 he was bedridden, but was still pleased to receive visitors. On May 12th he died and was buried in St. James' Churchyard next to the little Gothic church, which he designed in 1831.

It was said by some that he was a genius, and that his strength lay more in his bold conception and the impression his buildings gave as complete structures, than in Classical detail. His work sounded the last note of Classicism: he was eventually a man of the times, but it is perhaps not his sumptuous palatial designs but his country houses that really reveal him as an architect.

An architectural model, about 1826 designed by John Nash.

Bibliography:

J.C. Loudon (ed): *'Landscape Gardening and Landscape Architecture of the late Humphry repton Esq, being his entire works on these subjects'*, London 1840

Thomas Lloyd, Julian Orbach, Robert Scourfield: *'Carmarthenshire and Ceredigion, New Haven and London'*, Yale University Press, 2006

Richard Payne Knight: *'The Landscape, a didactic poem in three books'*, London, 1794

'An analytical Inquiry into the Principles of Taste', 4th ed London 1808

Michael Mansbridge: *'John Nash'*, Phaedon Press, 2004

Louise Nicholson and Richard Turpin: *'London, London, Francis Lincoln Ltd'*, 1998

Rutherford M. Platt: *'Land Use and Society - Geography, Law and Public Policy, Washington'*, Island Press, 2004

Uvedale Price: *'Essays on the Picturesque as compared wuth the sublime and the beautiful'*, Vol 1, London, 1810

Michael Southworth and Eran Ben-Joseph: *'Streets and the Shaping of Towns and Cities, Washington'*, Island Press, 2003

Richard Suggett: *'John Nash Architect, Royal Commission on the Ancient and Historical Monuments of Wales and National Library of Wales'*, 1995

John Summerson: *'John Nash, Architect to George the Fourth'*, George Allen and Unwin, 1935

John Summerson: *'The Life and Work of John Nash, Architect'*, MIT Press, 1981

Alan Tate: *'Great City Parks, Taylor and Francis'*, New York and London', 2001

Chapter Five
Robert Owen
1771-1858

Robert Owen.

Robert Owen was a man ahead of his time, he was a paternalist of the highest order; he came out of Newtown in Mid-Wales to stride the world with his enlightened ideas, which as a practical industrialist he was able to put into practice. He was a man of spirituality, who believed the poor deserved better, and he went about trying to improve their lot partially by challenging the accepted ideas of the time. In some ways he was a radical, although many at the time did not think he was radical enough. He certainly was driven not merely as a theorist but as a man of action, an idealist who had to temper his ideals to the real world, also had many glorious failures like New Haven but great successes too like New Lanark. He was one of a long line of a Welsh enlightenment that has not always been recognised.

Robert Owen was born in Newtown, a sleepy village in the centre of Wales. Both his parents were Welsh. But he left Wales at the age of ten and seems to have shown no interest in it for the rest of his very active life. At the end of his life, however, at the age of 87, he asked to return to Newtown and that is where he died and was buried.

His life can be easily divided into two parts, though they overlap in time. In the first he was a practical businessman, advancing from one successful under-taking to another; in the second he was a prophet, presiding over a succession of failed experiments but nonetheless inspiring thousands of people with the vision of a much better system of social organisation that could be obtained easily and without violence.

The first, financially successful part of his career sees him progressing from assistant shopkeeper to small manufacturer. Then he became manager of a large factory in Manchester employing some 500 workers, until in 1797 he took control of the great New Lanark spinning mill, near Glasgow, reputedly the largest factory of its day.

New Lanark was a village created by David Dale in a region of the Clyde Valley above Glasgow. The textile factories of the time had a bad reputation for long working hours in unhealthy - damp and hot - conditions. They attracted people in a state of desperation, many of them fleeing what had become impossible living conditions in the highlands. Most notoriously they used children, often, at the time, pauper children and orphans who had been taken from the streets and placed in the newly established 'foundling hospitals'. Some of the children at New Lanark came from the Town Hospital in Glasgow of which David Dale was a director.

When New Lanark started in 1786 there were around 80 children working there; by 1793 there were 273 and, according to Owen's account, by 1800 after he had taken charge, there were between 400 and 500. The total workforce on his arrival was between 1,700 and 1,800. Around two-thirds were women and children.

Responding to questions on conditions in the factory, David Dale said that each of the rooms in the mills held some 2,000 spindles and had around fifty to seventy-five children working in it. The youngest children were 6-7 years of age. They worked from 6.00 a.m. in the morning to 7.00 p.m. in the evening, with a half-hour breakfast at 9.00 a.m. and an hour at 2.00 p.m. for lunch. They had supper at 7.00 p.m. in the evening and, as soon as possible after that, teachers would arrive, mainly teaching them to read.

Owen's first important piece of writing - 'A New View of Society', published in 1813 and 1814 - lays out his dissatisfaction with New Lanark as he found it, and what he tried to do to remedy it. The emphasis is on the condition of the adults rather than the children and in particular on their moral condition:

'every man did that which was right in his own eyes, and vice and immorality prevailed to a monstrous extent. The population lived in idleness, in poverty, in almost every kind of crime; consequently, in debt, out of health, and in misery.'

Owen describes his work at New Lanark as a steady, patient encroachment on the vices of the workforce:

'Theft and the receipt of stolen goods was their trade, idleness and drunkenness their habit, falsehood and deception their garb, dissensions, civil and religious, their daily practice; they united only in a zealous systematic opposition to their employers.'

He emphasises that he never used punishment, that everything was done by patient and careful explanation, proving that better conduct led to greater happiness. As for the children:

'The system of receiving apprentices from public charities was abolished; permanent settlers with large families were encouraged, and comfortable houses were built for their accommodation.'

'The practice of employing children in the mills, of six, seven and eight years of age, was discontinued, and their parents advised to allow them to acquire health and education until they were ten years old....' though Owen thought twelve would have been a better age.

'The children were taught reading, writing, and arithmetic, during five years, that is, from five to ten, in the village school, without expense to their parents... Another important consideration is, that all their instruction is rendered a pleasure and delight to them; they are much more anxious for the hour of school-time to arrive than to end; they therefore make a rapid progress.'

While all this was being done:

'Their houses were rendered more comfortable, their streets were improved, the best provisions were purchased, and sold to them at low rates, yet covering the original expense, and under such regulations as taught them how to proportion their expenditure to their income. Fuel and clothes were obtained for them in the same manner; and no advantage was attempted to be taken of them, or means used to deceive them.'

The end result was that:

'Those employed became industrious, temperate, healthy, faithful to their employers, and kind to each other, while the proprietors were deriving services from their attachment, almost without inspection, far beyond those which could be obtained by any other means than those of mutual confidence and kindness.'

Owen had bought New Lanark with a group of proprietors who were first and foremost interested in it as a business investment. They were not averse to Owen's improvements so long as the business continued to yield a generous return, which it did, but by 1809 they seem to have felt he was getting too ambitious. Owen offered to buy the enterprise from them but to do this he had to enter into a new partnership. The 'New Lanark Company' was formed with himself as salaried manager and largest shareholder. The same problems, however arose, with the new managers complaining against the extravagance of Owen's plan for the education of children under ten who were not actually in employment. Owen then managed to put together a group of wealthy and influential supporters who, in 1813, bought the enterprise. They included the utilitarian philosopher Jeremy Bentham but also a group of Quakers, among them William Allen who would later turn out to be Owen's nemesis.

He was now free, or so it seemed, to develop his policy as he saw fit. Starting work on a new building which was completed by the end of 1815 and opened at the beginning of 1816 under the name of the Institution for the Formation of Character.

The Institution was open to all in the neighbourhood, not just the children of the mills. Music and dancing were taught, as well as military drill, since Owen argued that a society able to defend itself would have no room for a standing army. The children were given tunics designed to allow the free movement of the body - boys wore kilts, not trousers. During the Summer, there were excursions organised in the surrounding countryside, where Owen had arranged for paths to be laid out.

But Owen's vision for the Institution for the Formation of Character went far beyond the immediate project. The New Vision of Society argues that the whole of existing human culture had been based on a fundamental error which had to be rooted out if a just and moral society was to be established:

'From the earliest ages it has been the practice of the world to act on the supposition that each individual man forms his own character, and that therefore he is accountable for all his sentiments and habits, and consequently merits reward for some and punishment for others.... This error cannot much longer exist; for every day will make it more and more evident that the character of man is, without a single exception, always formed for him; that it may be, and is, chiefly created by his predecessors; that they give him, or may give him, his ideas and habits, which are the powers that govern and direct his conduct. Man, therefore, never did, nor is it possible he ever can, form his own character.'

His project, then was to remove children from the existing bad influences that were operating on them and introduce them to a new system that would be entirely based on a combination of kindness and reason. In particular, he believed, it was necessary to remove children from existing religious influences. The very last people who could be entrusted with the education of children are *'the official expounders and defenders of the various opposing religious systems throughout the world; for many of these are actively engaged in propagating imaginary notions, which cannot fail to vitiate the rational powers of man, and to perpetuate his misery.'*

We can understand why some of the more religiously minded among Owen's fellow proprietors were begining to wonder if they should be supporting this institution.

1815 - the year when Owen was building his new Institution - was the year of the Battle of Waterloo and the end of the Napoleonic wars. As Owen commented: *'On the day on which peace was signed the great customer of the producers died'* - meaning that the enormous demand created by the needs of the army suddenly stopped at the very moment when the labour market was glutted by the return of thousands of discharged soldiers. The result was a nightmare period in which the government engaged in a policy of repression - hanging, flogging, deportation and imprisonment - culminating in the 'Peterloo massacre' of 1819 when soldiers launched a sabre charge against a densely packed crowd which had gathered in St. Peter's Field, Manchester, to hear a radical orator, Henry Hunt, calling for parliamentary reform.

Owen regarded the demand for reform of the franchise as quite irrelevant. The intellect of the populace at large was, in his view, as deformed as that of the existing privileged aristocracy. The task in hand was to persuade men to act rationally and the aristocracy were probably more open to persuasion than a completely unformed rabble, subject to the maddening influences of poverty, insecurity and spirituous liquor. He was always anxious to dampen down strong feelings, and was in continual conflict with the radicals whose policy was to use the anger of the poor as a battering ram to widen the franchise.

Owen argued that where the ordinary mechanisms of the market - which he did not at this time challenge - could not provide for full employment, the state should intervene. In particular, he argued for the establishment of *'villages of co-operation'*, based mainly on a highly labour intensive agricultural work. When the House of Commons committee looking into the reform of the Poor Law refused to give him a hearing, Owen launched a huge publicity campaign which climaxed in two very well attended public meetings in London in August 1817.

A statue commemorating Robert Owen in Manchester.

One of his followers, John Minter Morgan, described something of the impact that he made:

'A more extraordinary sensation was never before produced by the proceedings of any single individual so little known to the public at large as was Mr. Owen at this period. Those who attended the meetings at the City of London Tavern in the autumn of this year, or noticed the wide circulation of the Reports of the meetings, can never forget the intense excitement that prevailed.'

It seems to have been about this time that trouble began to develop between Owen and some of his fellow proprietors, notably William Allen. Allen has had a bad press in the literature on Owen. The Russian essayist Alexander Herzen calls him and his fellow Quakers on the New Lanark board *'saintly shopkeepers'* and claims that had it not been for them *'there would be in England and America now hundreds of New Lanarks and New Harmonies; into them would have flowed the fresh vigour of the working population...'*

But Allen was a substantial figure in his own right, a leading campaigner against the slave trade and in favour of penal reform. He was a chemist and founded the pharmaceutical company, Allen and Hanbury. He helped to establish the Geological Society and was a fellow of the Royal Society and founder member of the Society for Diminishing Capital Punishment. His journal *The Philanthropist* had published the plan Owen submitted to Parliament for the relief of unemployment. He was involved with the *'Society for the purpose of encouraging the black settlers at Sierra Leone and the natives of Africa generally in the cultivation of their soil by the sale of their produce'*.

But he cuts a poor figure in the Owen story because his objections to Owen's system of education have a killjoy air about them. His main concern was to ensure a basic Protestant Christian education, but he also wanted the dancing master to be dismissed, psalm singing to be introduced, and that *'having considered the dress of the children, we are of opinion that decency requires, that all males as they arrive at the age of six years, should wear trousers or drawers : we agree therefore, that they shall be required to be so clothed.'*

This was part of an 'articles of agreement' with his fellow proprietors imposed on Owen in January 1824. Owen left New Lanark some months after this agreement was signed, but it would be wrong to think that in his absence the proprietors abandoned their idealism or even that Owen ceased to take a sympathetic interest in it. In 1833 Owen's own weekly paper *The Crisis* included this description:

'The cleanliness and well-ventilated state of the factories are also known and appreciated by every visitor; and indeed the blooming countenances of the girls, compared with those similarly employed in this quarter, speak volumes in favour of the New Lanark system of management.'

1824, the year when he had to agree to the conditions laid down by Allen and his friends, was also the year when he received Richard Flower, an Englishman living in North America, who was trying to find a buyer for 'New Harmony' - a large tract of land, some 30,000 acres, in Indiana, owned by the 'Rappites', followers of a German millennialist preacher called George Rapp.

Rapp had arrived in America from Würtemburg in 1803 and initially set up a community in Pennsylvania, under the name of 'Harmony'. There were soon about 600 members and around 1807 they decided to adopt a policy of strict celibacy. Thenceforth, like the Shakers, their numbers had to be replenished by new people coming in from outside.

In 1814 they moved to Indiana. Now they wanted to move again and were offering, according to the account by C.R. Edson: *'30,000 acres of land, nearly 3,000 of it being under cultivation and consisting of nineteen detached farms; 600 acres of improved land occupied by tenants; 15 acres of full-bearing vines; fine orchards; the village with regularly laid out streets, running at right angles to each other; a public square, around which were built churches, schools, and other public buildings, of brick; mills and factories, all for the sum of $150,000 a mere pittance for the property involved.'*

They wanted to move back to Pennsylvania, to a new site they called 'Economy', near Pittsburgh. It is rather sad to contrast the material success of the Rappites with Owen's effort which was, in the event, a fairly thoroughgoing failure. Edson, in an article published in 1892, tells us that:

'In less than five years from the time of their establishment at Economy, they had built factories for the manufacture of cotton, woollen and silk goods, and later on were controlling at Beaver Falls the largest cutlery establishment in the United States, and were noted for their extensive farming operations, orchards and vineyards...'

'and there they are to be found - what is left of them - today, millionaires, rich in their railroads, oil wells, coal mines, and other landed property.'

Owen accompanied Flower back to America at the end of the year and was lionised by the North American establishment, apparently very excited by his vision of a network of well-organised self-sufficient co-operative communities. Even before he established New Harmony itself he had inspired a Swedenborgian congregation in Cincinatti under Rev. Daniel Roe to establish a community in Yellow Springs, in Greene County, Ohio. He also excited the enthusiasm of William Maclure, a Scotsman who has been called the *'father of American geology'* and who introduced the Pestalozzi educational system into North America. Maclure gathered together a 'boatload of knowledge' with some of the best scientific minds in the country, to come to New Harmony and contribute to the educational side.

Advertisements were placed in the papers over the Summer of 1825 and some eight-hundred people soon turned up but, as Owen's son, Robert Dale Owen was later to complain, there was no attempt to secure references or any other information about them. In July, Owen left to return to New Lanark and did not return until January 1826 when he arrived together with Robert Dale about the same time as the 'boatload of knowledge'. He declared himself pleased with the state of the community as he found it and as a result decided to move on earlier than planned to the next stage of development - an equality of property. According to Robert Dale Owen:

'Under the new constitution, all members, according to their ages, not according to the actual value of their services, were to be "furnished, as near as can be, with similar food, clothing, and education; and, as soon as practicable, to live in similar houses, and in all respects to be accommodated alike..."'

This new constitution was adopted in February 1826 and those wishing to remain members were expected to agree to it within three days. The effect was disastrous. A process seems to have set in by which the community broke up into a number of different, more or less independent, smaller communities, and within the main community there was a tendency to divide into separate self-organising trades. One of the communities was formed under Maclure and had the name 'Macluria'.

Owen left again in the Spring of 1827. On his return in April 1828 he declared in a speech in Harmony Hall that the experiment had been a failure. From then on he had little more to do with it, though he continued to own most of the land. A large number of the original families continued to live in the area, and Owen's sons, David Dale Owen and Richard Owen, as well as his daughter, Jane Dale Owen, kept up their connection with it. David and Richard both followed Maclure in becoming geologists and, through David's influence New Harmony became in 1839 the centre of the United States Geological Survey.

After a brief attempt to persuade the Mexican government to give him Texas for his experiments, and a mammoth debate with a prominent American liberal theologian on the evidences of Christianity, Owen returned to England, where he became involved with the fledgling trade union and workers' co-operative movements.

We have seen that Owen was no democrat - at least in the present contemporary state of society when, he believed, people were so badly formed that they could not be trusted to look after their own interests. Essentially he seems to have seen society as a school in which the ruling elements acted as teachers to the rest - very bad teachers who were forming them in the ways of selfishness, dissipation and idleness. His policy was to improve the teachers - he had little confidence that the mass would be able to improve themselves of their own volition - the inability of men to form their own character was an axiom with him.

His arguments, however, contained the seeds of something more radical. He argued that instead of gold, labour should be used as the determining measure of the value of money. Workers should be paid in notes expressive of the value of their work, denominated according to 'hours'. The worker would thus be able to use them to obtain the equivalent of the value of his own contribution to the total social wealth.

Implicit in this was the idea that wealth is created by labour, in opposition to  the predominant idea that it was created by the investment of capital. A much more sophisticated version of this 'labour theory of value' had earlier been advanced by the economist David Ricardo. This idea that labour was the source of wealth was a great inspiration for the ideas of self-organisation that were gaining ground in the working class. Owen was thus adopted by - and tried himself to adopt - a tendency he had not initiated.

A large number of co-operative societies (for the most part very small scale trading associations) and trade unions or guilds (the distinction was not clearcut) existed throughout the country. The 'Owenites' saw these as having within themselves the potential for a complete restructuring of society and pressed for organisation on an ever larger, more national scale. Owen himself was not initially involved in this. On his return to England he had seen his main role as education. He was delivering regular Sunday morning lectures in London and founded a weekly journal, *The Crisis*. His first practical initiative was the establishment of an 'Equitable Labour Exchange'.

This was an attempt to realise the idea of a currency based on units of labour. One of his supporters offered him the use of a large building on the Gray's Inn Road, initially for the purpose of the lectures, but Owen quickly recognised its potential as a trading emporium. Workers - in this case presumably small independent artisans - brought the product of their work and were given notes in exchange which could then be used to buy other products deposited in the store. The notes supposedly represented the hours devoted to doing the work, but since the work of a skilled craftsman was rated more highly than the value of a day labourer it amounted in practice to a judgment on the part of the committee running the store.

All this time, dramatic developments were occurring in the trade union movement, centred on Birmingham, where there was another Equitable Labour Exchange and a great deal of interest in Owen's thinking. 1833 saw a major conflict between the Operative Builders Union and the building contractors, who were themselves combining and pledging themselves not to employ any members of the union. The Operative Builders Union was a relatively recent creation, bringing together a variety of smaller associations each of them representing particular crafts within the overall industry. Towards the end of the year it expanded again into the Grand National Union of Builders, with its own journal, *The Pioneer*, edited by James Morrison. *The Pioneer* first appeared in September 1833 as the voice of the centralising tendency within the union which aimed at an even greater scale of organisation, beyond the building trade - the Grand National Consolidated Trades Union, which finally emerged in 1834. Owen himself had been involved in the discussions that led to it but he had advocated a '*Grand National Moral Union of the Useful and Productive Classes of the United Kingdom*', which would have attempted to bring together employers and employees, masters and men, with the emphasis on a re-organisation of the whole economic system.

But Owen was out of phase with the mood of the times. The unions were faced with a policy of lockouts and an agreement among the employers to refuse to use workers unless they signed a 'document' renouncing trade unionism. The employers had the support of the government led by Lord Melbourne who was, as it happens, Owen's friend. In January 1834, Owen complained in a letter published in *The Pioneer* and in *The Crisis*:

'Sometimes you and your correspondents seem to have lost the spirit of peace and charity by which alone the regeneration of mankind can ever be effected. You have drawn a line of opposition of feelings and interests between the employers and employed in the production of wealth which, if it were continued, would tend to delay the progress of this great cause, and to injure those noble principles which you are so desirous of seeing carried into practice.'

But both *The Pioneer* and his own paper *The Crisis* were drifting away from him.

Since September 1833, *The Crisis* had been edited by a rather extraordinary figure called James Elishama Smith. Since June, he had been giving regular lectures in Owen's exchange building, arguing that the Christianity of the rich was Antichrist and that it was only now that the real Christianity, the Christianity of the poor, was beginning to manifest itself. He developed these ideas with great freedom in the pages of *The Crisis*.

A series of 'Letters on Associated Labour', almost certainly by Smith, appeared in Morrison's *Pioneer* at a time when Morrison was in an increasingly bitter dispute with Owen and the executive of the Consolidated Union. This was in the context of the arrest of six agricultural workers in Dorsetshire, held without bail for administering unlawful oaths, trying to form a branch of the Consolidated Union - the famous 'Tolpuddle Martyrs'. Owen was himself indignant at their treatment and had formally joined the Consolidated Union in April, but he was still trying to steer it towards a moderate policy of negotiation and compromise. Smith's *Crisis*, however complained against the inaction of the Union's executive and in the following issue expressed disagreement in a long letter in which Owen complained that his principles had been misunderstood and outlined the aims of the Union as he understood them - aims which contained nothing more radical than the elimination of drunkenness, the education of children and adults, and establishing proper relations between workmen and the government.

Smith wrote to his brother at the beginning of August to say he had left Owen's party and, a couple of issues later, *The Crisis* stopped publication. Morrison had resigned from the Union's executive in March, though he continued to publish *The Pioneer* in defiance of Owen's wishes. He died the following year.

In these conditions both the Labour Exchanges and the Consolidated Union collapsed. In November 1834 Owen launched a new journal - *The New Moral World* - with the emphasis on unity of interests throughout the country, and in May the following year he became the 'Social Father' of 'The Association of All Classes and All Nations.' The political initiative in working class politics passed decisively into the hands of the Chartist movement with its commitment to aggressive class warfare and its central demand for an extension of the franchise.

In 1839, another of Owen's 'societies' - The Society of Rational Religionists - took a lease on land in Hampshire for a new attempt at forming a community - Queenswood. With a population of nineteen people it fell far short of the ambitions Owen had had for New Harmony - not to mention Texas. The Rational Religionists also established 'Halls of Science', and employed lecturers, who included the atheist and lifelong champion of the co-operative principle, George Jacob Holyoake, the last man to be imprisoned for blasphemy on grounds of atheism. His friend, Charles Southwell who had been imprisoned just before him, was also one of the Rational Religionist lecturers.

Owen, meanwhile, was moving on to other fields.

Spiritualism had sprung up as a movement in North America in 1847, through the mediums, Margaretta and Catherine Fox. It had been introduced to Britain in 1852 by Mrs. Maria Hayden, who converted Owen in 1854, to the dismay of many of his followers. Owen passed on much of what he learned from the spirits - his parents, the Duke of Kent, President Jefferson, Shelley, Byron, some of the Old Testament prophets - but they seemed to bear a remarkable resemblance to his own ideas on the need to reform the world and unite the human race.

Some years after his death, he himself appeared to the medium, Emma Harding Britten, and revealed to her the 'Seven Principles of Spiritualism' later adopted by the Spiritualists National Union. One of the seven principles was 'personal responsibility' - whether we do good or ill is within our power and we may legitimately be given praise or censure depending on the choice we make, which implies that in the spirit world Owen somewhat uncharacteristically changed his mind. All his life he had taught that this notion of personal responsibility was the fundamental error at the root of all our social and moral ills.

In 1902, at the unveiling ceremony of a memorial raised to him in Newtown, his old comrade, G.J. Holyoake, chairman of the memorial committee, said he *'loved the Welsh people and the place of his birth'*. Perhaps the rugged old atheist had Owen's spiritualism in mind when he added: *'and it was well said of him that "his grave was too cold and damp for a soul so warm and true.'"*

Bibliography:

'Life of Wm Allen with selections from his correspondence', Vol II, Philadelphia, 1847

Max Beer: 'A History of British Socialism', London, 2 vols 1919-20

Robert Chambers: 'A Biographical Dictionary of Eminent Scotsmen', Glasgow, Edinburgh and London, Blackie and Son, 1855 (entry for David Dale in Supplement)

Margaret Cole: 'Robert Owen of New Lanark, London', Batchworth Press, 1953

Ian L. Donnachie and George Hewitt: 'Historic New Lanark', Edinburgh, Edinburgh University Press, 1993

C.R. Edson: 'Communism - Communistic Societies', xxii and xxiii (Bereans and Rappites) in Manufacturer and Builder, Volume 24, issue 10, October 1892 and ibid, issue 11, November 1892

'Communism - Owenites', xxvii and xxviii in Manufacturer and Builder, Volume 25, issue 3, March 1893 and ibid, issue 4, April 1893

Alexander Herzen: 'My Past and Thoughts', Berkeley, University of California, 1982

Briony Hudson: 'William Allen' in The Pharmaceutical Journal', Vol 378, 24th March, 2007

George B. Lockwood and W.T. Harris: 'New Harmony Movement', New York (D. Appletoin & Co), 1905

Debbie Matthews (ed): 'America Lane: In the footsteps of William Allen', Haywards Heath, 2001

Robert Dale Owen: 'A Chapter of Autobiography - Robert Owen at New Lanark', The Atlantic Monthly, Vol. 31, issue 185, Boston, March 1873, pp.311-321

'A Chapter of Autobiography - The Social Experiment at New Harmony', The Atlantic Monthly, Vol. 32, issue 190, Boston, August 1873, pp.224-236

'A Chapter of Autobiography - My Experience of Community Life', The Atlantic Monthly, Volume 32, Issue 191, Boston, September 1873, pp. 336-348

Robert Owen: 'The Life of Robert Owen Written by Himself', London, E. Wilson, 1857-1858

A New View of Society, Or, Essays on the Principle of the Formation of the Human Character, and the Application of the Principle to Practice, London 1813 (Essays 1-2) and 1814 (Essays 3-4)

Report to the County of Lanark of a plan for relieving public distress and removing discontent by giving permanent, productive employment to the poor and working class, Glasgow, 1821

Frederick Adolphus Packard: 'The Life of Robert Owen', Philadelphia, Ashmead and Evans, 1866

Sidney Pollard and John Salt (eds): 'Robert Owen - Prophet of the Poor', London, Associated University Press, 1971

William Lucas Sargent: 'Robert Owen and his social philosophy', London, Smith, Elder & Co, 1860

John Saville: 'J.E. Smith and the Owenite Movement' in Sidney Pollard and John Salt op cit, p.115 et seq

Chusichi Tsuzuki: 'Robert Owen and Revolutionary Politics' in Sidney Pollard and John Salt op cit, p.13 et seq.

Chapter Six
David Davies
1818-1890

The career of David Davies demolished the idea that all the influential coal owners were English, his seam in the Rhondda was one of the richest and he came to dominate parts of the coalfield to the extent where he even created his own port of Barry.

Llandinam, where David Davies was born and where he lived all his life, was in a remote part of Wales, lying between Newtown and Llanidloes. The Reports of the Commissioners of Inquiry into the State of Education in Wales, published in 1847, say of Llandinam:

'Llandinam Church School - A school for boys and girls, taught together, by a master, in the gallery of the parish church. Number of scholars, 62. Subjects professed to be taught - the Bible, the Church Catechism, reading, writing, arithmetic, English grammar, geography, and history... The gallery in which the school is held is, as usual, very inconvenient. The church itself is in very bad repair. The school furniture and apparatus are insufficient and in bad repair. The books are miscellaneous, being provided by the children. There are no out-buildings...

The master, a young man, aged 23, is a student at Trinity College, Dublin, and conducts the school during his vacations. He has no assistant and employs no monitors.

The girls receive no instruction in needle-work.'

This is where David Davies received what little formal education he had.

David Davies.

David's father, also called David, was a small-holder, eking out a living on the slopes of the hill Yr Allt Gethin, overlooking the village. He lived in a traditional Welsh long house called Draintewion, *'the place of the thick brambles'*. By profession he was a sawyer, taking commissions for sawing timber, and it was as a sawyer that his eldest son began to make a local name for himself, both for his strength and capacity for hard work, and for his ability to assess trees for the timber that they would yield. By 1841 the family had moved to a larger property, Neuadd fach, near the turnpike road that ran between Llanidloes and Newtown.

David Davies' career as a contractor began when Thomas Penson, County Surveyor of Denbighshire and Montgomeryshire employed him to build a bridge across the Severn at Llandinam, the first cast iron bridge in Montgomeryshire. The work was completed in 1846. Penson was impressed and gave him further contracts including, in 1850, a contract to build the Smithfield in Oswestry which was where he met Thomas Savin, the Oswestry draper who was to be his partner at the beginning of his railway building career. Also in 1850 he moved to a bigger farm, Gwernerin, 240 acres at the foot of the old hill-fort of Cefyn Carnedd, and in 1851 he married Margaret Jones of Llanfair Caerinion, near Welshpool, a fellow Calvinistic Methodist despite her parents' staunch commitment to the Anglican church. They would only have one child, Edward Davies, born in 1852. Edward would be the father of Lord Davies, Chairman of the Welsh National Opera, and of the Davies sisters of Gregynog, who gave an outstanding collection of French Impressionist paintings to the Welsh National Museum. Their grandfather was to be an important man in a wide range of fields but generally speaking the arts were not among them.

On Friday 28th September 1855 the *Shrewsbury Chronicle* carried an advertisement for the tender for the construction of the Llanidloes and Newtown railway. Seven tenders were submitted and the lowest came from David Davies. The projector of the Newtown-Llanidloes railway, George Hammond Whalley, of Ruabon in Denbighshire, envisaged it as part of a line that would stretch from Manchester to Milford Haven in Pembrokeshire. Work on the Llanidloes project was in the event deliberately delayed by Whalley in the hopes of joining up with another link in the Manchester and Milford chain, a line from Oswestry to Newtown. The first sod of the Oswestry-Newtown line was turned in August 1857 but through 1858 both lines ran into financial difficulties and work ground to a halt. Davies in partnership with Thomas Savin turned to another project, the Vale of Clwyd railway in the North, linking Rhyl, on the already established Chester-Holyhead railway, to Denbigh. Work began in August 1857 and the line - the first completed by Davies - was opened in October 1858. In November, with the Newtown-Llanidloes line still in suspension, Davies and Savin began work on a line between Newtown and Machynlleth.

By this time the Newtown-Llanidloes line had a new engineer, Benjamin Piercy, who was to play an important role in Davies' railway successes. Work began again at the beginning of 1859 and was finished quickly so that the line - the first he began but the second to be completed - opened, to great excitement in May 1859. The line passed through Llandinam and at a banquet given there by the contractors, the workers presented the sons of David Davies and Thomas Savin - respectively five and six years of age - with gold watches. In Llanidloes a banner was raised by the Lion Hotel proclaiming *'Welcome, Whalley, Champion of our Rights'*. In a speech at the opening ceremony, Anne Warburton Owen, one of the largest landowners of the region, suggested *'that the iron road is destined to act beneficently in the humanising of nations next only to Christianity itself.'*

The next project to be started was a further stage of the Mid-Wales line, aiming to link Llanidloes to Llandovery, passing by Rhayadar. The ambition of the company could be seen by its name - the Manchester, Liverpool, Swansea and Milford Haven Junction Railway. Behind it was the dream of opening up Milford Haven as the centre for a great transatlantic traffic. The £36,300 necessary to make an application to Parliament was put up by Davies and Savin and one wonders if Davies wasn't being seduced by Savin's grandiose ideas. There was, however, a quarrel with Whalley who was ousted from his chairmanship of the company by proxy votes wielded by Davies and Savin. An element in the confrontation may have been that Whalley was thinking primarily in terms of passengers while Davies and Savin were thinking primarily in terms of freight. In the event the extension from Llanidloes was not built by Davies and Savin and instead of heading west towards Llandovery, it moved eastward towards Builth Wells and Three Cocks.

Davies and Savin were now about to take on the daunting project of the Oswestry-Newtown line. This was in suspension largely because the company that had begun it was overcome with debt. There was no prospect of Davies and Savin being paid for the work and between them they had to raise £45,000 to settle outstanding debts to enable the work to begin. The arrangement was that instead of cash they would receive shares and debentures - their remuneration would depend on the success of the project.

Davies and Piercy were also taken up with the very challenging job of the line from Llanidloes to Machynlleth, a line that passed through the Cambrian mountains with an especially difficult passage at Talerddig where, to quote Herbert Williams' account. The passage, of about 400 yards, with walls on either side 115 feet high according to an account in the *Shrewsbury Chronicle*, took two years to complete and helped to establish Piercy's reputation as an engineer of international importance - much of his most important work was to be done in Italy, France and India.

But while Davies was working on the line to Machynlleth, Savin was planning a further development - an ambitious line following the coast from Aberystwyth to Portmadoc at the beginning of the Lleyn peninsula and then even further to Porth Dinllaen on the North side of the peninsula. The ports along the way would become tourist resorts and the railway company would offer holidays all inclusive of travel and accommodation. It seemed to Davies an absurdly quixotic project. The result was a protracted separation, made more bitter than it need have been by the intervention, on Savin's side, of George Hammond Whalley. It was a sad separation since there is something rather attractive about the alliance between the poetic dreamer Savin and the no-nonsense man of the people, Davies.

Savin set to work together with Piercy, and a line pushing north of Aberystwyth was constructed, passing round the formidable obstacle of the mouth of the river Dovey, where it connected with Machynlleth, and reaching up as far as Pwllheli, on the south side of the Lleyn peninsula. But after a period of exhilarating effort, Savin was bankrupted, together with many other over-ambitious entrepreneurs in a period of easy credit through the collapse of the Overend and Gurney Bank in February 1866.

By 1864, Davies had built four railways - in order of completion Vale of Clwyd, Llanidloes-Newtown, Oswestry-Newtown, Newtown-Machynlleth. As a result of the split with Savin he was no longer involved with the Llanidloes-Newtown or Oswestry-Newtown companies, though the Oswestry-Newtown took a lease on the line to Machynlleth which as a result had Savin's trains running along it. Davies was now a rich man and began buying up property round Llandinam. In 1862 he went on a trip to Sardinia accompanying Piercy who drew up a scheme for a railway system which was eventually to be completed in 1881. Davies built himself a large mansion, Broneirion, overlooking the Severn Valley, with a view of the Bethel chapel and of the station on the Llanidloes-Newtown line. It was completed in 1864. Davies never seems to have considered living anywhere other than Llandinam.

His career in railways was not yet ended. He was still to build the railway in the South West of Wales which connects Pembroke Dock and Tenby to the great

South Wales Railway (the railway that connects Carmarthen, Swansea, Cardiff and Newport before passing into England). This was completed in 1866. Then there was the line from Pencader through Lampeter to Aberystwyth, finished in 1867. And finally, in 1871, the little line from Caersws, on the Newtown-Machynlleth line, to service the lead mines in Van. The Van railway ran through some of his own recently purchased land. But by that time he was deeply involved in the project for which he is best remembered - the Ocean Coal Co. Ltd.

The Welsh coal industry had developed in conjunction with the exploitation of various metals - copper, lead and, most importantly, iron. With the development of the 'hot blast' technique from 1828 onwards it became possible to use the anthracite coal of the southern valleys rather than coke to smelt iron. The first large scale coal mines in this region served the great ironworks of the Guest family at Dowlais and the Crawshay family in Cyfarthfa, both near Merthyr Tydfil, and the ironworks owned by John Stuart, the second Marquis of Bute, in the Rhymney Valley. These became major producers of railway tracks throughout the world. In the early days, prior to the 1830s, the export of coal had passed exclusively through the Monmouthshire canal to Newport but with the opening of the railways and of the docks at Cardiff the export of coal became possible on a much larger scale. The coal in the valleys was 'steam' - relatively smoke-free-coal which was more suitable for use in steam engines than the smokey coal being produced in the main English centre of Newcastle-on-Tyne. In the 1850s, the Cynon Valley was the major centre for coal production. Coal was being exploited in the Rhondda Valley from 1815 onwards by Walter Coffin, later M.P. for Cardiff, but he himself had little confidence in its future. He opposed the building of a railway in the valley, believing that canal and road were sufficient for what could, realistically, be produced.

It was assumed that the Rhondda coal was too deep for exploitation. With the development of steam power, however, this was changing and, envisaging the possibility of future exploitation, the ironmaster Crawshay Bailey, nephew of Richard Crawshay in Cyfarthfa, had bought up large properties in the Northern part of the valley. In 1864 Davies applied to Bailey for a lease on a plot of land in the Rhondda. Herbert Williams tells us that Bailey's first reaction was to say - he did not enjoy dealing with 'speculators and adventurers'. Williams suggests that Bailey was just being playful - he must have recognised that Davies was the man to exploit the valley. However Davies was known mainly for building small single track railways in isolated parts of Wales and accepting to be paid in debentures - guaranteed interest bonds. It was a field depending on easy credit and dubious securities in which a spirit of speculation and adventure was rife and that was the light in which Davies himself saw his own partner, Savin.

The lease was signed in September 1864. Bailey drove an exceptionally hard bargain. Once coal was found, he required a rent of £1,500, rising to £2,000 a year for sixty years and royalties of 8d for every 2,520 lb of coal taken from the first mines. But for a while it looked as though his suspicions that no good would come of dealing with Davies would be justified. Two shafts were dug but there was no sign of coal. The story has it that Davies said to his men: *'Well boys, I am sorry to tell you that I cannot go on here any longer. I am sorry for I believe there is some grand coal here and that we are close to it.'* They then promised to work for him for a further week for nothing. On Friday 9th March 1866 one of the finest seams of coal in the world was struck in the Maindy pit at a depth of 220 yards. The story of the 'Ocean Merthyr' collieries had begun.

The Maindy pit began production in May 1866 but the event was little remarked in the confusion that followed, in the same month, the collapse of the Overend and Gurney bank.

This major event in the financial history of the United Kingdom followed a period of intense activity by Crawshay Bailey's 'speculators and adventurers', encouraged by a government fully committed to the ideal of 'free trade'. In the 1850s a series of government acts had established the idea of the limited liability company, under which shareholders - the national owners of an enterprise - were only liable in the event of a collapse to lose the cost of their investment. Under a system of unlimited liability they would be liable collectively for the whole debts of the collapsed enterprise. 'Limited liability' was a great encouragement to shareholding and therefore helped to produce an era of easily available credit and therefore of enterprise, judicious or injudicious. Credit was supplied by the new institution of finance companies who lent money much more freely than traditional moneylenders and at much higher rates of interest. The principle of limited liability encouraged them to take risks which the money lenders would never have dared.

The Overend and Gurney collapse spelled ruin as we have seen for Thomas Savin but not for Davies, and this has been seen as proof that Davies was right to break the connection and to see Savin's North West coast line as a quixotic and foolish adventure. Davies too, however, could have been broken by the Overend and Gurney collapse. Largely because of his investment in the Rhondda, he reckoned he was some £70,000 in the red. Now that coal had been found, however, his security was good - much better than it would have been if he had still been confined to railways. Hence the telegram from George Rae, general manager of the North and South Wales bank in Liverpool (in some ways at the time the capital of Wales): *'Go on STOP we will back you up STOP'.*

Four new pits after Maindy were opened in Davies's lifetime and by 1887 the enterprise had become so big that it was decided to form a public company to take over the business. The new company was called the 'Ocean Coal Company Limited' and David Davies was chairman. He guided the fortunes of the company until his death in 1890 and output rose from under 10,000 tons in the first year of production to nearly 1.75 million tons in the year of his death. A community of 20,000 people derived its means of existence from the great enterprise which he had created.

Davies often claimed that, given his background, he had a special insight into the feelings and aspirations of working men, and that these in no way contradicted his own feelings and aspirations as a great coal-owner. This became a major theme in his political career.

He first stood for Parliament in 1865, as liberal candidate for the county seat in Cardiganshire (there was also a borough seat for Cardigan). This election returned a liberal majority in Wales and marked the end of Tory domination but Davies himself lost, to his own surprise (*'It is an extraordinary thing. I am seldom beaten'*) and would have to wait until 1874 before he was elected, unopposed, for the Cardigan boroughs seat. On that occasion he said that he had been beaten in 1865 because he had been regarded as *'one of a class who were not thought respectable enough to be sent to Parliament'* but now *'it was admitted by nearly everyone that the working man had a perfect right to be represented in the House of Commons'*.

This idea that Davies was a representative of the 'working man' may have sounded oddly in the Rhondda valley coalfields where he was involved in a series of major confrontations with the rapidly growing trade union movement. In 1871 the coal-owners, in response to the depression that followed the end of the American civil war, resolved to cut wages by 5%. The result was a major strike organised by the Amalgamated Association of Miners, formed in Lancashire in 1869. The strike began in June and, after a period of terrible suffering, including the attempt to use strike breakers and the expulsion of miners from their homes; it was ended by arbitration in August. It was a victory for the strikers who obtained an immediate two and a half per cent pay increase, with a ten per cent increase the following February. But it was also a lesson to the coal owners. One of the reasons for the strikers' success was the solidarity of workers who agreed to continue working at the reduced rate but were willing to share their wages and sometimes their homes with the strikers. In 1873, the Monmouthshire and South Wales Coal Owners' Association was formed, representing some seventy-five percent of the total coal output of the region. This enabled the owners to confront trouble in a more unified manner. Its strength was revealed in the great dispute at the beginning of 1875 which followed a ten per cent wage cut, when the owners, Davies among them, organised a lockout preventing working miners from helping the strike. The result in April was a humiliating defeat for the workers, forced to accept a twelve and a half per cent pay cut.

At the same time, the principle was agreed of the 'sliding scale' by which wages would fluctuate according to the price of coal. The credit for devising this has been disputed between William Thomas Lewis, later Lord Merthyr, and Hussey Vivian, later Lord Swansea. Davies himself was doubtful about it, arguing that there was no necessary connection between the price of coal and the ability of the owners to pay wages. Davies declared in the context of the negotiations that he himself favoured unions in principle *'because it was easier to meet delegates than men individually.'* Nonetheless, the Amalgamated Union, which had boasted 45,000 members in Wales in 1873, was bankrupted and forced to dissolve.

It was replaced in the Rhondda by the Cambrian Miners Association whose full time organiser from 1877 was William Abraham, nicknamed 'Mabon' - the bard - because of his eloquence and fine singing voice. Mabon was a Calvinistic Methodist and a Liberal - he was elected in 1885 as the M.P. for Rhondda West. He believed in a community of interest between labour and capital and sat with Davies on the joint committee of owners' and workers' representatives set up to administer the sliding scale agreement. In 1879, when the Coal Owners Association introduced a 69 hour week instead of the 54 hour week that had been usual since 1869, Davies withdrew. He also introduced his own 'sliding scale', more generous than that of the Association. Believing that, in this respect, he had acted with generosity, he was very offended when his sliding scale was contested by the men in 1882.

It may be questioned whether, after the very earliest period of prospecting for coal, Davies had much personally to do with his collieries. From 1874 to 1886 he was a Member of Parliament, albeit a Parliament which assumed that most of its members, unpaid, had other lives to lead elsewhere. He was enjoying the life of a great landlord in the area round Llandinam and was very active in the life of the Calvinistic Methodist church, helping to finance a huge programme of church building. But his best known philanthropic venture was the support he gave to the University College, Wales, established in 1872 in Aberystwyth. Through this project he found himself once again entangled in the dreams of Thomas Savin.

The idea of a university for Wales had long been under discussion, especially by a group of Welshmen based in London. But it was a half hearted, unconvinced discussion, motivated by the feeling that since both Scotland and Ireland had universities, Wales should have one too. There was no very clear idea exactly what purpose such a university should fulfil. There was already a college for Anglican clergymen established in Lampeter, opened in 1827. The Presbyterians had a college in Carmarthen, originally established in 1704. A Congregationalist college had been established in Abergavenny in 1757 and had then wandered through Oswestry, Wrexham, Llanfyllin and Newtown before finally settling in Brecon in 1828. Should a Welsh University be an amalgam of the existing theological colleges? Was it a priority when there was no very adequate system of secondary education in existence?

What seems to have decided the issue was the sudden availability, at a very reasonable price, of a suitable building in Aberystwyth. The building in question was the Castle Hotel, built by Thomas Savin as part of his scheme for opening up tourism on the West Coast of Wales, on the site of the old Castle House, built by John Nash for Uvedale Price, theorist of the 'picturesque', in 1794. Savin saw Aberystwyth as the 'Brighton of Wales' and the Castle Hotel resembles nothing so much as a Gothic version of Nash's Brighton pavilion.

Savin had spent £80,000 on the hotel which was still unfinished at the time of his bankruptcy. It was now offered at £15,000 but eventually sold to the committee for £10,000. But they still had a lot of money to raise before the project could begin and they still seem to have had a very confused idea of what role it was supposed to fulfil.

The college opened in October 1872 with two professors, one in classics and one in natural sciences. It was at the opening reception that Davies, whose previous contributions had been unexceptional, offered an immediate £1,000 to be followed by £2,000 in

Aberystwyth University established in 1872 as University College Wales.

scholarships. In the 1880s a government report was published in favour of two Welsh colleges, one in North Wales and one in South Wales. It seemed that Aberystwyth was doomed when Bangor was chosen as the site of the college in North Wales. It was saved by another accident. In 1885 a fire swept through Savin's building, gutting the whole north wing. The outpouring of public support was such that the government agreed to give it an annual grant of £4,000, putting it on the same level as the new colleges in Cardiff and Bangor. Davies wanted to take the opportunity to move to a new site but the sentimental affection that had grown up for 'Savin's folly' proved too great for him.

By this time Davies had a reputation in the House of Commons for a style of plain untutored rhetoric that was both refreshing and rather irritating and repetitive. It is not easy to see why he should have been so anxious to pursue a parliamentary career. He was certainly part of the process by which Welsh nonconformity asserted itself within the Liberal Party but he was to be out of sympathy with the Welsh radicalism that began to appear in the 1880s with such figures as Tom Ellis and Stuart Rendel. His first speech was, understandably enough, to do with temperance, one of the great themes of his life. It was an attack on a proposal to reduce the price of beer by reducing the tax on malt:

'While the men were away drinking in the public house the roof of the working was cracking and the buttresses were giving way... the fact was that three out of every four men who were killed lost their lives from this cause - irregularity of working...'

Before dismissing this as the special pleading of an employer anxious to shift the blame for pit accidents on to his employees, we should remember that the dangers of excessive drinking were also an obsession with Robert Owen. In general, however, it seemed to be Davies's style to use his own experience of having been a working man to argue against measures that were designed to improve the conditions of the poor.

Davies's last important venture, however, involved a long hard parliamentary battle. The coal potential in the valleys had been largely unlocked by the initiative of the Second Marquis of Bute in building Cardiff Docks and the Taff Valley Railway. The Second Marquis died in 1848 the year after the birth of his son, John Patrick Crichton Stuart, third Marquis of Bute, who succeeded him on his coming of age in 1868. The third Marquis continued his father's work of extending the Cardiff docks but not fast enough for the huge trade that was now flowing through them from the valleys. In 1874 he had secured parliamentary permission to build a new dock at Roath but had been slow in following it up. In 1880, William Thomas Lewis, who had acted as mineral agent for the Bute family and managed their pit at Treherbert, became acting trustee of the Bute Estates, responsible for the docks. He proposed increasing the charges at the new Roath docks. This prompted Davies to push for the construction of a new docks at Barry, insisting that the volume of traffic was such that Barry would not in any way harm the interests of Cardiff, or indeed of Newport or Swansea. The bill to approve the new docks was passed against fierce opposition from the Bute family interest in 1884.

On the back of this triumph Davies was returned to parliament in the 1885 election, when his posters proclaimed him to be *'the working man's friend'*. He was however returned as a Liberal out of sympathy with the policy of the Liberal government on a number of issues that were popular with his own constituents - most obviously Home Rule for Ireland, but also the proposals for land reform in Ireland. Gladstone introduced his Home Rule bill in April, 1886 but was defeated through a rebellion in his own party. Davies was among the ninety-three liberals who voted against it. Parliament was

dissolved and a new election held in July. Davies was now, perhaps for the first time in his life, feeling in poor health and was tempted not to stand but was possibly too much aware that that was what many of his erstwhile supporters would have wanted. In the event he stood and was defeated, albeit very narrowly, by an unknown English lawyer, Bowen Rowlands, who supported Home Rule. Davies's old friend, John Gibson, editor of the *Cambrian News*, backed Rowlands as did the powerful Calvinistic Methodist ministers and the students at Aberystwyth. The boisterous opposition he experienced at the hands of the students put an end to his support for the college.

The Barry Docks opened in July 1889. Davies was present as Vice-Chairman of the newly formed Ocean Coal Company. Within a few years the traffic at Barry would exceed the traffic at the Bute Docks in Cardiff. The Ocean Coal Company had the largest output of any firm in South Wales - in 1893 it was producing one million tons more than its nearest rival. In the winter of 1889-90, however, Davies's health was declining sharply. He died in July 1890.

His grandson also David Davies was created the first Baron Davies in 1932. He raised and commanded the 14th Battalion the Royal Welch Fusiliers at home and in France until 1916 when he was appointed Parliamentary Secretary to David Lloyd George. His name is invariably connected with his two main public interests The Welsh Campaign against Tuberculosis and the International Crusade for World Peace. In 1911 together with his sisters the Misses Gwendoline and Margaret Davies of Gregyneg Hall he founded the King Edward VII Welsh National Memorial Association which under his direction developed into a nationwide scheme with many sanatoria and hospitals. From 1919

Statue of David Davies outside Barry Docks offices, Barry.

he was tireless in the pursuit of international peace. He was the founder of the League of Nations Union and wanted it to control the International Police Force. In November 1938 one of his ambitions was realised in the completion of the Temple of Peace and Health in Cathays Park, Cardiff. For many years he was the President of University College in Aberystwyth and amongst his numerous benefactions was the endowment of the Woodrow Wilson Chair of International Politics. This was the first of its kind in Great Britain. He was also President and a generous benefactor of the National Library of Wales.

Bibliography:
Blue Books of 1847 - texts available at the National Library of Wales website - http://www.llgc.org.uk/index.php?id=295
George Borrow: 'Wild Wales - its people, language and scenery', London and Glasgow, Collins, 1974 (First published London, John Murray, 1862).
Charles Frederick Cliffe: 'The Book of North Wales - scenery, antiquities, highways and byeways, lakes, streams, and railways', London, 1850.
Charles Frederick Cliffe: 'The Book of South Wales - the Bristol Channel, Monmouthshire, and the Wye, a companion and guide to the railways, watering places, shores, scenery, antiquities, unexplored regions, mineral districts, towns, and other objects of interest throughout the southern division of the principality', London, 1847
John Davies: 'A History of Wales', London, Allen Lane The Penguin Press, 2003
E.L. Ellis: 'The University College of Wales, Aberystwyth, 1872-1972', Cardiff, University of Wales Press, 1972
D. Emrys Evans: 'The University of Wales - a historical sketch', Cardiff, University of Wales Press, 1953
C.P. Gasquoine: 'The Story of the Cambrian - a biography of a railway', Wrexham and Oswestry, 1922
R.W. Kidner: 'The Mid-Wales Railway', Usk, the Oakwood Press, 2003
Herbert Spencer: 'Railway Morals and Railway Policy' from Herbert Spencer: Essays - Scientific, Political and Speculative, vol iii, London, 1891
James Taylor: 'Limited Liability on Trial - the commercial crisis of 1966 and its aftermath', paper from the University of Kent available on the internet
David Williams: 'A History of Modern Wales', London, John Murray, 1962
Gareth Williams: 'Tribute to the Rhondda' available on the Internet at http://www.therhondda.co.uk/
Gwyn A. Williams: 'Architect of Empire', New Welsh Review, no 18, (Vol V no 2), Autumn 1992, p.42
Herbert Williams: 'Davies the Ocean - Railway King and Oil Tycoon', Cardiff, University of Wales Press, 1991

Chapter Seven
The Morgans
of J.S. Morgan, J.P. Morgan, Morgan Grenfell, Morgan Harjes, Morgan Stanley and Morgan Guaranty

John Pierpont Morgan.

John Pierpont Morgan was one of the great robber barons alongside such men of influence as Carnegie and Rockefeller. The family came out of Wales but there is no direct evidence that he was concerned with his Welsh ancestry. It just seems a remarkable fact that out of a family of Welsh harness makers should come a banker who at one time held the destiny of America and its economic fortunes in his hands. He was a huge figure on the American political and economical scene of his time and all over the world. People bowed to his financial opinion and acumen. He was a larger than life character who loved the good things of life and was a great collector of many works of art and literature. We are left with the John Pierpont Morgan Library in New York which houses some of his collection and his legacy to New York.

John Pierpont Morgan Library in New York

Here is his story.

The great Morgan banking family of America has its roots in Wales. Young Miles Morgan came from a family which was based in Glamorgan in the 1660s. Miles was born in Llandaff, although his father moved to Bristol where he carried on his business of harness making. It is a remarkable story, how a small family from Wales became one of the biggest banking dynasties in the world. It showed what a land of opportunity America was and how minorities could take advantage of this.

In 1636, Miles and his two brothers, John and James, left an England torn by arguments over taxes and religion and sailed for the fledgling Puritan colony of Massachusetts. Miles was one of the original purchasers of land around Springfield, Mass in 1636. He prospered in Springfield, buying more land with profits from his farming and he was made surveyor of highways and sergeant of militia. In this capacity he fought the uprising of the Wampanoag Indians, and was rewarded when the attempt of the Indians to recover their territory had been put down. He continued to prosper and the Morgan family were established as one of the pillars of the community of Massachusetts.

Nathaniel, Miles' son, lived until 1752. His life was also prosperous if undistinguished. His son, Joseph became a soldier fighting against the French, only just surviving a famous massacre at Fort William Henry in 1757. He fought against the British in 1776 and when the war was coming to an end he was appointed to a special commission to consider the proposed form of government for Massachusetts and to draw up the state constitution. He was a farmer but his son, also called Joseph, developed a lively interest in the business side of things, travelling widely, buying and selling goods and land. He became a man of wealth and in 1812, he joined the Washington Benevolent Society in Northampton. At the same time he set himself up as a moneylender. Here was the start of the great Morgan banking tradition.

Joseph's involvement with the Washington Benevolent Society prefigures what was to become a major theme in the Morgan family's adventures. Although notionally a charitable society devoted to helping underprivileged boys, the Benevolent Society was actually a political movement, largely operating in secret and dedicated to the ideals of Alexander Hamilton, Secretary of the Treasury in the government established by George Washington under the new constitution in 1789. Hamilton argued for the 'federalist' position, also favoured by Washington, which entailed the building up of a strong unified country that would be able to rival Great Britain but would also resemble it.

As part of his programme, Hamilton in 1791 established a central bank with a twenty year charter. The bank was modelled on the Bank of England and four-fifths of its capital came from private investors. It was opposed by Thomas Jefferson on the grounds that it undermined the agrarian interest and concentrated financial power in the hands of a few very wealthy men at the centre. The period of the bank's charter came to an end in 1811 under the presidency of James Madison, who had changed from support for the Federalist position to supporting Jefferson. In 1812, in the context of the Napoleonic wars pitting the British against France, Madison went to war with the United Kingdom, which was trying to prevent the U.S. from trading with France. Although the Americans eventually won, Washington was sacked and the White House burnt to the ground in 1814.

The federalists of the Washington Benevolent Society supported what they saw as British as opposed to revolutionary French values, including a strong centralised financial power controlled by an aristocratic elite not subject to democratic control.

On 18th July 1813, Joseph's only son, Junius Spencer Morgan, was born. In 1834, he announced his engagement to Juliet Pierpont, the daughter of the minister of the Old Hollis Street church in Boston and in July of that year, he went to New York to learn the banking business. His social acceptability was increased by his marriage. Juliet Pierpont's father John was a well known Unitarian minister, one of the founders in 1825 of the American Unitarian Association. He was also a prominent campaigner against slavery, and a poet (his son, James Pierpont, was the author of the song 'Jingle Bells').

J.P. Morgan in his earlier years.

In the summer of 1854, Junius Morgan and his family went to London. Here he went into partnership with George Peabody, who had originally gone to London in 1837 to sell interest-bearing bonds on behalf of the state of Maryland. When the American Civil War broke out, Peabody and Morgan attached their colours to the Northern Standard. In this respect Junius was continuing his father's commitment to the Federalist cause. The Northern, anti-slavery, side favoured more central control in opposition to the states rights arguments supported by the South. When the Republican Party was formed in 1854 on an anti-slavery programme, it attracted the support of the major North Eastern industrial interests, seeing the possibilities of a great unified power that would be strengthened by the new territories being opened up in the West through the further suppression of the Indians and the spread of the railways.

Peabody and Morgan held considerable quantities of the securities, the new 'greenbacks' - a paper money not supported by gold - issued by the North under Lincoln. This investment paid off handsomely after the Northern victory. George Peabody was known as a generous benefactor in England, where he financed the

Peabody Homes for London's working poor and also in the U.S. where the Peabody Education Fund financed a huge scheme for schools in the South devastated after the Civil War. Peabody retired in 1864 and George Peabody and Co. became J.S. Morgan and Company, the foremost American banking firm in Europe and, crucially, the principal bank used by English interests wanting to invest in the United States. Later, in 1910, the bank was renamed Morgan Grenfell.

The Northern victory in the civil war had been followed by an immense expansion of the power of the industrial interests concentrated in the North-East and the virtual elimination of the old Jeffersonian ideal of an agrarian, small producer democracy. Although the break-up of the large plantations in the South and the opening up of the West still seemed to provide many opportunities for small scale farming, in practice the small men became increasingly dependent on the great railroad, steel and oil interests. They in turn needed capital and the major source of reliable, gold-backed capital was still Great Britain which put the J.S. Morgan bank in a very strong position.

Junius's son, John Pierpont Morgan, began his banking career with George Peabody in 1857 in London before moving to Duncan Sherman and Company, Peabody's representatives in New York. In the summer of 1871, he set up a new partnership with the Drexel family of Philadelphia. The idea was his father's - Pierpont had been considering giving up business altogether because of poor health and 'ennui'. At about this time, Drexel, through his agency, Drexel, Harjes & Co. in France, arranged the loan that enabled the French government to pay reparations to Germany imposed after the Franco-Prussian war. Astonishingly, the loan was repaid by the French within three years.

In 1869, before the connection with Drexel, J.P. Morgan gained control of the Albany and Susquehanna railway. Essentially he was saving it from the clutches of rival entrepreneurs who had launched a bid opposed by railway's president, but this was the begining of a long connection with the railway business which eventually, by 1900, left him in control of some 5,000 miles of track. He gave his name to the process of 'morganisation' - the process by which the bank would take over control of companies that were in financial difficulties. In 1889 and 1890 he organised two conferences among the most powerful railroad owners aimed to rationalise the industry and stop competition between them. This, of course, amounted to the creation of an anti-competitive 'cartel'.

Morgan's name was to become closely associated with that of the oil giant, John D. Rockefeller. Rockefeller had established a model of this way of operating in the so-called 'Cleveland massacre' of 1871-72. He had used his contracts with oil transporting railways to create impossible conditions for his rivals and as a result he had gained control of 22 of the 26 oil refineries in Cleveland. By 1879 his 'Standard Oil' controlled some four-fifths of the refining interests in the United States.

In the 1870s Morgan supported the experiments of Thomas Edison and his Edison Illuminating Company. Morgan's house in Madison Avenue was the first electrically lit private residence in New York. In 1891-92, he arranged the merger of Edison General Electric and the Thomson-Houston Electric Company to form the giant General Electric.

With the death of his father and of Anthony Drexel in 1890 and 1893 respectively, John Pierpont became the sole manager of the London and Paris operations. It was in this period that he pulled off his most ambitious commercial and industrial projects, and also became an important player in U.S. politics.

In the 1890s, the federalist, centralising tendency was faced with a challenge from a 'populist' tendency associated with the names of John P. Altgeld, governor of Illinois, and William Jennings Bryan, presidential candidate for the Democratic Party in 1896. The populists wanted cheaper, more easily available credit, either through a 'fiat' currency (the government printing paper money freely according to its assessment of what the market could bear) or through a currency based on silver as well as on gold. Morgan, whose power was largely based on his access to gold, put large sums of money into supporting the presidency of the Democrat Grover Cleveland, who remained faithful to the gold standard; and then, when Cleveland was replaced as Democratic standard bearer by Jennings Bryan, he heavily funded the successful campaign of the Republican, William McKinley.

Until 1899 Morgan had been largely involved in organising loans from Britain but in 1900 he secured for the first time a large loan from the U.S. to Britain in order to finance the Boer War - in which he had an interest since at stake was control of the gold mines recently discovered in the Transvaal. This could be seen as the beginning of the process by which the relative positions of Britain and the United States were reversed.

In 1904, J.P. Morgan & Co. and the former firm of Drexel, Harjes & Co - now Morgan, Harjes & Co. - in Paris arranged the purchase of the Panama Canal project, paying for it with U.S. government gold. It was a complicated operation. The Panama canal project had long been abandoned by its former French promoters and Congress in 1899 had voted to support an alternative route running through Nicaragua. The Panama project also required a spurious revolt in the area to separate it from Colombia.

Morgan was already heavily involved in the steel industry when, in 1900, he merged his own interests with those of Andrew Carnegie and others to form the United States Steel Corporation, at the time the largest combination in the world and the first company to have a capital of over a billion dollars. In 1902 he bought the Leyland Line of Atlantic steamships, which became the International Merchant Marine Co. and then the White Star Line, which built the Titanic. Morgan had a private suite on the Titanic and was due to sail on its maiden voyage in 1912 though in the event his failure to do so was of little benefit since he died in 1913.

There were many political efforts to control Morgan's activities. The huge monopoly holding company he formed together with his railroad rival, Edward S. Harriman - the Northern Securities Company - was opposed by the Republican President, Theodore Roosevelt, and broken up by a Supreme Court decision in 1904. In 1907, he combined with Rockefeller to stop the efforts of a copper magnate, F. Augustus Heinze, to break into the New York banking business. The result was the collapse of Heinze's banks and a disastrous crash which wiped out the savings of millions of people throughout the U.S. Morgan, champion of money strictly tied to gold, then 'saved' the situation by issuing $200 million in clearinghouse certificates - effectively a privately issued 'fiat' (or 'paper') money backed only by his own, albeit very considerable, credit.

In November 1910, a meeting of some of the most powerful interests in the U.S. was held under his auspices, in conditions of great secrecy, to plan the establishment of a central bank along lines similar to the privately owned German Reichsbank. Since the 1840s the federal finances had been held in 'sub-treasuries' directly under government control but, with a host of different banks chartered both at state level and at federal level with the right to issue their own money, the means of developing a policy for the supply of money at the federal level were very limited. What the industrial interests wanted was the ability to rationalise the supply of money and to set interest rates on a federal basis while keeping the whole process under their own control and out of the hands of the democracy.

The plan was opposed by the Republican President William Howard Taft who had, as a principled conservative, proved more effective in his opposition to trusts than the supposedly liberal, 'trust-busting', Theodore Roosevelt. As a result the banking interests financed their old enemy Theodore Roosevelt to stand against Taft, both within the Republican Convention and afterwards, when Taft had won but Roosevelt launched the new, short-lived, Progressive Party. The Progressive Party split the Republican vote and secured the election of the Democrat, Woodrow Wilson, whom the banking interests had also backed. The prize, in December 1913, though Morgan, who died in March of that year, did not live to see it, was the Federal Reserve Act. Since it established twelve regional reserve banks it did not look like a central bank but it functioned as a unity and had the all-important right to act as a lender of last resort and to set the discount rate, used as the reference for all banks when lending to each other as they have to do in order to maintain their own minimum reserve. The economic commentator and historian, Henry C.K. Liu, says of it that it is *an institution owned not by the people and controlled not by democratically elected officials but by political appointees acceptable to private bankers.*

In December 1912 J.P. Morgan had to give evidence to a sub-committee of the House Banking and Currency Committee chaired by Arsène Pujo, one of the numerous attempts in American history to regulate the inevitable tendency of capitalism towards monopoly. The Pujo Commission found that between them the Partners of J.P. Morgan & Co. and the directors of the Morgan-allied First National and National City Banks controlled *'In all, 341 directorships in 112 corporations having aggregate resources or capitalization of $22,245,000,000'.*

The Morgan tradition of centralisation, rationalisation, political manipulation and opposition to government interference with private enterprise was continued by John Pierpont Morgan's son, John Pierpont Morgan Jr., also known as 'Jack' Morgan, who took on his father's mantle in 1913 after experience working in his grandfather's bank, now Morgan Grenfell, in London. Under his leadership, the firm of J.P. Morgan & Co. continued to be a central player in the great events of the First World War, the 'roaring twenties', and the 'Great Crash' of 1929-32, though his efforts to oppose the

'New Deal' of Franklin D. Roosevelt - a distant cousin of Theodore's - were unsuccessful.

His achievement was less spectacular than his father's and we may question if he had as much personal power - his lieutenants, especially Thomas Lamont who would eventually succeed him in 1943, seem to have been very powerful figures in their own right. Nonetheless he did preside over the all-important moment when the U.S.A. was transformed from being a debtor in world financial affairs to a creditor.

In April 1915, Lamont gave a speech to the American Academy of Political and Social Science meeting in Philadelphia, pointing out the opportunity provided by the European war to take control of *'the development of private or semi-public enterprises in South America and other parts of the world which up to date have been commercially financed by Great Britain, France and Germany. If the war continues long enough to encourage us to take such a position, and if we have the resources to grapple with it, then inevitably we shall become a creditor instead of a debtor nation, and such a development would certainly tend to bring about the dollar, instead of the pound sterling, as the international basis of exchange.'*

Lamont argued that the United States could pay off its debts to Britain and France (debts largely negotiated by the Morgan Bank) by financing their side in the war. Wilson initially raised the obvious objection that this would be a violation of the principle of neutrality but he soon gave way. Not only was the money supplied by the U.S. but it was also used to purchase munitions from U.S. firms. By early 1917, however, it was beginning to look as if Germany might win. On 5th March 1917, the American ambassador to England - Walter Hines Page - wrote to Wilson to say that the United States government might have to contribute directly to the financing of the allied war effort which would of course amount to a declaration of war. Burton Hendrick's account of the *'Life and Letters of Walter H. Page'* explains that *'by April 6, 1917, Great Britain had overdrawn her account with J.P. Morgan to the extent of $400,000,000 and had no cash available with which to meet this overdraft. This obligation had been incurred in the purchase of supplies, both for Great Britain and the allied governments; and securities, largely British owned stocks and bonds, had been deposited to protect the bankers. The money was now coming due; if the obligations were not met, the credit of Great Britain in this country would reach the vanishing point.'*

The first $400,000,000 of the 'Liberty Loan' raised for the allies was used to pay off this Morgan debt and afterwards, when in the 1920s the European governments defaulted on their debts to the United States government, the bankers were paid in full.

Wilson's closest adviser at Versailles after the war was Thomas Lamont. Bernard Baruch, chairman of Wilson's War Industries Board, complained that there were so many Morgan men at the conference that it was apparent that they were running the show. The German reparations bill was set at $33 billion, a huge sum but still less than the British and French had hoped for. Morgan was personally involved in the schemes devised when, predictably, Germany defaulted - the Dawes Plan in 1924 and the Young Plan of 1929. Under the Dawes Plan an American consortium organised a loan to help Germany pay, charging 10% for underwriting it. The Young Plan, in the event undermined by the depression and the rise of Hitler, set up a Bank of International

Settlements as an International Central Bank only to be accessed by major bankers, doing for 'the world' what the Federal Reserve had done for the U.S. It was a forerunner of what was later to be the World Bank and the International Monetary Fund.

Morgan was also closely involved in a scheme designed to stabilise the pound and put it back on the gold standard. The scheme was largely worked out between Montague Norman of the Bank of England and Benjamin Strong, President of the Federal Reserve Bank of New York, most powerful of the Federal Reserves. Strong had been formed in the Morgan-dominated Bankers' Trust, and Morgan contributed a large loan to help in the stabilisation of sterling. The effect was to raise the value of sterling and depreciate the dollar, encouraging international investors to invest in the dollar rather than the pound. It was a key moment in the process by which the dollar replaced the pound as the principle medium of international exchange.

The high rate of the pound created difficulties for British industry and contributed to the causes of the 1926 General Strike. The low rate of the dollar and the easy credit it created contributed to the boom years in the United States and thus to the eventual crash. The whole process, and especially the effort to return the pound to the gold standard, was subjected to withering criticism by the British economist, John Maynard Keynes.

Morgan interests were dominant in all the administrations of the 1920s, all of them Republican, but especially that of Herbert Hoover at the time of the crash. Lundberg comments:

'*Morrow* [Dwight D. Morrow, formerly another senior partner at Morgan's. He left when Calvin Coolidge appointed him ambassador to Mexico in 1927] *and Lamont were Hoover's two principal advisers, and shaped the policies of his administration. The essence of Hoover's policy after the stock market tumbled and economic famine stalked the land was to* 'let the depression take its course.' *This was also, by a curious coincidence, the policy of J.P. Morgan & Co. and its newspapers, for the Morgan banks, alone of the nation's banking institutions, were almost 100% liquid, ie, had all their resources in cash or government securities. Every downswing in commodity prices, real-estate values, and securities quotations, enhanced the value of the liquid funds at the disposal of J.P. Morgan & Co, who grew more powerful every day that the nation as a whole became poorer.'* (p.184)

The Wall Street crash and its consequences inevitably produced a strong reaction of hostility to the power of the bankers and this was reflected in the irresistible popularity of F.D. Roosevelt and his 'new deal'. Roosevelt came to power in March 1933 and in May of the same year John Pierpont Morgan Jr. found himself having to give evidence before a Senate Committee whose chief counsel, Ferdinand Pecora, played the role that had been played in 1912 by Arsène Pujo. Morgan Jr., however, had to suffer a humiliation that his father had been spared. At the hearing on June 1st, Charles Leef, publicity agent for the Barnum and Bailey Circus, dumped Lya Graf, a circus performer who stood only 27" tall, into Morgan's lap. The resulting photographs did the tour of the world.

Morgan was also humiliated by the revelation that neither he nor any of his partners had paid any income tax in the years 1931 and 1932. This was basically due to the way in which the American tax system was organised - very substantial sums had been paid during the boom years - but it contributed mightily to the mood that enabled Roosevelt to push through his reforms, which included extensive regulation of the banking industry and of its ability to generate money on the basis of unreliable securities. Morgan was forced to break his bank up into two separate parts - J.P. Morgan & Co. became a straightforward commercial bank while Morgan Stanley was created as an investment bank (Harold Stanley, first chairman of the new bank, was a Morgan partner). According to Charles Geisst:

'Jack Morgan reportedly kept clerks busy simply cutting FDR's picture out of the newspapers so that he would not have to look at the president's face when reading the morning newspapers.' (p.231)

Morgan was involved in the formation of the 'American Liberty League' whose aim was to develop opposition to the Roosevelt reforms. Its chairman was Jouett Shouse, an executive of the Morgan backed General Motors, and its prominent supporters included the Du Pont brothers, associated with Morgan at least since the war, the Morgan lawyer, John W. Davis, Nathan Millar, a director of U.S. Steel and Alfred Sloan, chosen by Morrow while still a Morgan partner as head of General Motors in 1920. Despite great wealth (in 1935 the League raised as much money as the Democratic and Republican Parties combined) it proved in the end to be a very thoroughgoing failure. It supported the Republican candidate, Governor Alf Landon, in 1936, and also, within the Democratic Party, an opposition to Roosevelt under the name, the National Jeffersonian Democrats, which brings us back to old Joseph Morgan and his involvement with the anti-Jeffersonian, pro-Hamiltonian Washington Benevolent Society. The programme was still the same, thoroughly in the tradition of Hamilton, but it was now considered politic to call it 'Jeffersonian'.

In the event, the mood of 1936 was such that Landon's campaign - hopeless in any case - was harmed rather than helped by its perceived association with the big money interests behind the League.

Prior to the election, Morgan's activities had come under the scrutiny of another committee - the Nye Committee on the Investigation of the Munitions Industry, whose report was published in February 1936. This included a radical critique of what Morgan Jr. could well have regarded as his finest achievement - providing the allies with the means by which they could sustain the war and at the same time enabling the United States to overtake the United Kingdom as the financial capital of the world. Where the 1912 Pujo Committee had popularised the term 'money trust', the Nye Committee investigation popularised the term 'merchants of death' though the services of the merchants of death were soon going to be needed again as Roosevelt led the U.S.A. into the Second World War.

Edwin Hoyt, in his sympathetic account of the Morgan enterprise, shows Jack Morgan as effectively giving up the fight against the Roosevelt reforms and retiring into private life. He died on March 12th 1943. The Company became a corporation, eventually the Morgan Guaranty Corporation, the fourth largest bank in America. No Morgan was ever in the top listing of the officials of the new corporation though Henry Sturgis Morgan, Jack Morgan's son, was involved with Morgan Stanley.

The Morgan name lives on without the family. The J.P. Morgan Chase Bank was created in 2000, the year after the repeal of the Glass-Steagall Act, centrepiece of the Roosevelt period's effort to regulate the banks and to keep their different operations separate. It was formed through the merger of J.P. Morgan & Co. with the Chase Manhattan Bank which itself traces its lineage back to the Manhattan Company, founded on the initiative of Alexander Hamilton and Aaron Burr in 1799.

Thus a small family from Wales of the 1660s gave rise to a great banking dynasty which included two men with some title to be considered among the most powerful men in history. There is little evidence that they paid much respect to their Welsh roots, but they were a fact of life and gave them some sort of pull to the home country, even if it was the United Kingdom. It is interesting, too, that a family called Pierpont came over to Breconshire with Bernard Newmarch in the 1060s, but returned to Normandy as they did not like the climate.

Bibliography:

David R. Farber: 'Sloan Rules: Alfred P. Sloan and the Triumph of General Motors', Chicago, University of Chicago, 2002

Charles R. Geisst: 'Wall Street - A history from its beginnings to the fall of Enron', Oxford (OUP) 2004

Burton J. Hendrick: 'The Life and Letters of Walter H. Page', Garden City, NY, 1923

Edwin P. Hoyt: 'The House of Morgan', London, Frederick Muller Ltd, 1968

Henry C.K. Liu: 'Money, Power and Modern Art, Part 1: Ruthless empire builders', Asia Times, 15th December 1904

Ferdinand Lundberg: 'America's 60 Families', Vanguard Press, New York, 1937

Jean Strouse: 'Morgan, American Financier', London, the Harvill Press, 1999

William Morris.

William Morris was one of the great creative artists of the nineteenth-century; he initiated the Arts and Crafts Movement which became a great flowering outflow of the creative arts. He often harked back to his Welsh or Celtic ancestry which he felt not only gave rise to his dark moods but gave rise to his inventiveness and ingenuity. He came into contact with and collected around him a great company of fellow travellers. William was a thinker and a doer on a wide plain that harked back to medieval craftsmanship and the time before urbanisation and industrialisation. He felt the British needed to recapture their spirit and dig deep into their depths to do this; he was in many ways a master Celt who felt inspired by the history of this great country.

The Morris dynasty was essentially Welsh. His grandfather, who came from a small valley of the Upper Severn in the late eighteenth-century, was the first to drop the Welsh 'ap' from his name. William was intrigued by his Welsh roots and loved the sound of the ancient Welsh language. He attributed his dark hue and melancholy quality to his Welshness. In the middle of the 1870s he went out on a tour of Wales and loved places like Towyn in Merionethshire.

But he was born in Essex, on 24th March 1834. His father, also William, was thirty-six years old at the time of his birth, a senior partner in a discount office in the City of London. William Jr. was the third of his parents' surviving children, with two older sisters. There were six more children, who for the most part, unlike William, led a conventional life.

When he was six the family moved to Woodford Hall, a large Georgian mansion next door to Epping Forest. The estate for the most part was self-sufficient and many of their provisions were home produced. William became an avid fisherman on the small river near the house. He learnt at Woodford the value of community and mixing across classes - he liked the cosy kitchen best of all the rooms. William had his own garden, where he was first introduced to the wonderful world of flowers and scents.

In religious terms the Morrises were strictly Evangelical Anglicans. The religion of Morris's childhood was not questioning; it was accepted and he picked up from it many of the images he was to use in later life. He was a great wanderer in the countryside and often rode his pony through it, exploring as he went, becoming very fond of Epping Forest, loving its wildness and vastness and did much in later life to try and protect it. He was always observing and taking in scenes of old rivers and other forms of architecture, and was a great reader of books even from an early age. It is claimed that he had read all Walter Scott's books by the age of seven. He continued to love Scott, especially the romance, the chivalry and the ruggedness.

William Morris Sr. died suddenly in 1847, at the age of fifty. The firm he had been working for suspended business a few days later with huge liabilities and the family lost a substantial amount of money. William Jr. was ever after critical of his father and his perceived obsession with money. Nonetheless for much of his life Morris could always fall back on shares he possessed in the Devon Great Console mine, bought by his father before his death.

In 1848 he went to Marlborough College, in Wiltshire. The school had only been going for five years; there were over 500 boys with plenty of bullying and baiting of the younger boys. Staff morale was low. William detested many of the teaching methods used by Marlborough at this time - the rote learning and the cramming. But the school did have its advantages. There was little supervision out of the schoolroom, few organised games and, as a consequence, boys roamed around all over the town and countryside, and there was a decent library. He learned to appreciate books and would read much about the locality before he set out on his travels. William Jr. also enjoyed the school chapel, where he appreciated the music and could feel apart from the other boys.

In November 1851 there was a famous 'Great Rebellion' against the authorities at Marlborough. Morris does not seem to have played a great role in it, despite his own lifelong anti-authoritarianism, although it may have left him with some feelings of repugnance for the activities of a mob. He left Marlborough soon after this and spent the next year under a private tutor studying for the Oxford entry exam.

Morris took up his place at Exeter College in January 1853 where he immediately made friends with Edward Burne-Jones from the King Edward VI School in New Street, Birmingham. Although they looked very different, they shared many interests, including dressing up in an outlandish way. They were both very much attracted to the High Church ritual of the Tractarians. Also, the Victorian cult of King Arthur was reaching the height of its fashion when they arrived at Oxford after the publication of Tennyson's Lady of Shalott and Morte d'Arthur. William joined a set made up mainly of friends of Burne-Jones from Birmingham, who gathered together to share their love of literature and the arts.

In one of his vacations he made a three-week tour of Northern France in the company of Burne-Jones. The tour included visiting nine cathedrals and at least twenty-four non-cathedral churches. He was overawed by the magnificence of many of these French churches. Late one evening at the latter end of their French travel, Morris and Burne-Jones decided they would not go into the church but instead dedicate themselves to a life of art.

Morris attached himself to the Oxford based architect G.E. Street but although he originally intended to abandon his studies, as did Burne-Jones, he stayed on, passed his finals and achieved his BA. Burne-Jones meanwhile had sought out and became a disciple of Dante Gabriel Rossetti, whose studio was in an old house in Chatham Maze at the northwest corner of Blackfriars Bridge. Rossetti was six years older than Morris, and was a poet as well as a painter. He had already formed the Pre-Raphaelite Brotherhood in 1848, eight years earlier, with Holman Hunt and John Millais. Morris joined Burne-Jones in London, and, while still working for Street during the day, he went to a life class in the evening. Later, Rossetti, Morris and Burne-Jones became acquaintances of Robert Browning, widely regarded as the greatest living poet.

Morris and Burne-Jones soon moved to no 17, Red Lion Square, an early eighteenth century brick town house. The rooms were crowded with tapestry, brass rubbings and drapery. The furniture, much of it designed by Morris, was painted with medieval scenes by Burne-Jones, Rossetti and Morris. In 1857, with Rossetti and Burne-Jones, he returned to Oxford to engage in the decoration by mural of the

A self-portrait 1856.

Oxford Union. Morris's own panel as it appeared in the restoration of 1987 looks rather ungainly and amateur, especially compared with those of Rossetti and Burne-Jones.

In 1858 he fell in love with Jane Burden, eighteen years-old, a student and model of Rossetti's. She was from a poor background of agricultural workers. Her mother was illiterate and her own outlook on life was quite narrow but she was a classic Pre-Raphaelite beauty - tall, foreign looking and quite hollow cheeked. Rossetti was highly competitive sexually and took some delight in seducing his friends' mistresses. As it was he who had found Janey, he evidently felt obliged to have a relationship with her after she had married Morris.

Morris had been working solidly for some years on his poetry and in March 1858 published a book of poems entitled *'The Defence of Guinevere'*. His style was based mostly on that of Browning, whom the set very much admired. Many of his poems concerned the vulnerability of happiness. They were not received well by the cognoscenti, and this so upset Morris that he did not publish again for another eight years. His poetry, though, was not without its later admirers, notably Ezra Pound and W.B. Yeats.

Morris's wedding was held on 26th April 1859 in St. Michael's parish church in Oxford. At the age of twenty-five, he had a new home built, which came to be known as the Red House, designed by the architect Philip Webb, who had known Morris since his days working with G.E. Street. The site was at Bexley Heath in a small hamlet called Upton, ten miles from Central London. It was a fascinating house - plain and simple in many ways, with good conditions for the servants and with lots of interesting gables and arches. Burne-Jones painted some murals at the Red House, but most of them have now faded. Others joined in. Charles Faulkner, one of the little group of friends at Oxford, helped to paint the ceilings and Rossetti also contributed.

In January 1861, Morris and his friends first revealed their next venture to an old friend, George Price Boyce. They wanted to set up a shop where they would produce and sell painted furniture. 'The firm', as it became known, moved into no 8, Red Lion Square in April 1861, above a jewellers shop. Morris was appointed the business manager. The prospectus included mural decoration, carving, stained glass, metal work, jewellery and furniture. The young people all worked together - wives and husbands, lovers and mistresses and friends. It was a cauldron of ideas and creativity. By the end of 1862 there were twelve more employees, some of whom were recruited from the Industrial Home for Destitute Boys in Euston Road. They were very young, and had little skill when recruited.

The earliest design for Morris wallpapers was created in 1862. Morris's patterns included a sense of movement and fluidity which contrasted with the much more formalised patterns of the time. The commercial production of the wallpaper, however, was transferred to a manufacturer, Jeffrey and Co., in Islington. Morris, from then on, never manufactured his own wallpaper.

There is no doubt that Morris was a cult leader - his red tiles, blue china and all the rest led the market.

Morris's first daughter, named June Alice, was born on 17th January 1861 and on 25th March 1862 Janey gave birth to a second daughter, Mary.

Morris enjoyed being a father, and both daughters had very tender memories of their childhood. In 1865, the firm took a twenty-one year lease on a larger workshop, at 26 Queen Square. Morris decided to sell the Red House and move his family into the new spacious premises. Morris, as was his custom, expressed little sentiment at leaving Red House. The family were not so practically minded and found it a huge wrench from a place where they had been so happy.

Morris was still writing poetry and was engaged in the huge narrative, The Earthly Paradise, which was a homage to Chaucer, including as it did, twenty-four stories by different tellers. The writing mainly took place in the years 1865-1870 and reflected Morris's interest in the Norse and Icelandic sagas. Janey meantime had developed the ill-health, which does not seem to have been properly diagnosed, that plagued her throughout life.

The firm was consolidated in 1866 by the award of more commissions - for instance the re-decoration of the Armoury and Tapestry Room at St. James Palace. It was mainly thanks to a convenient friendship between the First Commissioner of Public Works and Rossetti that the Commission was won, but it was lucrative. Another good commission was to re-decorate the Green Dining Room in the South Kensington Museum.

Janey Morris had an inclination to live dangerously and began to develop a relationship with Rossetti for whom she had been acting as a model. Rossetti did a series of portraits of her, which made her into the personification of his sexual tastes. As he grew fonder of her his mockery of Morris was increased. Morris was aware of the relationship and it became the inspiration for some of his most deeply felt poetry, such as 'The Hill of Venus'. But despite the letters Rossetti and Janey exchanged there is no corroborating evidence that the relationship was consummated. Morris, never one to abandon friends or the Brotherhood, refused to confront Rossetti on the issue.

His financial position was becoming sticky. In 1868 a turnover of £2,000 at the firm had left a mere £300 profit to be divided among the partners and his private income from his shares was fairly static at £400 per annum. His standard of living seemed to require about £1,000 per annum.

In December 1870 the fourth and final part of Morris's 'The Earthly Paradise' was published. It had dominated five years of his life. It was while he was writing this poem that the seeds were sown of his devotion to socialism. He reflected again and again on the moral torpor and inactivity that surrounded him - the idea that the progress of industrialisation was inevitable and nothing could stop its debasement of the human condition.

After the 1860s which were the years of his epic poem 'Earthly Paradise', his illuminated manuscripts or painted books became his obsession. Between 1870 and 1875 he worked on eighteen manuscript books. The first was the beautiful 'A Book of Verse'. He did much to revive the arts of calligraphy and illumination, teaching himself Roman and italic scripts and learning how to gild letters. For the best manuscripts he used vellum. In the midst of all this artistic effort he was also looking for a house out in the country and eventually his eyes lighted on Kelmscott Manor, a beautiful stone grey building south east of Lechlade in Gloucestershire. He and Rossetti took a joint tenancy on the house.

William Morris made two journeys to Iceland, the first in the summer of 1871, the second two years later. He was there on both occasions for two months. The sheer barrenness of the land and the struggle to make a living gave him even more empathy with people living in poverty. His first sight of Iceland - the grey craggy volcanic cliffs - left an indelible impression on him. This was reflected in his poetry, especially in the poem 'Iceland First Seen'. He found the Scottish coast very drab after his views of Iceland which Morris often afterwards called his 'Holy Land'.

Morris returned to Kelmscott Manor, which became one of the great loves of his life; it is a very large house, Elizabethan, originally dating from 1570. He loved its entrances and exits, interesting views and the way the architect had juggled with its space. Kelmscott village was at that time a hamlet of 117 people, a close agricultural community. Morris saw Kelmscott as the centre of a spiritual phenomenon, a rural idyll based on centuries of history and tradition. He saw the network of rural communities and their accompanying values of friendship

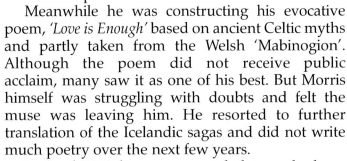

and self-reliance as some sort of ideal for a future socialist Utopia.

Meanwhile he was constructing his evocative poem, 'Love is Enough' based on ancient Celtic myths and partly taken from the Welsh 'Mabinogion'. Although the poem did not receive public acclaim, many saw it as one of his best. But Morris himself was struggling with doubts and felt the muse was leaving him. He resorted to further translation of the Icelandic sagas and did not write much poetry over the next few years.

In April 1873 he was persuaded to embark on his first expedition to Italy, though he had little sympathy for Renaissance culture. After his return he set off for Iceland again. This time he was to travel across, and be greatly impressed by, the black sands at Fljótsdalur. Sometimes they were in the saddle for nine hours. He found the journey exhausting and was glad to return to civilisation. It is about this time that Morris set out on a journey to Wales, his Fatherland as he calls it, perceiving that he could so easily live in a simple house there.

In his business affairs he set out with a new determination to take over and drive the firm. He paid £1,000 compensation to three partners - Rossetti, Brown and Marshall. The others - Burne-Jones, Philip Webb and Charles Faulkner - waived their claims. Morris took over as sole owner. He also gave up his connection with the Devon Great Console mine. To celebrate he ceremoniously sat on the top hat he had bought in 1871 when he had joined the mines board of Directors.

At this time, 1875-1878, William Morris became very interested in textile dying as a craft skill. He spent some time studying this technique in the small town of Leek in Staffordshire and was also able to observe the relationship between management and workers at first hand. Morris's socialistic leanings were increased by the patterns of work he observed - long arduous and repetitive hours of work and an overcrowded and polluted environment. He was convinced that standards would be greatly raised if he took control of dyeing his own fabrics and was far more interested in the old organic methods of dyeing than the new chemical ones.

After Leek he settled down in Turnham Green, South London, where he had moved from Queens Square and then, as if he wasn't already doing enough, he embarked on a translation of Virgil's Aeneid. Meanwhile, after staying with Rossetti in 1875, and posing for his portrait, the Astarte Syriaca, Janey decided that the affair with the artist was over, one of the reasons being his increasing reliance on alcohol.

Morris's daughters were growing up and they were sent to Notting Hill High School, a girl's day school considered quite advanced in women's education, for the time - they flourished there. But once Jenny, the more academic of the two girls, developed epilepsy, with all the social stigma attached to that disease, her promising academic career came to an end. Morris's gentleness and love towards her were inestimable, maintaining that she must be cared for within the family. It made Morris even more aware of the social ills around him and even more determined to do something about them.

Morris did not greatly enjoy serving on committees but he did so and was, for example, the honorary secretary of the Society for the Protection of Ancient Buildings. He conducted this society's affairs like a military campaign, pinpointing churches of all shapes and sizes that needed protection from the efforts of the flourishing restoration business. Morris was also a leading light in the Eastern Question Association, where he vehemently denounced Disraeli's support for the Turks in their efforts to put down a revolt in Bulgaria. Public speaking was not his forte but, like so many other skills, he was determined to master it.

After another holiday in Italy, when he began to suffer from gout, Morris in April 1879 moved into a house on the Upper Mall in Hammersmith which he renamed Kelmscott House. He was to live here until his death and spent about £1,000 on redecoration - his own income in the 1880s was to rise to roughly £1,800 a year. The house was not far from some of the London slums and Morris often looked out of his window and watched the poor urchins at play. His social conscience was pricked by this proximity.

After his obsession with dyeing in the mid 1870s he now moved on to weaving, employing Luis Bazur, a French weaver with his own mechanical loom. More weavers were employed, many of them rather ancient men who had been made redundant through the decline of the great weaving centre in Spitalfields. He revelled in the new designs in all kinds of material he manufactured with his weavers, then went further, moving into the design of hand knotted carpets and other floor coverings. His large carpets were a great success, bedecking many an English country house drawing room like the one now at Regent House Cambridge.

However despite all this attention to carpets it was tapestry he liked best. He taught himself how to create tapestries and it became an act of therapy with him. William loved his tapestry loom and in the spring of 1877, the Firm leased a shop at 264, (it is now 449) Oxford Street, which put it into the heart of the commercial retail district, and this contributed greatly towards its success. The shop could offer painted glass, embroidery, various carpets and tapestries, curtains, wallpapers etc; it produced a far greater range than any other equivalent outlet.

In the middle of the summer of 1881 Morris signed the lease for a seven-acre site at Merton Abbey in Surrey, thus obtaining more spacious surroundings for his workshops, in which over a hundred workers were now employed. Merton Abbey had been a silk weaving factory on the site of a priory that had been destroyed in the sixteenth century dissolution of the monasteries. A dye shop was put in the ground floor. The upper floor was dedicated to stained glass. There was a weaving shed. Across a timber bridge on the southern side of the river was the largest work shed, with the tapestry and carpet looms. Its top floor was given over to fabric printing.

On 9th April 1882 Rossetti, after a deterioration of his health, died, probably as a result of arterial degeneration. Sixteen months later Janey met her new lover, Wilfred Scawen Blunt. He was a poet and an explorer and very wealthy, also an opponent of the empire and a radical in many ways. Wilfred was a philanderer extraordinary and played with women, but he had been educated by the Jesuits at Stonyhurst and therefore was often burdened by his 'sins'. He was also a great enthusiast for everything Morris and Rossetti stood for. Morris had his suspicions about the relationship with Jane but knew also that Blunt regarded him with the deepest respect.

On 17th January 1883 Morris joined the Democratic Federation. The federation was basically aimed at uniting the working class against injustice. Although it had not said outright it was socialist, it was moving in that direction. It had been founded by Henry Mayers Hyndman, an upper class man who later wrote 'England for All', probably the most influential of any English book based on Marxist ideas. Morris, in his pursuit of socialism took to reading such books as Das Kapital and the works of William Cobbett to improve his knowledge. By May 1883 he was a member of the Democratic Federation executive. As part of his Democratic duties Morris spent much time giving talks on platforms throughout the country, bringing the message to the people. He was often joined by the Irish writer and playwright, George Bernard Shaw. In addition to more obvious social and political concerns, his lectures often discussed the nature and function of art.

Morris seemed to undergo a transformation of character as socialism took him over; he appeared like an Old Testament prophet, a figure of fearsome passion and foreboding. The name of the magazine of the Democratic Federation was 'Justice'. Morris was one of its leading contributors and was also very much involved with its finance. The Federation at this time was much rent with conflict and disharmony, which caused William to be much depressed in spirit. Finally the socialist movement split, with Morris walking out on Hyndman and helping to set up a rival body, the Socialist League. The League was formally established on 30th December 1884. Its aim was the realisation of complete revolutionary socialism; its magazine was The Commonwealth. The Fabian Society had recently been formed but was too middle class for Morris; he set about editing 'The Commonwealth' with his customary zeal and he was at it for the next six years with all the application and hard work that accompanied such a task. It included many famous contributors, including Marx's old collaborator, Friedrich Engels. Morris's daughter, May, now twenty-three, was becoming a great help to him both as director of the embroidery department in his workshops and in his political activities.

The Coach House attached to Morris's residence was the place where the famous Hammersmith Sunday lectures took place, where Socialists of all kinds were asked to speak, including the Webbs and Shaw. There was a lot of friction at this time between the police and the socialists and Morris was in fact charged with assaulting a policeman but established his innocence. After Morris's appearance in court the socialists, in league with many others, including people involved in the Free Church movement (calling for the disestablishment of the Church of England) and the Salvation Army, held a huge rally in Dock Street of about fifty-thousand people, which defied the police and defended the principle of freedom of speech.

1886 and 1887 were years of trade depression in Britain and Morris was right at the centre of the agitation for a better way of organising the economy. He travelled throughout the length and breadth of Britain propounding socialism and the idea of an economy based on co-operation rather than competition. But by autumn 1889 the Socialist League was in decline with ever fewer numbers attending meetings as members. They were certainly losing out to the burgeoning trade union movement. At the sixth annual conference there were only fourteen delegates. Morris was somewhat isolated by the appointment of anarchists to key positions. On November 21st 1890 the Hammersmith Branch under Morris cut its links with the League and was renamed the Hammersmith Socialist Society.

His final rejoinder to the League was the publication of the book 'News from Nowhere' which was a universally acclaimed futuristic novel about the implementation of a new socialist order. It was a book full of optimism about the possibility of a post-industrial society. It was translated into French, Italian and German and widely circulated in Russia before the Revolution. It became a seminal work for many future socialists.

By 1890 the Socialist League was split and its star waning fast. But, despite this, in many other ways Morris's star was still rising. The Kelmscott press was printing the first of its many volumes, Morris was writing prolifically and his business was flourishing. His ideas and those of the arts and crafts movement were spreading throughout the civilised world. In 1884, partly as a reflection of Morris views, the soon to be influential Art Workers Guild was founded and by 1890 membership had risen to 150. After the demise of the Socialist League, Morris returned with renewed vigour to his work in the crafts and was even more emphatic that a product should never be ugly, but have form and dignity. At this time he collected about him a large following of young men, artists and craftsmen in particular, whom he encouraged and who saw him as their mentor. Many communities sprang up throughout England in particular emulating the arts and crafts movement. His ideas also spread in America. Boston and New York, Chicago and California were among the main areas of activity.

In the early 1890s Morris's advocacy of socialism had taken a downturn but gradually it built up again. He energetically supported the great strikes in the coalfields in 1892 and in 1893 helped to form a Joint Committee of Socialist Bodies, though the newly formed Independent Labour Party was not asked to join. Artistic endeavour went on throughout this period including the six narrative panels of the Quest of the San Graal produced for William Knox D'Arcy in Stanmore Hall in Essex between 1888 and 1896. Knox D'Arcy, who made his fortune in gold mining in Australia, was later to buy the concession which opened up the oil industry - Anglo-Iranian Oil, later British Petroleum - in Iran.

Morris and Burne-Jones collaborated over the famous edition of Chaucer brought out by the Kelmscott press. But by early 1896 his health was deteriorating, although he was only sixty-two. In 1896 he was encouraged by the Queen's physician Sir William Broadbent to go on a cruise to help him recover, but his health got worse and eventually he began to have frightening hallucinations. He returned in August and died on Saturday 3rd October.

Most of the obituaries emphasised his achievements as a poet, some tried to assess his contribution to arts and crafts, but most of the capitalist press were dismissive of his attempts to promote socialism. The funeral, in Kelmscott parish church, was a simple ceremony without much fuss, a direct contrast to the recent funeral of Tennyson. Philip Webb designed the tomb, which was Nordic in appearance. A Welsh harp with a frame of purple flowers, presented by his Merton workers, was placed at the foot of his grave.

Bibliography:
Ian Bradley: 'William Morris and his world', London, Thames and Hudson, 1978
Jack Lindsey: 'William Morris - His Life and Work', London, Constable, 1975
Gillian Naylor (ed): 'William Morris by Himself - Designs and Writing', New Jersey, Chartwell Books, 2001
Fiona MacCarthy: 'William Morris - A Life for our Time', London, Faber and Faber, 1994
Nick Salmon: The William Morris Internet Archive: Chronology at www.marxists.org
E.P. Thompson: 'William Morris, Romantic to Revolutionary', New York, Pantheon Books, 1977 (first ed Stanford, Stanford University Press, 1955)

Chapter Nine

Frank Lloyd Wright
1867-1959

Frank Lloyd Wright's grandfather, Richard Lloyd Jones came over to the New World in 1844, arriving in Ixonia, Wisconsin, in 1845. With him was his family, including his daughter Anna. They moved to Hillside, Helena Valley probably around 1855-56, across the Wisconsin river from Spring Green. All told, there were eleven children, four of them born in Wisconsin.

The family prospered, becoming one of the most prominent families in the area. But they were Unitarians (opponents of the teaching that Jesus, as Son of God, was equally God with God the Father). They came from a part of Cardiganshire that was known to Calvinists as the 'black spot' because of its concentration of Unitarian chapels. That was why the family needed their own chapel, the 'Unity Chapel', the first building young Frank Lloyd Wright is known to have worked on. But between his birth in Wisconsin in 1867 and his helping to build the chapel in 1885, a great deal of wandering and turbulence had intervened.

Frank Lloyd Wright.

Anna's husband, William Russell Cary Wright, was the superintendent of the school district in which she worked as a teacher. The date of their marriage, after the death of his first wife is given as 1865 or 1866. He had trained both as a Baptist minister and as a musician, and he made his living from preaching, lecturing and music.

But he had a restless disposition, moving from one position to another. Everywhere he went he was liked and his lectures, preaching and music were appreciated but not sufficiently to assure him a stable living. He was essentially impractical with money and did not realise the impossibility of some of the tasks he had taken on. The marriage was not a happy one with Anna always having to scrimp and save, and William treating money with the most cavalier and irresponsible attitude.

Anne claimed to have foreseen that her son would build beautiful buildings and to have decorated his room with pictures of them when he was small. She had herself been greatly influenced by the ideas of the early nineteenth-century German educational theorist Friedrich Froebel. He believed children were highly creative creatures with great potential, which had to be encouraged, and welcomed. Anna had been introduced to these ideas when she had visited the Centennial Exhibition in Philadelphia in 1876 and, together with Froebel's toys - basic brightly coloured interlocking blocks designed to encourage an aptitude for construction. They were also to have a great influence on her son.

In the autumn of 1881 the family had some good financial news when, on the death of Frank's grandfather on his father's side, they inherited a life insurance policy. But about the same time Anna left her husband's bed saying she no longer loved him; in fact she loathed him. A couple of years later he left and applied for a divorce in the summer of 1885. He took with him a few bits of furniture and some musical instruments and renewed his links with his first family. Frank never saw him again.

In 1887 Frank took up a job in Chicago, in the office of J. Lyman Silsbee. Silsbee was an architect who had been employed in 1885 to build a church for Frank's uncle, Jenkin Lloyd Jones, a leading figure in the Unitarian movement, though he was to drop the name 'Unitarian' believing that the emphasis on ethical Christianity - social improvement and opposition to war - transcended theological boundaries. He had then been commissioned to design a family chapel for the Joneses in Hillside, Wisconsin. This was the 'Unity Chapel' and there is evidence that a large part of the work was actually done by Frank. Silsbee, was a fashionable architect who specialised in work for the nouveaux riches. He was very much involved with the 'Aesthetic Movement in America', which was a rejection of high Victorian Gothic architecture in favour of the simpler 'colonial' style, evoking the early history of the European settlements in North America. Henry Hobson Richardson had initiated the 'Shingle style' of architecture on the East Coast, which was a variety of styles united by the use of wooden shingles for walls and roof. Silsbee was a devotee of Hobson and Frank could not help being influenced by his employer, especially coming from a background where the idea of 'art for art's sake' had been taken for granted as part of the normal order of things.

By early 1888 his mother had found work at the Hillside Home School, founded by her sisters, Frank's aunts, Jane and Ellen, and Wright himself had moved to the prestigious Adler and Sullivan firm of architects, one of Chicago's largest. Meanwhile he had fallen in love with the young Catherine Lee Tobin known to all as Kitty. He met Kitty at Uncle Jenkin's church in Chicago. The Tobins were well off and socially acceptable; they were Unitarians. Kitty was the only girl in a family of four therefore much adulated. She reached her eighteenth birthday on March 25th 1889 and Frank was almost twenty-two when, in the teeth of his mother's opposition, they were married.

By 1887 eight-hundred thousand people lived in Chicago and by 1893 a million. A great fire had broken out in 1871, which destroyed seventeen-thousand buildings and left one-hundred thousand people homeless. It led to a huge work of rebuilding which attracted many architects and builders to the city. One of them was the young Louis Sullivan. Later, at the time Wright was working with him, he designed the Wainwright building in St. Louis, Missouri, in 1891, a ten-storey building often seen as one of the first 'skyscrapers'. He coined the well-known phrase: *'form follows function'* - the utility of function should be put first.

The Wrights moved into their first house in March 1890 just before the birth of their first child, Frank Lloyd Wright Jr., on March 31st 1870. In the office Wright was by now chief designer and was in charge of a group of thirty draftsmen. Adler and Sullivan built very few private houses, although Wright believed these to be his own forte - he was never happy in a room or house until he had re-arranged everything to his own liking. In the early summer of 1893 he went into private practice, which he had been doing for some time out of hours. He was in fact kicked out of Adler and Sullivan for extensive moonlighting, which was against his contract and contrary to the rules of the profession. By this time he had a second son, John, and Catherine was expecting again. The third baby, Catherine, was born in early 1894.

Even before the break with Sullivan, Wright was becoming interested in the revival of imitated Renaissance and classical forms which was being made popular by Eastern architects like the firm of McKim, Mead and White. One of his own designs, the James Charmley house of 1891, exhibited all the influences of classical design. The William Winslow house in River Forest, one of his first commissions after leaving Sullivan, also showed his mastery of the classical form. Despite Sullivan's dislike of this style Wright's great period of classical design started in 1892-93, his last year of employment with Sullivan.

In 1889, soon after his marriage to Catherine, he had begun to build his own house in Oak Park, then a village lying to the West of Chicago. The house demonstrated the evolution of his ideas. By 1895 he was moving from a rather eclectic artistic approach to one which was unified, bold and quite stark. In the same year, with the coming of a fourth child, he concentrated on building a giant playroom. This was entered by way of a long low corridor so that when one went through the door into this high vaulted room, one had an enormous impression of space and release. It was a device he was to employ over and over again in the years to come.

Wright became interested in the Arts and Crafts Movement championed in England by William Morris and his circle. He was encouraged by the publication in 1893 of a new London-based magazine called *The Studio*, which introduced the ideas of the movement to many in America. In 1897 the *International Studio* began publication in the United States and in the same year, Wright was involved in the establishment of the Chicago Arts and Crafts Society. In his designs he particularly emphasised the importance of the hearth and home, a reflection of what had been lost in industrialisation. He also began to experiment with open plan houses and get away from box like rooms, becoming famous for his low-hanging, massive roofs; he also used built-in furniture and broad, low doors. He liked to insist on natural materials though he disagreed with the Arts and Crafts movement over their principled opposition to the use of machines. In addition to the Arts and Crafts he developed interests in graphics and topography, and also became fascinated by photography.

Frank was an expert at self-promotion and waltzed into meetings wearing a broad rimmed hat, cane and swirling cape. The outfit became known throughout the circles he moved in. Between 1894 and 1911 he built 135 buildings and was the acknowledged leader of the new Chicago school. He had a number of sponsors such as Charles Roberts, a millionaire, also of Welsh origin who was one of his neighbours in Oak Park. Roberts was chairman of the committee that employed Wright to build a new Unitarian Church in Chicago - the 'Unity Temple', which had a glorious interior wonderfully lighted up by many and ample skylights. Like the play-room in Wright's Oak Park house, it had a complicated access, which ended with a lovely inner space, bathed in light.

In the autumn of 1903, the Wrights' sixth and last child was born, to be named Robert Llewellyn. Catherine and Frank were growing apart all this time. She was much given to criticising him and his eyes began to wander. He developed a relationship with Martha ('Mamah') Borthwick Cheney, whom he had met in

1903 while working on a commission for her husband, Edwin Cheney, one of his Oak Park neighbours. In 1909 he suddenly abandoned everything, his wife and family and burgeoning practice, and eloped with Mamah to Europe, where he was in the process of negotiating the publication of a book on his work by a Berlin publisher, Ernest Wasmuth. Preparing the elaborate illustrations to the book was his main occupation while in Europe, helped by, among others, his son, Frank Lloyd Wright Jr. (preferring simply to be known as 'Lloyd'), but it was a complicated business, accompanied by a stimulating encounter with European culture. Mamah meanwhile was translating the works of a Swedish feminist writer and educational theorist, Ellen Key - her translation of Key's *The Woman Movement* was published with an introduction by Havelock Ellis in 1912.

Frank returned to the United States in October 1910 to try to sort out his financial and personal affairs. He had a clear plan of what he wanted to do - to divorce Catherine, to turn the studio in Oak Park into a house suitable for his old family to live in, to adapt his house to be rented out as a source of income, and to build a new house - 'Taliesin' - in the Lloyd home country of Hillside, Wisconsin, as a home for himself and Mamah. Catherine however refused him the divorce he wanted (it was only finally granted in 1922) and in his acute financial difficulties he was reliant on help from old clients, in particular Darwin Martin, who had secured him the commission of the prestigious Larkin Administrative Building, built in 1906 for the soap manufacturer and mail-order pioneer John D. Larkin in Buffalo, New York. Martin was a devout Christian Scientist who strongly disapproved of the escapade with Mamah and Wright was reduced to pretending that it was over and that he was returning to his family.

Larkin Administrative Building, 1906.

In 1912 and 1913 his commissions reached an all time low as his unpopularity hit his own work in Chicago but he was rescued later on by the grant of a contract to redesign a new hotel in Tokyo that would cost £17 million. He was also asked to construct the Midway Gardens in Chicago - an area the size of an entire city block that would serve all the year round as a pleasure garden. His two sons, John and Lloyd, joined him in the partnership. Mamah had by this time moved to Taliesin.

In Taliesin Wright had employed a black servant and his wife, Julian and Gertrude Carlton and although this man was efficient there was something sinister about him. One day he splashed gasoline across the rugs in Taliesin and set the house alight then plunged a hatchet into the brain of Mamah Borthwick and also killed her son and daughter, John and Martha as well as several others. Seven people died as a result of burns and the attack. A posse was formed which included Frank's Uncle Jenkin but Carlton was quickly found near the house. An attempt to lynch him was forestalled and he was incarcerated in jail where he starved himself to death. His motives were never explained. Wright was told in his office in Chicago and rushed immediately in a state of shock to Taliesin.

After this Taliesin became a life force for him: *'I turned to this hill in the Valley as my grandfather before me turned to America - as a hope and a haven.'* The tragedy drew him closer to his own Lloyd Jones family. His sister Maginel was a great support encouraging him to rebuild. Anna his mother returned to the centre of his life, a formidable but supportive figure who rarely left his side for the next nine years before she died.

The next woman in his life soon came along - Maude Miriam Noel, an aspiring sculptress, who wrote to him a letter of commiseration after Mamah's death. It looked like love at first sight, but Frank, with his usual impetuosity, had fallen for a woman who was a morphine addict and pre-occupied by self delusion. She adored him, making him the object of her constant praises and devotion, and she eventually moved in with him at 25 East Cedar Street in Chicago. Then she found he was not easy to live with, criticising her for her extravagant clothes and for smoking. Despite all this they continued to live together for the next years.

From 1916-1922 Wright was engaged on the huge project of building the Imperial Hotel in Tokyo. There were endless small tenancies. Every bedroom in the two huge wings seemed to be different from every other. It was highly ornamented and refined. The ceilings were of many different heights; there were hidden doorways and large garden courts with ornamental parapets. It was uniquely Wright and in the end it would cost four and a half-million dollars. He received a 10% fee for it all. In his own quarters he was provided with a five-room apartment and a grand piano; he also had a car and his own chauffeur. He always asked to be extremely comfortable when he was working. Miriam was totally involved in his work and supported him throughout.

Just as it was about to open, in September 1923, there was a devastating earthquake. Over 90,000 people were killed and Tokyo and Yokohama were all but flattened but the Imperial Hotel withstood it all. Wright had designed it to withstand earthquakes by 'floating' it on steel and concrete piers embedded in 70 inches of mud. The device was new and the Japanese architects of the day regarded it with scepticism but in the event Wright was more than convincingly vindicated.

In 1922, he at last obtained a divorce settlement from Kitty, giving her a cash settlement of $10,000 plus possession of the household furnishings and $150 per month. Their estrangement had lasted thirteen years. In November 1923, after his divorce became final, Wright married Miriam Noel at midnight on a bridge over the Wisconsin River but in May 1924 Miriam left him. They had only been married for about six months.

Within a short time of Miriam's leaving him, Wright entered into the last and most durable of his love affairs. This time the object of his affection was Olga, called 'Olgivanna', Hinzenburg, née Milanov, born in Montenegro in 1898. Her grandfather was Marko Miljanov, a poet and hero of the Montenegrin and Serb resistance to the Ottoman Empire. She had been largely brought up in different parts of the Russian Empire and in Turkey and, while still in her teens, she had married Vlademar Hinzenberg, an architect ten years older than herself. In 1917, in Tiflis, in Georgia, she met and became a disciple of Grigoriy Gurdjieff, who taught a controversial doctrine of restoring harmony and consciousness to a humanity he believed was half asleep. With Gurdjieff she escaped revolutionary Russia and she lived for a time in his 'Institute for the Harmonious Development of Man' in Fontainebleu, where among much else she was charged with looking after the desperately ill novelist Katherine Mansfield, also a Gurdieff disciple. Mansfield died in Fontainebleu and some of her friends blamed the eccentric regime Gurdjiff had imposed on her.

Olgivanna arrived in New York in late October 1924. She met Wright at a ballet performance in Chicago in November and they were instantly attracted to each other. She moved into Taliesin early in 1925, it was to be her home for the next sixty years. It was about this time in a thunderstorm that Taliesin caught fire again and was nearly destroyed. Much of Wright's priceless collection of Orientalia and other objets d'art was ruined but at least fortuitously much of the structure was saved and of course it was rebuilt, as Taliesin III.

On 1st January 1925 Wright moved his office back to Chicago again, this time to 19 Cedar Street. He was attracting more attention in Europe. Ernest Wasmuth had reprinted the Ausgeführte Bauten und Entwürfe von Frank Lloyd Wright in 1924 and in 1925. A Dutch architect, Hendrikus Wijdeveld, devoted a series of seven consecutive issues of his journal Wendigen to him, then gathered them together in a single volume. It included articles by Lewis Mumford, Robert Mallet-Stevens, Erich Mendelsohn, H.P. Berlage, J.J.P. Oud, all of them very distinguished names in the world of architecture in England, Germany, France and the Netherlands. It was all highly encouraging but perhaps made it all the more obvious that nothing equivalent was being done in the United States.

At this point, the details of his personal life reach a level of complexity that defies caricature.

On Thanksgiving Day 1925, Miriam announced publicly that she was filing for divorce and that Wright had beaten her on two different occasions. This was the first public revelation of his problems and the press flocked to Wisconsin where they soon discovered that he was living with Olga. This was news to Miriam as well, who now rejected the offer Frank had made for settling the divorce. In November, Wright renewed a charge of desertion he had made against her and she responded by lodging a complaint of misconduct against Olga. In December 1925, Frank and Olga had a baby daughter, Iovanna.

The following year, in August 1926, Miriam filed a suit of $100,000 against Olga for alienating her husband's affections. Then Olga's own former husband, Vlademar Hinzenberg, appeared on the scene. He had granted her a divorce without much difficulty but he now claimed custody of their daughter, Svetlana, born in 1917. He issued a writ of habeas corpus for Svetlana and also obtained a warrant for the couple's arrest under the 'Mann Act' - an act initially introduced against 'white slavery', but which had been expanded to cover any man and woman crossing state borders for what were judged to be sexually immoral purposes (Charlie Chaplin had also been pursued under it). At about this time Wright and Olga disappeared. Pictures and descriptions of them, together with Svetlana and even of the infant, Iovanna, were circulated by the Sheriff of Sauk County, Wisconsin.

The Bank of Wisconsin foreclosed on the mortgage Wright had taken out for the rebuilding of Taliesin. It took possession of the house and all its contents and obtained an injunction preventing either Frank or Miriam from entering it. Hinzenberg offered a prize of $500 for Frank's arrest. A building firm in Madison, Wisconsin, sued him for $4,000 owing in repairs. Hinzenberg sued him for $250,000 for alienating the affections of Olga and Svetlana. He was eventually found with Olga and the children hiding in a cottage near Minneapolis. They spent a night in jail.

Eventually a divorce from Miriam was obtained in August 1927 and exactly a year later to the day, in August 1928, he married Olga, but not before Miriam had broken into a house he was renting in La Jolla, California, and smashed up the furniture.

The financial difficulties were solved, or at least improved, by a group of his friends and supporters, including the ever-faithful Darwin C. Martin. They persuaded him to turn himself into a jock stock company - Frank Lloyd Wright Incorporated - and then bought shares in him. The bank was paid off, as was Miriam, and he could return to Taliesin and resume work, but everything was now owned by the shareholders.

By 1929 his prospects looked reasonable again with plenty of work to hand. Miriam died on Friday January 3rd 1930, which rather relieved his finances. Her entire estate was valued at four dollars. He received five-thousand dollars from the Trust Fund set up to pay for her monthly instalments, and this was very welcome at this time. He was also being helped by the intervention of his cousin Richard Lloyd Jones, Uncle Jenkin's son. Richard was a successful journalist, owner and editor of the somewhat reactionary *Tulsa Tribune*; he had asked Frank, partly out of charity and family solidarity, to build him a house. He soon fell into the inevitable trap when he kept advancing Wright money despite his dissatisfaction with the way the house was developing. Westhope, much criticised at the time, is now in the National Register of historic buildings. It turned out to be too hot in summer and too cold in winter and the flat roof leaked almost immediately. Richard Lloyd Jones despite this was very happy with it.

Wright now turned his attention to the founding of a fellowship at the site of his aunts' old school in Hillside, near Taliesin. Soon the school's kitchen had been restored and so also had the dining room. A number of students had enrolled. The object of the fellowship was to collect together a band of willing and enthusiastic young men - young women were only the exception to the rule, though in practical matters Olgivanna was very much the hub round which the Fellowship turned. It may originally have been her suggestion and there was a whiff of Gurdjieff's Institute for Harmonious Development about it.

It was a highly organised day. Wright himself was up at four-thirty and there would be a choir practice straight after breakfast. Wright loved variety and so the students regularly had to switch activities during the day. Parties often took place to celebrate all sorts of things, including Hallowe'en and birthdays. Meal times were often changed to stop the students from falling into a rut. Everybody had to dress formally for dinner on Sunday evenings and there was much - often musical - entertainment afterwards. During the day he had amplifiers stationed around the house and garden so students could be serenaded by the classics - especially Bach - wherever they were working. Many of the jobs were rotated although people who were perceived as being very good at particular tasks tended to get stuck with them. The Wrights were exacting and quite pedantic to work for. Despite this they inspired tremendous loyalty and there was a great feeling of team spirit among all at Taliesin.

All this time commissions were coming in and, helped by his fine assistant Jack Howe - a quick and accurate worker who assimilated Wright's designs much more easily than other pupils - Wright was able to build a successful practice again. One of his most famous commissions was for Edgar J. Kaufman, owner of a department store in Pittsburgh whose son was, briefly, one of Wright's pupils. In his usual way Wright had pretended his design was completed, then, when Kaufman suddenly announced he would be arriving in a few hours to see it, Wright exploded into action in front of his astonished pupils. In two hours he had managed to execute the design, such was the beginning of one of the most beautiful houses  in America - Fallingwater, as it was called, eventually cost $110,000 and was very similar to Taliesin. It was a house of great contrasts, large open spaces, hidden entrances and narrow staircases, called Fallingwater because it was built over a waterfall.

In 1936 he designed the S.C. Johnson & Sons ('Johnson's Wax') Administration Building and by this time, with his usual perpetual inventiveness, he adopted a new style of 'streamlining', all to do with sleek lines and rounded edges. The building was organised with rows of slender columns around the central work place and surrounded by curving tiers of balconies attached to offices where the middle management would work. One entered through a low shiny reception hall, which hardly suggested the cathedral like space above. Air-conditioning was an innovation, as was the glass tubing in the walls and roof. Johnson was so pleased with the result he asked Wright to build him a house. Its name was Wingspread and was the biggest Wright had built. He did it in a cruciform pattern with the living room as centre and the other rooms branching out from it in four wings. Unfortunately the house, like Westhope, leaked.

Wright was also at this time obsessed with the idea of building interesting and beautiful houses for ordinary people without the huge financial resources of his usual clients. His designs and the devices he used for what he called his Usonian (United States of North America) houses were adopted by building contractors and cheap home catalogues. Open plan interiors and exterior patios were the order of the day.

In the winter of 1936 at the age of seventy, unusually for him, he was ill, contracting pneumonia. It was touch and go, but he pulled through. However he realised how difficult it was to heat Taliesin in the bleak Wisconsin winter, and he began to think of having a place further south. He bought about eight-hundred acres of land in Arizona in the McDowell Range of hills overlooking Paradise Valley outside Scottsdale. There was no water at first but Wright persevered and it was found. Here, over a period of years, he built Taliesin West.

After a trip to Moscow in 1937 Wright, in collaboration with the philosopher, Baker Brownell, wrote *Architecture and Modern Life*, which emphasised the benefits of decentralisation and the sterility of centralisation as practised in Nazi Germany and Soviet Russia. Wright was becoming a man of distinction in the United States. Universities began conferring honorary degrees on him. In 1940 the Museum of Modern Art mounted a retrospective exhibition dedicated to his career and in the same year the Royal Institute of British Architects presented him with the Gold Medal award for Architecture.

When the Second World War arrived again he again took an anti-British, accusing the British of entire self-interest in the preservation of their Empire. His friend and fellow Welshman, Clough Williams Ellis, complained about his attitude. When America entered the war, he was very keen to hang on to his assistants and found himself being investigated by the F.B.I. for sedition and possibly helping them to avoid the draft. His political sympathies, despite the emphasis on decentralisation and individualism, were generally with what he saw as the international socialist movement and the victims of Imperialist exploitation.

After the war years he had many projects including a hotel, shops and theatre complex called Crystal Heights in Washington D.C.. His major commission, though, was a museum in New York to house the modern art collection of the copper magnate, Solomon R. Guggenheim.

Within Taliesin, as the practice grew so did the formality and impressiveness of the guest lists for his parties and dinners. Wright was very much at the height of his fame. As Wright's energy and powers waned so Olgivanna took over much of the running of Taliesin. Some left the fellowship feeling that she was too manipulative and too inclined to intrude into their private life. Others however praised her thoughtfulness - she was a second mother to many. There is no doubt that, despite inevitable clashes of temperament, they had a deep and constant love for each other.

In the spring of 1949 he was given the gold medal of the American Institute of Architects. His acceptance speech lived up to expectations. It was full of criticism of his fellow architects and the cities they had built which fell so short, in his opinion, of the opportunity afforded them. He surprisingly received a great reception and had become a star in America, people recognised him in the streets; trains were held back so he could catch them.

One of his favourite commissions in his last years was the nineteen-storey skyscraper he built for Harold H. Price, as the administrative centre for his international construction company, which specialised in oil and gas pipelines. It conveys an impression of sculpted delicacy. Other projects included a synagogue in Philadelphia, a Unitarian church in Madison, a Greek Orthodox church in Milwaukee and so it went on. During the last nine years of his life he received three-hundred commissions. A hundred and thirty-five of them were built. He travelled extensively and eventually, in 1956, he visited Wales, where he accepted an honorary degree from the University of Wales and visited Portmeirion, the fanciful town designed by his old friend, Clough Williams Ellis, who had accompanied him on a visit to the U.S.S.R. in the 1930s.

The Museum of Non-Objective Art (it became the Solomon R. Guggenheim Museum in 1952, after Guggenheim's death in 1949) finally opened in 1959 with its great spiral ramp, enabling the art lover to walk slowly downwards watching the pictures. The walls sloped outward - it has been described as resembling an inverted tea kettle. It was a moulded space full of flow and movement. The evolution of the design ran into many problems, for example with the authorities on the grounds of transgression of building regulations but also with the new director, James Johnson Sweeney, a figure almost as confident in his own abilities and judgment as Wright himself. Wright wanted the building lit primarily by natural light from above. Sweeney installed fluorescent tubes. Sweeney also insisted, in accord with the modernist ethos Wright abhorred, on brilliant, dazzling white walls. And he devised, contrary to Wright's intention, a system enabling the paintings to hang vertically on Wright's slanted wall. The relationship was not helped by Wright's lack of respect for modern painting. The museum was refurbished in the 1990s and its directors claim to have returned more closely to Wright's original intentions.

The arguments over the Guggenheim raged to and fro, and Wright himself became ill with Meniere's syndrome, a problem of pressure in the ear that produced nausea and spells of dizziness that often lasted as long as a month. His first wife Catherine died in 1959, one day short of her eighty-eighth birthday. On Saturday 4th April Wright was admitted to hospital. He had an operation on Monday April 6th and died on Thursday April 9th not living to see the opening of his Guggenheim Museum.

Bibliography:

Anthony Alofson: 'Frank Lloyd Wright - The Lost Years, 1910-1922', University of Chicago Press, 1993

Maginel Wright Barney: 'The Valley of the God-Almighty Joneses, Spring Green', Unity Chapel Publications, 1986 (1st ed, 1965)

Phillips G. Davies: 'Welsh in Wisconsin. Madison: State Historical Society of Wisconsin', 1982

William R. Drennan: 'Death in a Prairie House. Frank Lloyd Wright and the Taliesin Murders', Madison, University of Wisconsin, 2007

Finis Farr: 'Frank Lloyd Wright: A Biography', New York, Charels Scribners and Sons, 1961

Brendan Gill: 'Many Masks: A Life Of Frank Lloyd Wright', New York, G.P. Putnam and Sons, 1987

Peter Hughes: Richard Lloyd Jones, Dictionary of Unitarian and Universalist Biography, Unitarian Universalist Historical Society, http://www25.uua.org/uuhs/duub/index.html

Donald Langmead and Donald Leslie Johnson: 'Architectural Excursions: Frank Lloyd Wright', Holland and Europe, Greenwood Press, Westport, Conn, 2000

Meryle Secrest: 'Frank Lloyd Wright: A Biography', University of Chicago Press, 1998

Cathy Tauscher and Peter Hughes: Jenkin Lloyd Jones, Dictionary of Unitarian and Universalist Biography, Unitarian Universalist Historical Society, http://www25.uua.org/uuhs/duub/index.html

Robert C. Twombly: 'Frank Lloyd Wright, His Life and Architecture', New York, John Wiley and Sons, 1987

Frank Lloyd Wright: 'An Autobiography', New York, Longmans Green, 1932

Chapter Ten

Lord Camrose
1879-1954

William Ewert Berry.

NOTE: Hartwell's biography, the *Dictionary of National Biography* and the *Dictionary of Welsh Biography* all spell Berry's middle name as 'Ewert'. Many of his acquaintances, however, spell it 'Ewart'; the publishing firm he created with his brother Seymour was called Ewart, Seymour and Co. Ltd, and we can perhaps safely assume that he was named after William Ewart Gladstone.

William Ewert Berry was born at 73 Thomas Street, Merthyr Tydfil, Glamorgan on 23rd June 1879. His father, John Mathias Berry, came from Camrose, in Pembrokeshire, from a family of tenant farmers on the estate of Golden Grove. He worked on the railways and, with his wife, Mary Ann Rowe, he moved to Merthyr where he worked on the Taff Vale Railway. Later he gave up the railways and became a salesman, dealing in tea. He was a Freemason and became Grandmaster of the Merthyr lodge as well as Mayor of the town. Four children were born in the marriage - Beatrice, Seymour, William and Gomer, in that order.

Later he decided to settle down, giving up the life of a travelling salesman and starting his own firm as an auctioneer, estate agent and accountant. Seymour joined him and through his drive and initiative the firm became the largest of its kind in North Glamorgan. One of his most memorable coups was to sell Cyfarthfa Castle - home of the great ironmaster, William Crawshay - to the town corporation in 1909.

Later, in 1916 Seymour took over the numerous business interests of D.A. Thomas, Lord Rhondda, who had just joined the war cabinet. As a result he became within three years director of over sixty companies. The most important of these was the steelworks, John Lysaght and Co., which later folded into Guest, Keen and Nettlefold (GKN). He bought Lysaghts in conjunction with his brother William and others in what has been seen as the biggest industrial transaction in the history of Wales. In 1926, he was created first Baron Buckland of Bwlch, named for the home he had bought in 1922.

William, meanwhile, joined the *Merthyr Times* on Tuesday 2nd May 1894, aged thirteen years and ten months. At the age of sixteen he apprehended the manager, who had run off with the petty cash, and was rewarded by being given his position. He witnessed the Merthyr riots in 1898. In July of the same year, he answered an advertisement in the *Daily News* for a journalist on the London financial weekly the *Investors' Guardian*. He got the job and moved to London but in the event he only stayed with them three months. In the middle of October 1898, he was fired, apparently over a difference of opinion. He tried to create the impression with his parents that he was still working, although he was out of work for four months. He then became sub editor for the Mercantile Press Agency at 18/- a week.

Around the turn of the century William replied to an advertisement for the post of manager at the 'Kennel Publishing Company', owned by a wealthy Anglo-Australian women by the name of Mrs. Whiteman, or Weightman. She had made her fortune in Australia through exploiting what the professionals had believed to be a worked-out gold drift. Her son at the same time had discovered a talent for entertaining the miners with scenes from Shakespeare. He came to London and launched a stage career under the name of Sydney Carroll and was soon joined by his mother, who bought a successful magazine called *Our Dogs*. She then established a companion journal called *Our Cats*, with Sydney as editor-in-chief. The Kennel Publishing Company was responsible for *Our Cats* and for the *Journal of the Ladies' Kennel Club*, but not for the much more successful *Our Dogs*. William worked for the company until suddenly, round about 1901, Mrs. Whiteman sold it and both William and Sydney found themselves out of a job.

He now decided to start up, in collaboration with Carroll, his own monthly advertising magazine, the *Advertising World*. Soon afterwards his brother Seymour gave him £100, which was placed in a new publishing company, Ewart, Seymour and Co. Ltd. This was to keep going for twenty years, publishing books in association with William's various periodicals.

William was a jack-of-all-trades; he canvassed for advertising and collected the information, staying up most of the night, drinking endless cups of coffee to keep to the appropriate deadlines. He even took up smoking and was determined to make a success of this project and persuaded his brother Gomer (later Lord Kemsley) to join him in London. In the second half of 1904, it was clear that the magazine was taking off. Unfortunately, just at this time, Seymour contracted tuberculosis. William whisked him off to the Tregenna Castle Hotel at St. Ives in Cornwall and worked out a healthy and hearty regime for him, which involved among much else exposing him to fresh air by removing all the windows, as well as the consumption of large quantities of cream.

While they were there, they met a Dubliner called Thomas Corns, who, on their return to London, invited them to his house. William fell in love with Mary Agnes 'Molly' Corns's daughter. She had developed an interest in Theosophy and especially in the views and principles of its Anglo-Indian theorist, Annie Besant. Much to her parents' annoyance, she insisted that the wedding should be at a registry office. William's parents did not attend, nor did her father. It was only eighteen months later that she relented and allowed a full Anglican service.

William's next venture was to buy the magazine *Health And Strength* on 12th March 1906. He had noted the great success of physical culture in the United States and saw it making advances in the U.K. He soon reduced the price and printed it on a weekly basis attracting many more readers. With articles on such subjects as 'Are women growing taller?' and 'Training for a long distance walk by a famous vegetarian pedestrian', *Health and Strength* was a success.

In late 1909 William sold the *Advertising World* for the then enormous sum of £11,000. The brothers as a result were able to move out of London to houses in the country. William's house stood in two acres near Weybridge and had its own tennis court. Later in the year he launched a new journal, *Boxing*, capitalising on the growing popularity of the sport. *Boxing* was a twenty-four page, small, half sheet paper with a few poorly printed photographs. By 1914 he was printing 250,000 copies of the magazine, and although he said it never made a profit, it gave him much enjoyment. Eventually in 1920 he sold it, together with *Health and Strength*, to Sydney Carroll for £1,000.

In June 1910 he bought the *Penny Illustrated* paper from the Illustrated London News and Sketch. This was a thirty-two page weekly, a mishmash of entertaining features, cartoons and bland political comment, with no very obvious target audience. William began by sharpening the quality of the writing and the edge of the satire - his contributors included G.K. Chesterton. But it was in 1915, and almost by accident, that he made his move to the centre of the newspaper world. He was lunching at the National Liberal Club with an estate agent and boxing promoter called James White. White was engaged in a major real estate deal in Covent Garden with Sir Joseph Beecham, the famous pharmaceutical manufacturer, pioneer of popular advertising and father of the conductor Sir Thomas Beecham. He was approached by a friend wanting to know if Beecham would be interested in buying the *Sunday Times*. The proposition was taken up by William, though Beecham helped him (the deal included free advertising for Beecham's pills). Hartwell believed that the brothers managed to buy it for £50,000 though Camrose himself had said he had to pay £75,000. Where they got the money from is quite a mystery but there is no doubt that many friends and old business acquaintances rallied around.

By 1915, the *Sunday Times*, founded in 1822, was suffering in comparison with its great rival *The Observer*, founded in 1791. *The Observer* had been taken over in 1905 and put on a firm footing by Lord Northcliffe, who also controlled the *Daily Mail* and *The Times*. The paper had become highly successful under the editorship of J.L. Garvin, one of the leading 'scaremongers', arguing that the rise of Germany posed a threat to British interests that had to be confronted. In 1911 Northcliffe had quarrelled with Garvin and abandoned the paper to William Waldorf Astor, who had kept Garvin as editor. In 1915, in the context of the war Garvin had done so much to promote, *The Observer* had a circulation of around 200,000 as against something like 30,000 for the *Sunday Times*. In 1915 the *Sunday Times* made an overall trading loss of over £2,000.

Like *The Observer* it was Conservative in its politics. Other prominent directors or shareholders included Esmond Caillard, brother to the Finance Director of Vickers arms manufacturers; Dr. Jameson, recently Prime Minister of Cape Colony in South Africa and famous for the 'Jameson Raid' against the government of Paul Kruger in the Transvaal, which helped to spark the second Boer War; and Sir Arthur Steel-Maitland of the Conservative Central Office. Berry's contract included a clause stipulating that the paper's political policy would not be changed without the consent of the directors.

From the start William, initially calling himself 'managing editor', took on the role of chief sub-editor for the *Sunday Times*, a role which he enjoyed and to which he attached great importance. Leader writers for the *Sunday Times* included Lord Sydenham and G.K. Chesterton. Lord Sydenham was an administrator and military engineer who as Governor of Bombay had acquired a reputation for the somewhat brutal repression of dissent. Chesterton, who had written for Berry's earlier venture, the *Penny Illustrated*, had already published a comprehensive statement of his political views, *What's Wrong with the World*, as well as the *Father Brown* stories, though he had not yet formally entered the Roman Catholic church.

Berry's old friend Sydney Carroll contributed theatre reviews. Shortly after the end of the war the *Sunday Times* acquired the services of two of the most famous critics of the age - Edmund Gosse and Ernest Newman. Gosse at the end of the nineteenth-century had introduced Ibsen to an English audience but by 1918, when he started writing for the *Sunday Times*, he was best known as the author of *Father and Son*, his account of his relations with his father, the marine biologist Philip Gosse, and of his upbringing among the 'Plymouth Brethren'.

Newman joined in 1919 after working briefly for *The Observer*. He is best known as the biographer of Richard Wagner but he had also, in 1911, translated Albert Schweitzer's book on J.S. Bach. He continued writing for the *Sunday Times* until shortly before his death in 1959.

Progress was slow during the war, partly owing to the difficulty of obtaining newsprint, but by 1920 circulation of the *Sunday Times* had risen to 80,000 and by 1923 to 110,000.

In November 1919, he bought the *Financial Times*. Like so many of his deals there is some mystery as to how he raised the money which amounted to about £300,000. Shortly afterwards he bought the not very successful tabloid, the *Daily*

Graphic and in 1920 he took over *Kelly's Directories* and also the Associated Iliffe press, publisher of specialist trade magazines. This brought him into relations with the Conservative M.P., Edward Iliffe who soon became a third partner with William and Gomer, especially important in the context of the soon-to-be-formed Allied Press.

The Berrys were beginning to be noticed by men of political substance. He was made a baronet under Lloyd George's government in 1921 and began to be invited to the Prime Minister's 'breakfasts'. He was to be made a peer in 1929 with the title Lord Camrose. His importance was heightened by the purchase of the publishers Cassells for around £500,000. Hartwell suggests that he may have seen this venture into book publishing as complementary to the *Sunday Times*, which had developed a specialisation in serialising the memoirs of important people.

The next big deal William attempted was the purchase of the Manchester based empire of Sir Edward Hulton - two dailies, three Sundays and one evening paper, described by the *Financial Times* as *'embracing two thirds of the population and wealth of industrial Britain.'*

By this time Lord Northcliffe had died (in 1922), and his holdings, Associated Newspapers, which included the *Daily Mail*, the *Evening News* and the *Sunday Dispatch*, had been taken over by his brother and collaborator, Lord Rothermere. Rothermere sold the jewel in Northcliffe's crown, *The Times*, to Astor, and the publishing company, Amalgamated Press, to the Berrys. Rothermere already had papers of his own, including the Glasgow-based *Record*, the *Leeds Mercury* and the *Daily Mirror*.

Max Aiken, Lord Beaverbrook, was becoming an important player with the *Daily Express*. Hulton, whose properties included the very desirable *Evening Standard*, disliked Rothermere and wanted to sell to William Berry. A price of £6 million was agreed with an immediate down payment of £300,000 but at the last moment Beaverbrook intervened offering an immediate down payment of £1 million, *'the biggest newspaper deal that Fleet Street has ever known.'* However, Beaverbrook himself had little interest in the Hulton empire; he was primarily interested in the *Standard* and in using the coup as a means of establishing influence within the Rothermere empire. He went on to share it in a complicated arrangement with Rothermere who, in turn, was to sell the Manchester papers to the Berrys for a price approaching what they had earlier proposed paying for the whole collection. To finance the purchase, a new company - Allied Newspapers - was formed, which also took control of the *Sunday Times*.

William now had a collection of Manchester newspapers as well as the *Sunday Times*. More newspapers were acquired in Newcastle, Glasgow and Sheffield and Rothermere finally decided to sell him the London based *Daily Sketch* and *Illustrated Sunday Herald*.

In May 1928 William and Gomer were shattered by the death of Seymour, their financial wizard of a brother. He was thrown by his horse and his skull was broken against a telegraph pole near his home at Buckland in the Usk valley. As a result of his death, William and Gomer took over his extensive industrial interests, which included the coal mines of another of the Welsh entrepreneurs discussed in this book, David Davies. William, however, claimed that they did not gain much from these interests - that in fact they lost money trying to keep open unprofitable mines in the Merthyr area.

Although Rothermere appeared to have out-manoeuvred the Berrys by selling them the provincial part of the Hulton collection, he began to develop a fierce feeling of rivalry against them with the result that in February 1928 he published a plan to establish a provincial empire of his own. Circulation wars broke out, especially viciously in Newcastle, but the whole process came to an end with the Wall Street crash of 1929. Rothermere lost some $40,000,000 and had to call off his war of attrition, withdrawing from the field. It was a sound victory for the Berrys, who had kept their heads throughout.

Rothermere's jealousy of the Berry brothers may have been inspired by their purchase in December 1927 of the *Daily Telegraph*. In the nineteenth-century, under its founder, Edward Lawson - who, as Lord Burnham, was the first of the great 'press Lords' - it had been a pioneer of a new style of lively, even chaotic news reporting. The paper was still in the hands of the Lawson family but it had been undergoing a long decline and by 1927 its circulation was down from around 300,000 at the beginning of the century to more like 84,000.

The Telegraph was William's first attempt at a quality daily newspaper. He knew that, though he did not want to make any changes in the personnel, he would have to take some direct control himself if he was to prevent further decline. By February 1930 circulation was rising to 100,000. In November 1930, the decision was taken to reduce the price to a penny. Sales almost doubled overnight and by December 1932 had risen to 264,000. In January 1937 they reached 520,000.

The partnership of the Berrys and Edward Iliffe was now one of the most impressive publishing groups in Europe. In January 1937, it split, possibly as a result of Gomer's new wife who may have wanted to see her husband - recently, in 1936, raised to the peerage - established as an independent force not as a perpetual second-in-command to William - the division was friendly. William kept control of the *Daily Telegraph*, the *Financial Times* and the *Amalgamated Press*. Gomer, now Lord Kemsley, took Allied Newspapers, including the *Sunday Times*, though William was deeply sorry to see it go. Edward Iliffe kept *Kelly's Directories* and also acted as Gomer's deputy chairman in Allied Newspapers.

Meanwhile William was still adding to his empire. In 1937 he bought the very High Tory *Morning Post*, amalgamating it with the *Telegraph* in October. The *Post* had had a chequered career. It was the oldest daily paper in Britain and in the early nineteenth-century had included Coleridge, Southey, Charles Lamb and Wordsworth among its contributors. It had been edited for generations by various members of the Borthwick family and still had a large and faithful following. Despite the amalgamation, the 112,000 or so readers of the *Morning Post* went over to the *Telegraph*, whose circulation went up to about 630,000.

William talking on his phone in his office at the Daily Telegraph.

Domestically in the 1920s and 1930s William's life changed. By 1923 he had a family of eight and they were close, giving him much pleasure and enjoyment. In 1936 they moved to Hackwood Park in Hampshire, which was a grand house with 3,000 acres and a wonderful spring wood attached to it. He also bought a lovely house in St. James Place. The manager of the Kennel Publishing Company had come a long way.

He had become a close friend of the maverick Tory, Lord Birkenhead who in 1926 had invited him to join the Other Club, which met once a fortnight around a single table. It had been formed in 1911 when Birkenhead and Churchill had both been blackballed from an old dining club called simply The Club. The Other Club now included, apart from Birkenhead and Churchill, such figures as Lloyd George, Beaverbrook, Rothermere as well as artists like William Nicholson and Sir John Lavery and authors such as Arnold Bennett and H.G. Wells.

Ownership of the *Telegraph* made Camrose an important political player through the whole period which includes the depression, the coalition government, the rise of Hitler, the abdication crisis, appeasement, Munich and the outbreak of the war. In all this excitement, however, he cuts rather a dull figure, especially when his initiatives are contrasted with the antics of Rothermere and Beaverbrook. In the early thirties discontent over Britain's unpreparedness for war was initially stirred up by Lord Rothermere and it was initially Rothermere, not Camrose, who provided Churchill with an outlet in the popular press. At the same time Rothermere was corresponding with and visiting Hitler and was a leading advocate of 'appeasement'. As Churchill commented in a letter to his wife; *'He wants us to be very strongly armed and frightfully obsequious at the same time.'*

Churchill took up the issue of rearmament in conjunction with Hugh Montague, first Viscount Trenchard, often characterised as the founder of the R.A.F. As Hartwell points out both Churchill and Trenchard believed that the future of war lay with a tactic of heavy bombing of industrial centres. Hartwell claims that Camrose backed them without comprehending that Trenchard's idea of the next war was a competition in killing civilian populations. When in 1935

Hitler revealed that Germany had developed an air-force in defiance of the Versailles treaty it was the *Telegraph*, possibly acting on a tip-off from Churchill's extensive private intelligence network, that reported his other claim, suppressed by the government, that he had achieved parity with Britain. In this latter respect, of course, Hitler was bluffing, and, contrary to Churchill's predictions, the main emphasis in the development of German air power was on fighter aircraft rather than bombers. Although he was accused of ignoring the issue, Baldwin, who swept back into power in November 1935, launched a programme of tripling Britain's air force capacity, again with the emphasis on fighter aircraft.

On 12th March 1938 William was in South Africa when he heard the news of Hitler's Anschluss with Austria. He had gone partly to explore the country and partly because he thought the climate would relieve the awful gout he was suffering. When William returned from South Africa he was greeted by a letter from Churchill offering to write a fortnightly article in the *Telegraph*. Churchill had finally been sacked from Beaverbrook's *Evening Standard* after making a speech in which he advocated a 'grand alliance' of England, France and the Eastern European countries against Hitler (he was still not ready to propose an alliance with the U.S.S.R.). Camrose accepted straightaway, initially for six months though in the event the articles continued for fourteen months, almost to the British and French declaration of war.

The *Telegraph* boasted that it had more foreign correspondents and therefore better coverage of foreign affairs than any other British paper and at a time when the Chamberlain government had set accommodation with Germany as a main priority it may have drawn more attention than, say, the Rothermere press to atrocities within the areas under German control. After Munich, though, the seizure of Prague produced widespread revulsion. It was after Prague, in an article in the *Telegraph*, that Churchill at last began to talk of a possible alliance with Stalin, though by this time Stalin, giving up on the possibility of an alliance with the western democracies, was already considering the possibility of a deal with Hitler.

The *Telegraph* began campaigning for a Ministry of Supply to bring about a mobilisation of the workforce for rapid rearmament. It also argued for the inclusion of Churchill in the government. From this point onwards its support for Churchill became continuous, right through the war and afterwards, until his death. Churchill was later to tell Robin Barrington-Wood, editor of the *Times* that when he read the newspapers he always left the *Telegraph* to the last *'because I know it will be all right'*.

Although Churchill, soon after he became Prime Minister, had Camrose created a Viscount, he was never offered any government work except briefly by Chamberlain at the beginning of the war, when he became Chief Assistant to Lord MacMillan in the newly created Ministry of Information. Churchill had brought Beaverbrook in as Minister for Air despite their old enmity, probably in the hopes of neutralising him, though the Beaverbrook and Rothermere press continued to be highly critical (Harold Harmsworth was succeeded as Lord Rothermere by his son, Esmond, in 1940). The press campaign against Churchill became especially virulent as the Empire in the East crumbled before the onslaught of the Japanese in the early days of 1942. Churchill's whole strategy turned on the United States but in the early stages of their involvement the

Americans had their hands full in the Pacific. It was in these circumstances that Camrose became one of Churchill's closest personal confidants, so close that he was actually dining with the Churchill family on V.E. day, accompanying him when he went out to face the cheering crowds.

After the windows in his St. James House were shattered in the 1940 blitz, Camrose took up residence in the Dorchester Hotel. Outside London, his country house, Hackwood, was requisitioned as a Canadian hospital but he rented nearby Audley Wood. There one of his neighbours was Churchill's long-time collaborator, Brendan Bracken, with whom he struck up a friendship, partly on the basis that both of them were compulsive long distance walkers. One result of this friendship was that towards the end of the war he sold the *Financial Times* to the owners of the rival *Financial News*. Bracken had been chairman of the *Financial News* until his appointment as Minister of Information in 1941. The sale was finally completed in May 1945.

This helped bring about a deterioration in his relations with Gomer, Lord Kemsley, who would have liked to have taken the *Financial Times* himself and believed he had a right to first refusal under the terms of the division of interests in 1937. Gomer's papers did not share William's unalloyed enthusiasm for Churchill, and William disliked the note of personal aggrandisement his brother had introduced - Allied Newspapers were renamed Kemsley newspapers, their headquarters was called Kemsley House, the masthead of the *Sunday Times* referred to it as *'a Kemsley newspaper.'*

In April 1947, the *Daily Telegraph* briefly achieved a circulation of over a million, but had to fall back under the pressure of the fuel shortage of the time. The circulation breakthrough finally occurred for good in April 1953, the year before Camrose died. But perhaps the greatest coup of his last years was the publication of Churchill's memoirs. This involved an elaborate scheme for circumventing income tax and death duties. The Churchill papers were placed in a trust in favour of his children. The trust signed a contract with a supposedly independent publisher who then employed a supposedly independent writer to use them for a book. The publisher in question was *'Churchill and Telegraph Publications.'* As for the writer, Churchill said to Camrose rather plaintively: *'Bill, I do hope you'll think of me.'*

Eight days short of his seventy-fifth birthday he died of heart failure. At his death, the diplomat and author, Harold Nicholson, wrote of him *'He showed that one could be a Press Lord and a gentleman. He was an example to the newspaper world.* Churchill said *'In dark and uncertain times no man could be more steady and persevering.'*

It might be worth adding that both Seymour and William Berry, his brothers, were generous contributors to Merthyr charities in an age long before the welfare state hence the statue to the former there. Seymour had an excellent sense of humour by all accounts. When conducting an auction for charity (his early profession being auctioneer) he decided the winning bid was inadequate so he started the auction again!

Bibliography:
Lord Hartwell: *'William Camrose, Giant of Fleet Street'*, London, Wiedenfeld and Nicholson, 1992
Keith Robbins: *'Politicians, Diplomacy and War in Modern British History'*, Hambledon Press, London and Rio Grande, 1994

Chapter Eleven

Clough Williams Ellis
1883-1978

Clough Williams Ellis was a bit of a maverick; although he had no recognised architectural qualification, he went on to make an creative living out of his architecture. He was also eventually inspired by the Wales he had been brought up in and where he returned to live. Portmerion was the ultimate in entrepreneurial activity and speculation, and today stands as an unique legacy of Clough's imagination. He did not start from nothing but was motivated by an enlightened up bringing to bring some of his fashionable and slightly bizarre tastes to his homeland. Clough saluted the magnificence of Snowdonia in particular and brought his patriotism to bear in unending enthusiasm for Welsh National Parks in particular. In many ways he was an opportunist and out of this came his creativity.

Clough's father was John Clough Williams Ellis M.A., J.P. who was for twenty years fellow and Tutor of Sidney Sussex College, Cambridge and 10 years Rector of Gayton, Northants before he retired to Glasfryn near the small village of Llangybi in the region above Cricieth and Chwilog in Caernarfonshire. Mabel his mother was from a Birmingham family who had invested in the slate quarry in Blaenau Ffestiniog, the source of the family's wealth. John and Mabel had four surviving sons of which Clough was the second. Clough was born in Gayton on 25th May 1883. It is interesting that although Clough was brought up in this devout family he was never pious and was particularly a rationalist in outlook. As a boy he was accident-prone but his *'easy come, easy go'* style of upbringing brought about especially by his mother was one based on common sense and freedom.

Clough Ellis Williams at Portmeirion in 1961.

On his father's retirement to Glasfryn, he encountered a rather bleak country area but Clough took to country pursuits and in particular he enjoyed hunting. Clough was quite proud of his lineage; his paternal grandmother, for instance, was descended from Sir Richard Clough of Plas Clough in the Vale of Clwyd, who had been Queen Elizabeth's agent in the Netherlands. The Williams side also is said to have been around in the sixteenth-century living in Plas Brondanw.

His early education was conducted by a governess and from the start he had a healthy disregard of religiosity. He was extremely proud of his Welsh ancestry but had little in common with the local boys as he spoke only very poor Welsh. Despite his Victorian upbringing he was essentially a free spirit. He became a man of independence and self-reliance; he was very much his own man, and the roots of this were created in his boyhood. One of the things he was concerned about was outward appearance and style and he often disapproved of those who fell out on both counts.

He was in his teens beginning to be fascinated by architecture and the shape of buildings, although grand ones were few and far between in the area. Tanrallt, his Aunt Hilda's residence was one of his favourites and they got on extremely well. At fourteen he was dispatched to a famous public school in Northamptonshire called Oundle. His headmaster Frederick Sanderson was a man of liberal views against the established and pervading ethos of late Victorian times.

Clough saw in Sanderson and especially his science lessons a fellow traveller and although he was unhappy with much of Oundle, he seemed to have engaged its headmaster. He spent much of his time trying to get out of the school environs, which is why he formed the photographic society and even joined the choir for its outings. Clough ended up as a bit of a philistine, certainly in academic terms only achieving one per cent in his final French exam.

One of his most lasting impressions of the Oundle area was the Elizabethan ruin of Kirby Hall, which he adored and was quite lyrical about in later years. Sometime during his latter years at Oundle he passed on a tram through the smoke and slums of London's East End; this again was to leave an abiding impression on him against bad architecture. He left Oundle in 1900.

University seemed to offer no choice; the family had always gone to Cambridge; because of the architecture it had to be Trinity. In order to get in he had to study Greek and Latin, which was drummed into him by paternal enthusiasm, which was not reciprocated. Once he got there he soon realised he was not really a drinking man, the latter being characteristic of so many contemporaries, but he was one of the pioneers of driving in the city at the time. At Cambridge where he was supposed to be studying science, he spent most of his time reflecting on architecture filling note books with drawings; as a result he was soon persuaded temporarily to work for his brothers' new electrical manufacturing company as a laboratory assistant as he determined how to become an architect. The electricity industry could have been the making of him as a future industrialist, but he knew what he wanted and was not to be sidetracked. He quickly gave up, found himself on the streets, but was rescued by his parents and an allowance of £160 per annum, which provided him with board and lodging.

He found in the London telephone directory an entry for the Architectural Association in Tufton Street, Westminster to which he hurried at once. The Principal and Clough took to each other and he found himself enrolled on a course after the long vacation. He went off to one of his many remote cousins A.H. Clough who owned a number of properties, which he was keen to develop. This is where he really got his hands dirty, doing all those practical jobs necessary for the building trade. His first effort at design was a porch on one small house, which gave him some satisfaction as a first achievement. He was also engaged in surveying and measured drawing, particular skills for one wanting to be an architect. The builder himself was a great influence on Clough, giving him insight and a good training. Clough went back to the Architectural Association and he enjoyed in his second term the extraordinary luck of being given a commission to design a country home for a charity in Oxfordshire for which he was paid ten guineas. Connor Cottage was completed in 1904. His habit of taking his builder into the college and thrashing out details was said to be disruptive and he and the college parted company after three months. He was not one to let this get him down and carried on with the practicalities of architecture regardless, with his normal self-confidence.

In design itself at this time great things were taking place with Frank Lloyd Wright in America, Charles Rennie Mackintosh in Glasgow and Comet in Spain. These seem to have little effect on Clough who harked back to the beautiful ruin of his schooldays. The English country house was his love and tutor.

He was eclectic in his copying of styles taking from Palladian, Baroque and Modernism, but he did not seem that interested in the architects of his own time, although William Morris earlier arts and craft movement was an influence on him.

He had now moved in with his elder brother in 1902 in Cork Street; both were family impecunious but Clough was still able to have a good time and he installed himself in a drawing cubbyhole near Grays Inn and set himself up as an architect. Enjoying a number of small commissions which helped him accumulate know-how. He moved in 1906 to Arnold House on the Embankment to a series of attic rooms where he even invented an electrical switch, which he patented and sold, in order to keep the money coming in. Clough had without doubt, like many Welshmen, an eye for the main chance and was in genious at making connections and getting by with his work. Though living alone, he did well with the many invitations he acquired as quite an eligible available bachelor. He was born into the right time with the Empire at the height of its confidence; there was plenty of building work available. The round of parties continued and, Clough an attractive tall and rather eccentric individual had his admirers. At this time in 1908 he was given ownership of his father's property of Plas Brondanw in Meirionydd and a love affair started which went on for many years. In 1910 he met Lawrence Weaver editor of *Country Life* who became almost his mentor and put a number of commissions his way. Two years later he was commissioned by the Bishop of Bangor to build a parsonage at Pentrefelin near Cricieth, which is to be seen today. His round of balls and country house parties continued giving him many useful connections although in the heady days of his twenties he was determined not to get romantically entangled. He engaged and almost revelled in Edward society with its self-confidence and eccentricity.

Plas Brondanw.

At about this time he met Amabel Strachey daughter of St. Loe Strachey, editor and proprietor of the *Spectator*. She had been brought up in a house full of the great and the good toing and froing; she loved poetry and became the literary editor of the *Spectator*. She joined the Labour Party and she indulged in much scientific journalism. He fell for her despite his determination not to become entangled. At this time the seeds of his future love for the National Parks and Trust were sown and he bought the peak of Cnicht that overlooked Brondanw and the two summits of the Moelwyns; it was to stop anyone spoiling the view of this country and it showed he possessed an 'aesthetic conscience'. An influence on Clough was Peter Thorp a man who had trained for the Jesuit priesthood, who had a vision of clearing Britain of the grime of the Industrial Revolution. Thorp was an active member of the Design and Industries Association of which Clough was a notable member and later took over as chairman; it finally mutated into the Design Council. A visit to Glasgow just before the Second World War heightened Clough's awareness of the awful problems of the slums and the necessity for amenities and town planning. He was continuing as a man of many parts, trying to be an accomplished ice skater which fitted in with his appreciation of the art and grace of dancing and he had a tendency to trespass and was often pottering around old buildings, restoring them without their owners permission.

It was in 1912 that he met in a railway compartment Mr. Archibald Christie who commissioned him to rebuild Llangoed Hall. It was a complex structure which he built with a Tudor feel to it. I do not have space here to go into its finer details, but it was built of Gwespyr stone, a superb honey coloured sandstone from North Wales. It was superb and a tribute to its architect's self-confidence and eye.

By 1914 he had safely established himself for what looked like a successful career in architecture. Clough was thirty-two when the war broke out. He was virtually dismissed as too old for recruitment but he persevered, feeling it his duty to enlist. At the start he was enlisted into the Imperial Light Horse, which mutated into a battalion of the Royal Fusiliers. Meanwhile he had become engaged to Miss Strachey. The call up seemed so chaotic and he heard almost immediately the Welsh Guards had been formed and signed up. He asked permission to marry and for a wedding present from his fellow officers asked for money for a ruin, which was eventually built on a hilltop behind Brondanw. After the marriage he took his new wife to Wales, where despite her Home Counties background she seemed to take to the diverse habits of the Welsh. She writes in 'All Stracheys are Cousins'; *'Living in Wales is better than living in most places'*. Four days were all they were allowed before Clough was despatched to the front-line. Clough admits after his time in the war like many other artists, he was fatalistically critical. He found plenty of boredom in trench life, and spent time sketching and learning Welsh when not fighting. He also wrote reviews of books for the *Spectator* sent to him by his father-in-law. He heard at this time that Amabel had borne him a daughter, Susan. His sketching activities were noticed and he was withdrawn from the trenches to survey and sketch enemy positions sometimes even from a balloon.

Clough spent much of the rest of his time roving and reconnoitring, from aeroplanes and from the ground but, at least, he was billeted at Brigade H.Q. not the trenches. Soon he became interested in tanks and managed to arrange a transfer to the Third Tank Brigade. There he quickly had to take over from his immediate superior Major Boots Hotblack and when the tanks penetrated the line at the second battle of Cambrai, Clough was awarded an M.C. for his bravery. He arrived home by persuading the authorities that he needed Amabel's help to write the history of the Tank Corps, which he had been ordered to do. The book was successful enough to be serialised in the *Daily Telegraph.*

He became very much at one with Owen and Sassoon, *'War is the most disastrous madness for all concerned, and my abhorrence of it inevitably led me to take an interest and even some small part in politics.'*

After the war and a brief period of inaction in the Civil Service, Clough went back to private practice and Amabel and the three children (Susan b. 1918 - d. 2007, Charlotte b. 1919 - d. 2009, and Christopher b. 1922 - d. 1944), moved into a house in South Eaton Mews. Cloughs practice flourished and he himself became a great agitator for town and country planning. In the 1920s he chaired the Design and Industries Association and continued his advocacy of proper planning. His great crusade was making and preserving a proper environment in which people could live. One of the largest commissions at this time was to convert Stowe into a passable public school, which took many years and many ups and downs.

Many have criticised Cloughs additions and alterations, but on restricted time and purse, Clough could be said to have done a good job.

It was at this time that the phrase 'to Clough up' a building became known which was about his concern to inject some fun into the elevation of a drab building. This commission led to many more conversions and revivification of many a country house. His practice flourished in London and in Wales, and even in the Cotswolds at Cornwell Manor there is a fine example of his work.

Amabel meantime had taken to leftist politics and their house was full of people like Aneurin Bevan, H.G. Wells and Sir Stafford Cripps. Clough helped to design Lloyd George's resting place. There is no doubt that Clough resembled another of our entrepreneurs in many ways, Robert Owen; they both believed, probably quite rightly that good environment has a positive effect on character and behaviour.

By and large Clough, in his political dealings voted Labour. He was in many ways a perfectionist and found it difficult to live with the mess created by humans.

In 1930 Clough moved to George Romney's old house in Hampstead, a lovely Georgian house which was improved by many artists of a modernist inclination, but Clough chose to ignore their ideas being much happier with the delicately balanced Palladian style.

Throughout this time in his writing and other public advocacy, he pursued a relentless campaign against environmental scandals and appalling buildings. Amabel and Clough were still mixing on the fringe of the Bloomsburg group and the aristocracy; their intermediaries of the former were June and H.G. Wells.

Clough was primarily concerned with domestic architecture and rarely expanded into public works, although he was offered a sort of architectural commissar's position in Russia after he had spoken to the Central Committee on his observations of that country. He eventually refused, realising how long he would have to be out of his own country and how he would be paid in unexportable roubles. On one of his trips to Russia he met Frank Lloyd Wright whom he had to help out at a customs post.

Clough kept up his unending struggle against British Philistinism throughout the inter war years. Our couple wrote the Pleasures of Architecture as their main entreaty to the masses to consider and appreciate their environment. In 1928 Clough had written and published 'England and the Octopus', one of the initiatives that led to an upsurge of interest in preserving the environment. It was a diatribe against the inadequacies of much of urban and industrial planning. His criticisms even stretch to lack of control of litter, which he blames partly on teachers for not educating their charges. In many articles he seeks to protect the natural environment especially his beloved Snowdonia. Clough was a prolific writer of books and also lectured all over Europe; a little book written with John Sorrenson 'Architecture Here and Now' showed he was not entirely averse to modernism. His great interest in architecture was accompanied by many others, including a great love of sailing., and he had his own 15-ton ketch, 'Scott', which he took on many expeditions even across the channel. He experienced many exciting escapades on boats and inevitably was always saved from disaster by his extraordinary luck, an adventurer and loved to explore the islands of the Mediterranean and often based himself in Southern Europe to launch these expeditions; he could never be accused of parochialism.

Now we come to Portmeirion, situated on the peninsula Aber Iâ which he bought; there he determined to build a village for the discerning visitor. It had to generate a profit to pay for itself otherwise Clough could not afford to maintain it. The village is a thoroughly eclectic mixture of all styles, including Victorian Gothic; it was five miles distant from Plas Brondanw and on a beautiful peninsula. The site was surrounded by two estuaries that of Traeth Mawr and Traeth Bach, Clough bought this from an uncle by marriage Sir Osmond Williams. The village is pure Clough, the Town Hall owes most of its existence to the demolition of Emral Hall in Flintshire; at the sale Clough enthusiastically bid for items such as the ballroom ceiling, which he then installed in the Town Hall after arduous transportation in 100 pieces across the nearby mountains. The Town Hall has since been named probably more aptly the Hercules Hall.

Portmeirion Square.

The Second War arrived and Clough gave his blessing to the unofficial use of his village as a rest and recuperation centre for the veterans. Portmeirion was established to give its residents a feeling of privacy and to provide quietness and rest for its visitors, hence cars only for residents and deliveries. One of the first things to be seen, as one enters the gateway is Battery Square with high on its right the Pantheon or Dome. The Dome is in many ways to provide aesthetic pleasures, as is the Belfry, both of which can be spotted from a long way off.

Clough's financing of Portmeirion was helped by the advice of his son-in-law Euan Cooper-Willis and not much was done on mortgage and re-mortgage, shrewdly in fact.

What are we to make of Portmeirion? Lewis Mumford in the New Yorker in January 1962 called it *'an amusing array of politely incompatible, argumentative, but elegantly phrased buildings... It is the fantastic collection of architectural relics and impish modern fantasies.'* Portmeirion is a gay, deliberately irresponsible reaction against the dull sterilisation of so much that passes for modern architecture.

There is no doubt that the film for television *The Prisoner* put this rare village even more on the map; before that a whole host of writers had used it as a place  of retreat. Susan, his daughter, was responsible for the retail outlets and established the pottery in 1960; it has since become known all over the world, the main export markets being firstly the U.S.A. and secondly South Korea. War broke out again in 1939 and at the age of fifty-seven Clough volunteered his services only to be turned down on age grounds; he went on to become a local in the home guard, having let Romney House and returning full-time to Brondanw, where he gave sanctuary to many children from Liverpool. Clough was hardly idle during the War, spending much time on extra mural education for students and other forms of education. His son Christopher was killed in action before Monte Casino in Italy in 1945.

It is interesting after the War, when rebuilding was all the vogue, that a man with Clough's record on conservation would back the pleas for a Butlins camp at Pwllheli and also take on the task of chairman of the committee for the new town at Stevenage. He was even a hardheaded realist over such matters, and both developments eventually did not cause a lot of offence. Clough when he was in Wales spent much of his time protesting against any despoilation of his beloved Snowdonia.

1951 was a very bad year; Plas Brondanw suffered a terrible fire, in which, had Clough not set his alarm for 5 a.m., he and Amabel might have perished. It was thanks to Clough's indomitable persistence and enthusiasm that it was rebuilt in two years. To have lost a son and a house in five years and still retain his optimism shows the tremendous fortitude of the man.

During all this time he served on a number of National Committees including the Welsh Committee of the Festival of Britain, he advised Government Planning on reconstruction of Wales and served on the Hothouse Committee on National parks.

Clough and Amabel after the Second World War spent much of their time in touring abroad, going to Egypt, Damascus and of course America, where he saw Williamsburg, a fossilised Portmeirion. Another book published at the time *On Trust For The Nation* described his appreciation and approval of the National Trust and Britain and was a journey throughout the land describing properties and traits of land belonging to the Trust. Although at times in this book, as with many others, he seems to put the beauty of buildings above the need of people, he comes down eventually on the Lallas side saying *'The best things that are left to us must now clearly be guarded not from the people but for them.'* In 1958 to cap a

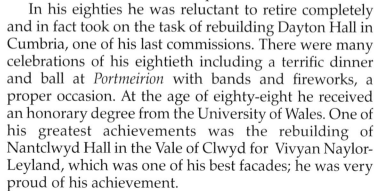

lifetime of service to the country he was made a Commander of the British Empire.

In his eighties he was reluctant to retire completely and in fact took on the task of rebuilding Dayton Hall in Cumbria, one of his last commissions. There were many celebrations of his eightieth including a terrific dinner and ball at *Portmeirion* with bands and fireworks, a proper occasion. At the age of eighty-eight he received an honorary degree from the University of Wales. One of his greatest achievements was the rebuilding of Nantclwyd Hall in the Vale of Clwyd for Vivyan Naylor-Leyland, which was one of his best facades; he was very proud of his achievement.

In his nineties he took to broadcasting like a duck to water; he was remarkable for his aristocratic voice and long yellow stockings, not to mention his tallness of stature. Even at ninety he still travelled, going to Mexico and then New York, and after that Los Angeles, where he was well-entertained. He went off to India and was remarkably unimpressed by such wonders as the Taj Mahal. His early nineties passed with much celebration including Amabel and Clough's Diamond Wedding in 1975, but he was getting frailer, and he found the winter of 1977-78 very difficult; in fact he slipped on ice and fractured his femur; he recovered but was much weaker, but much to some people's expectation declared himself at this late stage 'an atheist'. He died in 1978, much loved, himself a great lover of Wales, of beauty in nature and buildings, a colourful character possessed with great Celtic insight and intuition. He remains a favourite of the author's, because of his boldness, his creativity and love of nature and his country. Amabel survived another six years, exploring Buddhism, writing her autobiography *All Stracheys are Cousins* and mourning the man she had been married to for sixty-three years.

Bibliography:

'Clough Williams-Ellis, The Architect of Portmeirion A Memoir', Jonah Jones, Seren Books, Bridgend, 1996
'Architect Errant, The Autobiography of Clough Williams-Ellis', Clough Williams-Ellis, Golden Dragon Books, Portmeirion, 1971

Chapter Twelve

The Brewing Industry in Wales

Col. S.A. Brain.

Everyone in Wales seems to know Brains Brewery and they also know the famous slogan *'It's Brains you want'*. The brewery on its old site can trace its origins to 1713. On the takeover of Phillips and Andrews by Williams and Andrews in 1844, the site in Saint Mary's Street became known as the Old Brewery. This area was ideal in a way as a deep well had been sunk to reach the water bearing gravel subsoil. Cardiff in 1841 was still a small town, less than half the size of Merthyr, but in 1839 the port and railway to the valleys had been opened up and iron and coal were pouring in. By 1901 the population had exploded from 11,400 in 1841 to 164,300. In 1885 eighteen breweries were listed in the city. In 1862 the old brewery was taken over by established brewers, the Thomas family from Frederick Street. They developed a number of pubs including the Golden Cross in Custom House Street. Their sister Francis Elisabeth Thomas married Samuel Arthur Brain, a descendant of a well-known Gloucestershire family. Samuel Brain had trained as a scientific brewer and had come to Cardiff in 1863. After the debacle for brewers of the Welsh Sunday Closing Act, the Thomases resolved to sell the brewery and who should be waiting in the wings but Samuel Brain. His uncle, a wealthy Bristol banker, supported him with capital. Samuel was ambitious and determined to expand; in 1887 he erected a new brewhouse on land behind the existing one. It was a massive investment and made Brains a leading brewery in South Wales. The brewing capacity was vastly increased. Samuel, backed by his wealthy uncle, bought pubs galore. When he took over, the old Brewery had eleven houses; by 1900 Brains owned or leased eighty. Despite the Welsh Sunday Closing Act of 1881 a large number of private licensed clubs opened to get around the Act, and Brains supplied them. By 1896 Brains were producing 1,400 barrels of beer a week. Samuel Brain was a very clever businessman; he transformed a small brewery into a major city business, his name being remembered by the famous brew SA. He was made Mayor of Cardiff and he turned the firm into a limited company SA Brain and Co. Ltd. The old brewery continued to brew the draught beers and a new brewery was erected to cater for the growing bottle trade.

The new brewery had been built on a site between Nora Street and Helen Street. Brains is unique for the high concentration of their houses in one city. Christopher Brain, the present chairman and great-grandson of the founder admits the brew is an acquired taste; you either love it or hate it - there is not much in between. Some of Brains licensed houses were built by notable architects. The Birchgrove and the Westgate were rebuilt in the late 1920s by Sir Percy Thomas. There were many famous licensees including the famous flyweight boxer Jim Driscoll, who ran the Duke of Edinburgh.

Buckley's Brewery of Llanelli was built up by an extraordinary entrepreneur called Henry Child, who came to the town in 1760. He leased the Talbot's Head and also bought an old malt house and pub called the Falcon. From the profits he leased the Carmarthen Arms in Wind Street in 1791 and built the White Lion nearby. The pubs brewed their own beer and so there was a market in malt and he also leased farms to grow his own barley; he liked to nurture his beer from cradle to grave. After John Wesley's visit to Llanelli in 1769 Henry Child became a Methodist, and in 1798 the Rev. James Buckley from Oldham in Lancashire married Child's daughter Maria. Childs died in 1824. Buckley found himself running the brewery. When he himself died, his son James took over the brewery. He was a figure who was determined, had a high moral approach but was relentless in his pursuit of profit. After his death when Buckley's Brewery was formed in December 1894, the company owned or leased 120 pubs and many others were tied on loans. It had agencies selling its beer throughout South-West Wales. The ultimate seal of approval was fixed to the business, when it was granted a Royal Warrant of Appointment as brewers to the Prince of Wales. After

the First World War in which the firm proved most useful by sending a whole fleet of motorized drays to help in France, the firm again expanded into Cardiganshire and the Swansea and Neath valleys. When the drinking trend changed from draught to bottled beers between the wars, Buckley's main brand was their Special Welsh Ale, which was known around the world. It was sent to Argentina, South Africa and Australia. As time progressed, we now find ourselves in the 1970s when Colonel Kemmis Buckley the great, great-grandson of the Reverend James Buckley was chairman of the firm. He oversaw a major redevelopment of the company but then control passed outside the family to Griffith Phillips a stockbroker; profits began to fall by 21% in 1983 mainly owing to costs incurred by large-scale refurbishment. Two groups looked greedily at Buckleys; Tony Cole of Westwood and Whitbreads were circling like predators. Cole was seen off and his stake was sold to Peter Clowes and Guy Von Kramer. Clowes' empire was in serious trouble and Buckleys had to be put up for sale. Guinness in conjunction with the Club brewery, Crown of Pontyclun formed a joint company. In 1990 Guinness took control of Crown Buckley, the new owners recruited Mike Salter to take over as managing director. In 1993 he negotiated a management buy-out of Crown Buckley from Guinness and the company was again an independent brewery. In 1997 Brains took over the brewery, A scion of the Buckley family, Simon Buckley has successfully set up Evan Evans brewery and has a number of pubs and hotels in Wales including the George in Brecon successfully run by the manager Robert Jones.

David John was the founder of Felinfoel brewery, which started when he bought the King's Head in the village of that name as a sideline from his tinplate and ironworks. In 1878 he erected a large brewery which was built next to the river Lliedi. The brewery built up trade throughout the counties of Cardigan, Pembroke and Carmarthen and was registered as a private company in 1906. David John's daughter Mary-Anne married John Lewis, a compulsive gambler, who shot himself after one gamble too many. His formidable wife carried on the business taking her big stick to the brewery - which she actually used on slackers. The next momentous occasion for Felinfoel was the introduction of canned beer for which the brewery was one of the pioneers in the U.K. spurred on by the large tinplate industry in South Wales. It produced this canned beer from 19th March 1936. When the war arrived canned beer was made almost exclusively for the troops, shipped out by the N.A.A.F.I. Despite the popularity of canned beer, after the war Felinfoel found it hard to compete with the big boys. In 1965 the John and Lewis family had a falling out when Buckleys put a bid in for the brewery; the John family decided to sell-out. The Lewis family held firm and despite its tiny majority of shares it held on to control the 1970s under one John Lewis; a modernization process was started. In 1976 after much hard work, its premium bitter Double Dragon won the Challenge cup for the best cask beer at the Brewers Exhibition in London, also its standard bitter won first prize in its class. Head brewer Fred Cheesewright must take the main credit for this achievement. The Company has survived many challenges and changes constantly and is still at the forefront of the Welsh brewing tradition.

The Rhymney valley was famous in the early 19th century for its ironworks, Benjamin Hall, the son-in-law of Richard Crawshay of Cyfarthfa, ran the Union Ironworks until 1820, Also in the valley was an ironworks owned by the Marquis of Bute. One of his most successful managers was a Scotsman Andrew Buchan, who was instrumental in setting up the brewery as a commercial opportunity to quench his men's thirst. By 1878 it was brewing 12,500 barrels a year and owned 29 tied houses. In 1902 one of Pontypool's main breweries, Crown Brewery was taken over by Rhymney. Known as Andrew Buchan's Brewery, it broke the links with the ironworks in 1929. As time progressed there was to be a link-up with Whitbreads. In 1959 under Col. Harry Llewellyn's leadership they took over Ely brewery and changed the name to Rhymney. Col. Llewellyn had won an Olympic Gold Medal at show jumping in the 1952 Olympics, he was also an experienced industrialist. He had also been decorated

RHYMNEY

by General Omar Bradley for the part he played in planning D. Day and the campaign in Europe as Field Marshall Montgomery's liaison officer. He recognized the potential for lager long before many other people. By 1961 Rhymney was recording profits of £500,000 and was a 700 pub concern and was now even buying hotels like the Angel in Cardiff. Rhymney was a leading innovator introducing tank beer brought in by road tankers. Although things looked quite rosy, in 1964 there were worrying trends on the horizon especially the trend to drink in clubs. Rhymney lacked the mega money to compete and also expand out of the depressed valleys. Whitbread saw their chance for a complete takeover, which was accepted by the shareholders led by Julian Hodge. After Whitbread's takeover of Evan Evans Bevan of Neath the following year, the companies were merged in 1969 to form Whitbread Wales under the Chairmanship of Harry Llewellyn. The company's Welsh roots began to disappear except for the introduction of a low gravity brew called Welsh Bitter. The company did chose to build a huge modern brewery at Magor next door to the M4 and between Cardiff and Newport taking advantage of the huge supply of water pumped out of the Severn tunnel. It was built in 1979 at a cost of £51 million across 58 acres of land; here it brews Welsh Bitter.

Evan Evans had been born at Ynysmaerdy near Briton Ferry in 1794. By 1830 he had become a licensee of the Grant Arms in Neath High Street; he gained a lucrative appointment as the local agent for Guinness. His entrepreneurial spirit was quickly recognized. With partners in 1846 he bought two ships which were partly used to run pleasure cruises to Devon. His Neath brewery in the High Street soon expanded with travellers being employed to extend the business far and wide. He bought out his rival the Vale of Neath Brewery and this gave his enterprise so much more room. By 1866 he was employing 200 workers, and was so much more than a brewer; he became Mayor of Neath, helped establish an efficient fire service and formed the 17th Glamorgan Volunteer Rifle Corps. Evans was shrewd enough to keep on the right side of the Church as the temperance movement grew. In 1864 he bought land outside Neath for coal mining; his son-in-law David Bevan was a great asset in this venture, being a surveyor and colliery engineer. The two of them ended up owning four mines and 800 tons of coal a day were being exported. This large business was taken over when Evan Evans died in 1871 by his equally talented son-in-law David Bevan. He was happier with the coal side of the business, which he expanded and he also was a great pillar of the community, being Mayor of Neath twice. After his death in 1888 his only son Evan Evans Bevan took over. He bought and built pubs at a great rate. By 1919 the company owned 148 houses. On his death in 1929 he was the main colliery owner in Wales with seven mines, and he was said to be the largest single employer in Britain. He also owned large estates in Breconshire. His only son took over, David Evans Bevan, and in 1935 the brewing side was turned into a limited company with 207 pubs. In 1947 the coal mines were nationalized so David concentrated on the brewing side. More pubs were bought and hotels commissioned, output at the brewery was trebled. In 1954 Sir David Evans Bevan's son Martyn became a director but in 1967 they decided to sell-out to Whitbread. Apparently the deal was done on a train journey from Swansea when Col. Bill Whitbread met Sir David and agreed to buy the brewery. Before the deal was completed there was a huge fire at the brewery; this destroyed the bottling plant and keg store. However, much of the operation was moved to Cardiff and in 1969 Evan Evans Bevan and Rhymney Breweries were merged to form Whitbread Wales.

Today, lager accounts for more than half of the beer brewed in Britain. In 1960 very few brewers bothered with lager, but it was at Wrexham that some of the first lager was brewed. Some wealthy immigrant men from Germany and Czechoslovakia came to register their new company in Wrexham on 6th May 1881 and gave it the name The Wrexham Lager Beer Company which was limited to £50,000 in 5,000 shares. They found the right brewing water at Millpond Meadow, and engineers from Austria worked on the plans for the brewery. Initially Wrexham Lager had to content itself with distant business through private hotels and restaurants and despite its claim to be the first British

lager brewer, it didn't go back as far as the Austro-Bavarian Brewery and Crystal Ice Factory of Tottenham in London. By the turn of the century, 80% of Wrexham's output was for export. Robert Graesser was the leading light in the company in 1904 and he had built one of the first purpose built lager breweries in Britain and one of the first to install refrigeration. There were many barriers to its expansion in North Wales, and in fact it was easier to find Wrexham Lager in London in top venues like the Carlton and constitutional clubs. It also hung onto the Cunard Liner trade and was supplied in small quantities to many small British breweries. Just before the

2nd World War it broke into local trade by buying all 23 houses belonging to Beirnes. By 1945 with little opportunity for investment, the brewing plant was run down to such an extent that it was too costly to re-equip and the company sold out to establish Burton Breweries Ind and Coope and Allsopp in 1949. This firm became part of the giant Allied Breweries and a new brewhouse was commissioned in Wrexham at a cost of £2.5 million which opened in July 1963. Wrexham was now brewing foreign lagers such as the American Budweiser for sale in this country. In 1982, the brewery celebrated its Centenary by brewing its famous dark lager and won in 1990 the Championship Trophy for draught lager at the Brewing Industry International Awards in Burton-upon-Trent. Three years later, the Wrexham concern was linked up with another well-known lager when Allied Breweries merged with a Danish Brewery to form Carlsberg-Tetley.

Whisky was just one of the spirits distilled in early Wales; we can go back as far as Reaullt Hir of Bardsey, who in the 4th-century created a spirit known as gwirod, which was a mix of barley, yeast and honey. In the 19th century there was a distillery at Frongoch near Bala. However with the advent of the religious revival, and the increase in temperance, that distillery closed down. The Welsh Whisky Company at the turn of the century won a gold medal at the great Chicago Exhibition of 1901. It had been a very large enterprise with an issued share capital in 1890 of £100,000. The Bala Distillery closed because of the onset of prohibition in the United States and the advance of the Temperance Movement in Victorian Wales. Interestingly, the building was later used as a camp for Irish dissidents during the 1st World War. The whisky was patronised by Queen Victoria and the Prince of Wales and had its own rail link to the Midlands and to Liverpool. In Henry VIII's time and later, there had been a scattering of small farm distilleries, certainly a couple in Pembrokeshire from 1491-1547. The word 'chwisgi' was first heard in about 1784, in the small industry then existing in Wales. In 1643 an excise tax was imposed on distilleries which drove the movement underground. In 1781 the government banned private distillation and all means of creating distillation was subject to confiscation. Money was given to those handing in old pieces of distilling equipment. Duty trebled in 1793 to help pay for the war with France. A man from Dale in Pembrokeshire went to the United States and founded the Evan Williams Distillery in Bardstown in Kentucky in 1783. This was the first distillery in the Louisville area and is still a major brand in America. Thomas Jefferson the famous Welsh American granted settlers 100 acres of land in Kentucky where they could grow corn and the excess was turned into whisky. Jack Daniel can probably be associated with origins in Cardiganshire. His forebears were thought to have emigrated to New York where he was born in 1846. He left home at an early age and went to work for a Methodist preacher and distiller by the name of Dan Call. Eventually he went to Lynchburg in Tennessee where Jack Daniels Distillery was first registered. It was the original distillery in America. It is interesting that although there were many Non Conformist Welsh there and the area was dry, much of the whisky was sold outside the county. Jack Daniel never married or had any children. Lem Motlow his favourite nephew took on the business when Jack died from blood-poisoning.

Dafydd Gittins, a man from Brecon in 1974 saw an opportunity in a market and having decanted raw whisky from two oak casks which had been imported from Glasgow, filtering it and adding an appropriate amount of Brecon water and having special bottles and labels designed, selling Swn-Y-Don as Welsh Whisky. In 1976, Dafydd got a loan from the Welsh Development Agency. Brecon Brewery Ltd. was set up in the old brew house at the back of the Camden Arms. They had a compounders licence from HM Customs and the stocks were kept in a bonded warehouse in Cardiff. In 1982 they leased two units from the W.D.A. at the Ffrwdgrech Industrial Estate. In 1991, they moved to far larger premises on the estate and opened a visitor centre in 1992. However things went very wrong after this; the Scotch Whisky industry brought a court case against the Welsh Whisky because it wasn't distilled in Wales but in Scotland. A new type of still had been designed at the University of Surrey and was used in the new Gwalia distillery in the village of Penderyn at the Southern edge of the Brecon Beacons. Distilling commenced on 14th September 2000. The wash is produced at the Brains Brewery in Cardiff. Gwalia, unlike either Scottish or Irish malt whisky distilleries, it does not have a set up with a separate wash and spirit still but has only one still on which the whole process from wash to new make takes place. The fresh spirit is first matured in barrels that contained Evan Williams bourbon or Jack Daniels Tennessee whisky and are finished in ex-Madeira casks. Tasting-wise, it has fragrance of toffee and vanilla with the slightest whiff of leather and fruits (apples and lemons).

Despite the contraction of the brewing industry, in the 1970s and early 1980s, 300 new breweries came to life across the U.K. which added plenty of variety. In Wales, there were beers like Master-Blaster (Afan Brewery), Druids Ale (Gwent Ales), Piston Bitter (Monmouth Fine Ales) and Snowdon Strong (Gwynedd Breweries). However, by the 1992, the brewery trade was so sown up by the big six (Allied Breweries, Bass, Courage, Scottish & Newcastle, Watney & Whitbread) that out of eighteen of the new breweries that were set up in Wales, only two were left. Although there is heightened consumer power with the founding of CAMRA, the Campaign for Real Ale, the most successful and long lasting of the new breweries in Wales were those linked with complimentary businesses such as Powells and Newtown. These concentrated on wholesaling other brewers' beers in Mid-Wales and were able to revive Sam Powells Beers which although it has gone out of trading, are still brewed by Woods of Winstanstow.

Few other really local breweries survived the cull.

Bibliography:
'Loyalty Pays, A History of the United Clubs Brewery' by Brian Glover, Alan Sutton Publishing Ltd 1995 Stroud
'Prince of Ales, The History of Brewing in Wales' by Brian Glover, Alan Sutton Publishing 1990

Chapter Thirteen
John Lewis and John Spedan Lewis
22nd September 1885

John Spedan Lewis.

John Lewis's stores epitomize Britain's shopping culture today; they cater for all tastes and still have their reputation for variety and not being undercut. They are an unique partnership organization which is a terrific incentive to their staff and their success is largely due to their dynamic founders, John Lewis senior and John Spedan Lewis. They took under their wing the Peter Jones store and although the Lewises were for long based in Somerset, they never forgot their Welsh ancestry; the company could be described as a Welsh concern especially as it has just opened a flagship store in Cardiff, Wales's capital city. The two men's enlightenment could be compared to the paternalism of other of our entrepreneurs like David Davies and Robert Owen.

John Spedan Lewis was born on 22nd September 1885, the son of John Lewis, a West Country draper who had come to London over twenty-one years before, started a small shop in Oxford Street and never looked back. What was the Welsh connection? Spedan Lewis was fond of saying, *'My father was Welsh through and through'*, although the Lewises had come from Pennard on the Gower coast to near Shepton Mallet in Somerset in the 1660s. John Lewis senior was born in 1836 and his family had been craftsmen and shopkeepers in Shepton for more than a century.

John Lewis Oxford Street c.1885.

John Lewis senior was orphaned when he was seven and the family of six was brought up by an aunt Mrs. Ann Speed. In his early forties he grew a large beard, which covered a face which was self-assured with a sensitive mouth, a very round head; he also had large hands and was quite muscular.

At the age of fourteen, after three years at the local grammar school, he left to be apprenticed to a draper called Tasken in Wells six miles away. He left Wells and went on to Bridgewater, still as a draper and thence to Liverpool, and eventually to London. He worked, to start with, in Peter Robinson's and soon became the buyer of silks and woollen dress materials. He got on well with the head of the firm, Mr. John Robinson and it looked as if he might eventually get a junior partnership. However he was desperately keen to be his own man and bought an old tobacconist shop with the help of money from his sisters.

At this time you would only need a pound to rent a shop in Oxford Street but you needed to be known by the wholesale trade in order to establish a line of credit. There were plenty of employees to be had as the labour force was plentiful; their wages were low which made more money available for investment in capital and there was a great flow of money at the time initiated by Victorian businessmen who were doing so well.

John Lewis started his own business in 1864 and remained the sole proprietor for the next forty-two years. He concentrated on building up two or three major departments and collected much money in the process.

He didn't marry until his forties and then married a sister of the founder of the drapers Baker, Baker of Bristol. She had been to Girton at Cambridge and had a good mind although she didn't read much. The family lived in Spedan Tower, a large Victorian house in four acres of ground in Hampstead. She was a convinced Christian, he a confirmed agnostic. He was opposed to baptism for their three sons so she had to arrange it clandestinely.

John loved his garden, taking much time and effort to establish it especially the rockeries, but disliked games and many forms of sport; he quite enjoyed occasional visits to the theatre and the opera and liked to listen to classical piano music. He had a great sense of fun and was extremely inordinately kind, especially towards young children and animals.

Business wise he often grossly underpaid his best employees. Being determined that he would never be poor and that his family would always be well-cared for, he was extremely careful with money.

He was an earnest liberal and a republican although a bit of a snob. He was desperately keen on his rights, so much so that on one occasion he spent a short term in Brixton Prison as a result of his pursuit of them. John hated Trade Unions and at the age of eighty-four was involved successfully in beating a strike of his own employees. He did not have much time for democracy and social justice in his own shop. He was a man of many contrasts who built a business carefully and studiously which his son John Spedan was able to develop.

John Spedan Lewis went to Westminster School where he was a Queen's scholar. At the age of nineteen he went into his father's business and, at twenty-one, was given 50,000 capital plus a quarter of the profits of the Oxford Street shop. Soon afterwards he was placed on the board of Peter Jones, which was at the time a failing store, which his father had purchased the year before. While Spedan was at Westminster school, the Marquis of Salisbury formed the last great aristocratic administration in 1895. As he was being made part-owner of his father's business, the celebrated Liberal government of 1906 with figures like Lloyd George, Asquith and Churchill was taking office and the newly formed Labour Party had 30 seats.

John Lewis general departments, 1899.

Spedan was a creature of his time; he lived as liberalism took over from conservative imperialism at the beginning of the twentieth-century. From these roots his ideas of partnership began. He realised the discrepancy between his fortune and the crumbs the employees of his father earned and never really explained why he set up his partnership. For more than forty years he devoted himself to developing the Partnership, which he started in Peter Jones in 1915, started experimenting with sharing power with his staff as early as 1905 and established the first element in the extensive partnership system of democracy - the Committees for Communication which still function today. Times often became difficult and when they did so he did not hesitate to sell his home and estate in Harrow to move into an apartment, forego his salary and even sell some of his investments to keep the partnership going. In 1920 he started sharing the profits the business made. Every member of staff became one of the owners, with a say in how the company was run and a share in the profits. Today the John Lewis Partnership is one of Britain's leading retailers. Turnover in 1995-96 reached £2.8m and profits stood at £150m before tax. John Lewis at this time operated 23 department stores across the United Kingdom and 113 Waitrose supermarkets. John Lewis offers almost everything for the home and their haberdashery departments are some of the most extensive in the country. Their slogan for 60 years has been, *'We are never knowingly undersold.'* The democratic nature of the partnership was continually reinforced and Spedan Lewis in 1950 established a written constitution for the business and transferred his rights of ownership to the trustees.

A total of 167 people were employees in Waitrose when the John Lewis Partnership acquired the business in 1937 inheriting a turnover of £150,000. Waitrose started a transition from counter to self-service in 1950 (following the American trend) and opened its first supermarket in Streatham in 1955. Waitrose in 1996 employed 14,040 partners who all have a share in the profit and a say in the running of the business of the John Lewis Partnership. In 1996 the cash share of the profit for each partner was 15% of annual pay.

John Spedan Lewis was an impressive man. He had a very long chin and body, shortish legs, an intelligent face and was dynamic; at 6ft 2", he was a strong man, a charismatic figure, and was always superbly turned out. His genius was partly in the shrewd selection of his employees; he adopted early the idea of central buying and the power it gave a business in terms of discount and credit. The purchase of Waitrose and Selfridge Provincial stores in 1940 was a clever move, the key to the whole organisation was the Central Council. Four-fifths of this was elected by the partners; up to one-fifth are appointed by the Chairman. It represents the partners, elects three trustees of the Constitution *John Spedan Lewis in 1906.* through whom the council can remove the chairman; it then elects five directors to the Central Board. If three of these directors so wish, they can require the Board to consult the Council on proposals to liquidate more than 5% of the Partnerships fixed assets, commit the Partnership to increasing its total capital by more than 5%, close a branch or a specialised department of twelve or more partners. Articles and rules are only amended with the Council's agreement. It controls a budget entitlement of 1% of pay sheet for own and branch council spending, and is consulted on any other use of Partnerships profits. Chairman and other Executive Directors make annual reports to Council and answer questions. It has power to discuss any subject and make recommendations to the Chairman and Board.

It is interesting that among the young men Spedan Lewis recruited was Bernard Miller, who had done Economic History in the Nineteenth-Century and who had been very taken with Robert Owen's experiments, another of our Welsh entrepreneurs. People did not feel they were a part of a money-making machine under John Spedan Lewis's management; they were very much part of a team. Sir Bernard Miller who was his personal assistant for some time said that one was swept along by Spedan. One of his great attributes was the clarity with which he argued and put his views across. One of Spedan's other great qualities was to pick the right and bright men more so in those days than women for the job. Spedan was very widely read which helped in the parallels he drew upon for argument; he really did care for people, although he was also desperately concerned with efficiency. He did make mistakes, including hanging on too long to too much stock just at the beginning of the Korean War when prices went very high and then fell back extremely sharply. He wasn't very good at owning up to his own mistakes, but he did take them to heart. A superb retailer and shopkeeper, he just had a knack with prices and seemed more interested in building the structure than seeing it function. He was excellent at detail and in his recruitment for fast stream management he was only really interested in those graduates from Oxford and Cambridge, the two universities he recognised. His interests included skiing holidays, but he was not very good at skiing and much better at tennis, which he played a lot; he also played a lot of cricket but was not much good. Chess was one of his joys and he also enjoyed the opera but his main love was chamber music. His idea of partnership was on a par with some of Owen's innovative ideas and he was, in many ways, of the same sort of stature.

There were many other aspects to Spedan's character. For instance he loved wild flowers. His knowledge of plants and even things like bugs and beetles was enormous. He also had a big collection of waterfowl and other birds on the estate at Longstock. Possessing a very keen brain, which impressed all around him, he turned it to both his leisure interests and retailing especially his idea of partnership, which became a lifelong obsession. Spedan picked many people for the upper echelons of the partnership and although he was generally a kind man, he was quite ruthless if their contribution was not up to the mark.

In terms of the retail business he started off by getting Peter Jones back on to its feet about 1927 or 1928. Although the profits were not spectacular they were built on a firm foundation and he made sure the key people in the organisation were very able. The partnership principle obviously attracted many of them in.

After the re-establishment of Peter Jones he began to experiment by, for instance buying three out of town branches. He was one of the first retailers to institute central buying. The purchase of Waitrose in 1937 and that of Selfridge Provincial Stores in 1940 were brave and successful leaps into the dark, partly as four out of the six main shops existing before the war had been badly bombed.

Consolidation occurred after the war and a strong and flourishing organisation was built. In terms of the stores' own factories it was decided never to manufacture as a firm if John Lewis could get precisely what it wanted elsewhere.

One of his ideas was to promote sailing in the partnership as a team sport and also to give people the chance to sail in a yacht who might not be able to otherwise. The yacht was called after Spedan's aunt Ann Speed. Geoffrey Suage who arranged the building and commissioning of a yacht for the Partnership became an integral part in writing the *Gazette*, was its editor, the partnership newsletter. It is interesting that Spedan never stopped a letter being printed in the Gazette, a very enlightened approach for an owner at that time; although his employees respected him, his managers were quite fearful of him, but underneath it all he was appreciated as a kind man.

Spedan had an extraordinary eye for detail, which he often coached in others. In the trade itself his expertise was buying and this is what he concentrated on. He established one of the best teams in the trade although he did have an uncontrollable temper and when he was just fishing flew into a rage when a trout got off his line, threw down the rod, stamped on it and broke it and never fished again. Spedan was, however, extremely caring to those people who did not have a lot and didn't want to leave his profits to a foundation or even his family but wanted it ploughed back into the Partnership. He continually ferreted around for people's opinions on others in the Partnership especially their superiors, which did not lead to a very relaxed atmosphere.

Spedan was apt to blame in public and tended to overcomplicate things. He had been a good boxer in school and as with all the sports he tried, he only enjoyed golf if he was winning. He was totally immersed in the work of the Partnership and holidays to him were always an inconvenience; he was a great believer in giving people enough rope to hang themselves and was one of the pioneers in trying to attract graduates into trade. His integrity was absolute, but he was excitably vital and had terrific energy.

In 1955 Spedan Lewis retired, nominating Mr. O.B. Miller to succeed him as chairman. Mr. Miller had joined as a graduate learner in 1927 and married another learner Miss Jessica Ffoulkes. The re-building of John Lewis Oxford Street began and the first purpose built Waitrose supermarket opened in Streatham with floor space of 2,000 square feet. For some years after the war, John Lewis traded from a temporary shop; one section of the store facing Cavendish Square had been rebuilt pre-war but had survived the bombing.

1959 - there was the creation of two Directorates of Training, Waitrose as the Directorate of Training for Food was separated from the department stores for the first time. 1960 - the rebuilding of John Lewis Oxford Street was completed 1963 - John Spedan Lewis died on 21st February 1963. At the same time a new central service building for department stores opened at Stevenage housing the Partnerships first computer. 1964 - Was the Centenary of the Oxford Street business and the 50th anniversary of the start of the partnership with Peter Jones. In 1968 the Central Council Committee was set up to examine the sharing of power. Its recommendations were implemented in 1969 leading to some adaption to the roles of Chairman, Central Board and Central Council. 1970 - Weekly communication half hours were re-introduced, and also the first wholly cash payment of Partnership bonus. 1972 - Sir Bernard Miller retired and Peter Lewis the nephew of Spedan became Chariman. 1974 saw the introduction of the first electronic cash registers. 1975 - Metric training began in Partnerships stores. 1976 - John Lewis and Waitrose branches opened in the new Brent Cross Shopping Centre, the partnership's first venture into an out-of-town site. In 1979, the Partnership bonus was 24% and John Lewis and Waitrose branches opened in the shopping centre at Milton Keynes, their first venture into a new city. Long leave was introduced giving 6 months holiday after 25 years service. 1981 - the premises of Lewis's in Bristol was re-opened as John Lewis Bristol. 1983 - was the year the partnership reached 1,000 million pounds turnover in a year.

1984-85 a weeks annual holiday was introduced for all partners after 3 years service. It is important to note that, at last, a John Lewis store has now come to Wales, in Cardiff to take the family back to its roots.

Peter Jones

Peter Rees Jones was born in Monmouthshire in 1893, the son of Thomas Jones, a quite successful manufacturer. After a private education, it was decided he would go into surgery. He served his apprenticeship in Carmarthen and then in 1864 with the sum of £14 in gold in his pocket he deliberately set out for London to make his fortune. It is said that he entrusted his money to a young man from Staffordshire whom he met on the train, who kept it safe for an appropriate time. Peter started off working in Newington but soon moved to the Hackney Road where he bought his first little tailor shop. In 1868 he suffered two great tragedies in his personal life, his twenty-five year old wife Anna died and his two-year-old baby child; he was devastated refusing to leave his wife's grave for some time. His surviving daughter was cared for by relatives in Wales. Peter moved to a shop in Southampton Row, Bloomsbury and remarried a Miss Amanda Cochayne, and in 1871 moved again to Chelsea which was still quite working class in its make-up and then leased two small shops at what is now Draycott Avenue, or Marlborough Road as it was then called. He knocked the two shops into one.

On 14th March 1872 misfortune hit again with the party wall between the two shops collapsing. One young apprentice was killed and Mrs. Jones trapped under a beam for some time. It was said that Mr. Jones was well compensated, as the contractor and foreman were heavily criticised. He then began to expand his business and by 1874 his turnover was £8,000 and total salaries came to £230 a year. By 1884 turnover stood at £40,000 and the number of staff had climbed from 30 to 150 assistants. The number of staff doubled again in the next ten years. Chelsea was beginning to become more fashionable and Peter Jones's clients wealthier.

Mr. Jones himself was a man of great application and diligence, one of the first in in the morning and the last to leave at night. He was a terrific organiser always open to ideas from his workforce and continued extending his shop until 1890. The shop became enormous, built of brick, five-storeys high and crowned by a turret. It had plate glass windows and high show rooms; the umbrella department had marble pillars and had mirrors throughout, and a

Exterior of Peter Jones store.

lovely walnut staircase existed. It was one of the first big shops to have electricity.

Many of the staff lived above the shop. Peter Jones made sure they were looked after with a decent library, piano and billiard tables. They all received a good Christmas bonus and seats were provided in the shop for the female assistants. The shop was floated as a public company; it had profits of £10,802 and peaked in 1902-03 when turnover reached £157,000 with profits of £12,000.

Mr. Jones was chairman of the Board of Directors. This was not so successful from then on; his two fellow directors, his sons were said not to be so interested in the business.

The firm were buying too much cheap bankrupt stock with not too many sales. Mr. Jones was devoting less time to the business and more to his art collection. On 31st August 1905 he died of a chill and stroke. His funeral was large and well-attended by local traders for few had not received favours from him. He was a highly intelligent man with terrific energy and initiative. Peter genuinely cared for the welfare of his workforce; he was a liberal through and through both in thinking and in politics. He never intentionally injured the feelings of his fellow men as the *Drapers Record* wrote at the time of his death. His shop went on to be bought by Spedan Lewis; another enlightened Welshman, from whence it went from strength to strength.

Bibliography:
John Spedan Lewis 1885-1963 published by the John Lewis Partnership, printed in Rugby
The Merchant Princes by Carol Kennedy, Hutchinson 2000 London

Chapter Fourteen
Julian Hodge
1904-2004

He was born in London on 15th October 1904, his earliest ancestors were tradesmen from the town of Barnstaple in Devon. One of them called John Hodge was a clockmaker; many of the family learned this particular craft. Julian's father Alfred was born in 1881 and lived to the age of seventy. He came to know a Miss Jane Simcocks through his interest in amateur dramatics and fell in love with this rather formidable young lady.

Despite slight social inequalities the families had Roman Catholicism in common. After service in the Boer War, Alfred married Jane in January 1902. Alfred returned to his old business of plumbing but things were so tight that for the birth of their second child Julian the family had to return to her mother's house in Cold Harbour Lane, Camberwell. Early in 1909 they moved to South Wales where plumbers were said to be needed and in short supply. The family moved to Hengoed in the industrial Rhymney Valley, where Alfred became a plumber for the local council. He also worked part-time running a cinema in the evenings. After a short time they eventually rented a four-room end of terrace house in Sir Ivor's Road, Pontllanfraith. One of the advantages of the village to Julian's mother was that it had a Catholic Church.

Julian Hodge.

The name Hodge formed a large part of the congregation. Jane was determined to see her flock educated and supplied her off-spring with books from the local library. The avid readings of Dickens turned the young Julian into a youngster of socialist leanings. The Hodges were very hard up and even experienced hunger at times. Julian had short employment in a chemist's shop and then found a job as a junior clerk at Pontllanfraith Station where he got paid 30s a week. The Swansea - Pontypool line on which the station stood was part of the main Great Western system. Julian was determined to succeed; he desperately wanted to escape poverty and also not to be broken by it like his father. His father and Julian's mother Jane carried the burden of the family. At the age of eighteen Julian found himself the main provider for four children. He found himself keeping chickens as a source of income and food.

Julian was promoted to the Divisional Superintendent's Office at Pontypool Road; he had passed his matriculation since leaving school and as a hobby read novels in French. In the Great Western's exams he came first in English and in Railway Operation and Railway Law. Although he didn't pass first in accountancy he became an enthusiastic amateur at this stage of his life. He enrolled with the Association of Certified Accountants in 1925 and embarked on five years of exams.

He worked furiously only taking one night off each week to go to the cinema. Julian Hodge qualified as a Certified and Corporate Accountant in 1930, then enrolled as an external student at London University for a B.Comm.; he came up against science, which he had little aptitude for so he failed to complete.

Julian turned down promotion from clerical to management grades at G.W.R.; he did not want to leave Wales. Although he did nail a brass plate to his mother's home *'Julian S Hodge, Certified Accountant'*, this did not attract many punters and he resorted to selling life insurance in the evenings.

A quite successful venture, he banked £430 by 1934 with which he bought for cash the lease of a local house. It was semi-detached and had four bedrooms with a large attic. He recruited some part-time staff as the business took off and the files in the house were bulging with information. By the mid 1930s he had a full-time clerks job on the railways, some accountancy work and a flourishing life insurance business.

His first venture into entrepreneurial activity was to go into partnership with a Station Master to set up a chemist's shop in the main street in Blackwood. The initial window display was far too ambitious but things took an upturn when bulbs were sold in pots at Christmas time; even a lending library was added but tension rose between the manager and his employees and the shop was sold. He started to play the stock-market but ended up owing £1000, a lot of money at the time and he could well have been bankrupted. His bank manager Russell Thomas bailed him out. With Russell's encouragement he then took out a solid portfolio of stocks with a baker called Wyndham Smith. Through this gentleman he came to the notice of the well-known Withers family; one of them a Jackson Withers owned a cinema chain, and Julian began to manage his affairs. Julian was left to construct the formation of this man's cinema interests with one company. Despite lack of any real knowledge of how to go about this, he found out the mechanics and did it successfully, after which he was employed as their accountant for £500 per annum. The network eventually grew to forty-eight cinemas.

At the beginning of the Second World War Julian was in two reserve occupations, railway official and accountant. In the previous capacity he was fully stretched in the Divisional Superintendents' office organizing trains for the troops. He did offer himself for service, but with flat feet, weak eyes and very low blood pressure he was deemed unfit for duty. Meanwhile he had been introduced to the Carpanini family who had bought the New Continental Restaurant in Queen Street, Cardiff; with the advent of war they were interned on the Isle of Man and Julian was given power of attorney over their business, which he happily improved when he returned it to them.

Julian was also invited to take over as internal auditor to the Cardiff munitions company Currans; to do this he resigned from G.W.R. He re-established his firm in 31 Windsor Place, and discovered much about the stock exchange after he pumped Norman Harry the Cardiff stockbroker for information in the early part of the war. Not long after the end of the war his mother died.

Even after the Second World War Cardiff was a fairly disastrous area for business. Much of the work, which might have emanated from the City of London, did not because of the fear of trade union militancy in South Wales. However, he did persuade after much cajoling Abbey National to allow him to represent and in the first twelve months as their agency wrote more than one million pounds of good business. He had also made friends with Roy Mathews a director of Abbey National who later became very influential. Hodge was to come up again and again against the City's prejudice against Cardiff.

After the war one of his other major moves was to form Hodge & Co. (Insurance Ltd). He also set up an industrial holding company the Gwent and West of England Enterprise Ltd., which was a private company with an authorized capital of £5,000. The initial shareholdings were owned by Hodge & Co. Insurance Ltd. The seeds of his future empire had been sown; the holding company began with the acquisitions' of a number of garages with money borrowed from the bank. Higher purchase was only in its early stages but Hodge, having an eye for opportunity, bought a Newport-based firm of Anglo Auto Finance Ltd., which later became a major part of his own empire.

Julian gathered a good team around him including his old friends Archie Davies and Lawford Yeates in the accountancy practice and Ronald Taylor who was very involved in Gwent's garages. The team often worked an eighteen-hour day. Sam his co-tenant's younger brother, was particularly useful to him as was Donald Walters, a young barrister.

There had been a large number of frauds in the hire purchase business and Julian was keen to avoid such pitfalls. At the beginning he would only lend to established dealers; he always maintained a small force of investigators to make checks on clients. One of the ways he attracted depositors was to offer them high interest rates; as such he made enemies with other Finance Houses, which kept him out of the Association for some time.

In the early years of Anglo Auto Finance the company dealt with garages, motorcar dealerships and used car sales all within the car area. The company also kept a tied connection, whereby it kept control in one form or another of the source of the hire purchase business. It was an obvious step to buy a car new or old from a Hodge garage under a hire purchase agreement from a Hodge firm and was insured through Hodge & Co.

Julian had worked so hard he had little time for his private life. A young woman half his age Moira Thomas had worked with him on the accountancy side and he gradually realised he was in love with her and although she resisted him for five years they were married at St. Peters Roman Catholic Church, Cardiff on 31st December 1951. He had by the 1950s made such a name for himself that the bankers granted him a loan of £1 million, and joined the board of a largish firm called Avana Associated Bakeries in August 1951. He persuaded the board that an expansionist policy was best and purchased two other companies. One of the subsidiaries of these companies was a jam factory in Ledbury which was nearly bankrupt; Julian persuaded Lloyds to lend him £75,000 in order to stock Marks & Spencer with raspberry jam; he was lent this by Lloyds and the relationship never looked back. From this transaction Julian developed a productive relationship with Marcus Sieff of Marks & Spencers. Julian took over the chairmanship of the Board of a temporarily ailing Avana and thanks to his contacts with Marks & Spencers was able to restore the firm's finances. Eventually £11 million pounds of business was done through the two companies.

During the first six years of Julian's chairmanship before tax prospects of Avana rose from £128,000 to £434,000, the assets employed almost trebled. Hodge began to make pronouncements on companies outside his orbit, which did not add to his popularity in some quarters.

In 1956 he formed an organisation called Investors Protection Facilities Ltd., partly to provide advice and to protect minority interests in companies. Hodge and his colleagues Sam Taylor and Donald Walters would often appear at shareholders meetings armed with extensive research and really put the board through their paces. Investor Protection Facilities was never unsuccessful and over time it gained about £20 million for the shareholders it represented. It helped to protect many vulnerable individual shareholders, of which there were a lot more then than there are now. Hodge however did lose money on the concern, but he did gain prestige and loyalty as a result of his efforts.

Hodge's own business consisted of a heavy connection between the motor distribution and retail interests and hire purchase interests. To this he was also adding cinemas, stores, caravans, engineering, transport and banking. Gwent & West of England Enterprises was keen to become a group of nine quoted companies ultimately responsible to Gwent, on whose board each would be represented. By the early 1960s the group's garages were selling nearly 15,000 new vehicles per year. Hodge also began an incursion into the caravan market; St. Donats Holiday estates owned and managed a chain of holiday sites throughout South Wales.

The Hodge group transport interests were completed by Gomm's Commercial Motors and Reliant Motors. He bought Reliant primarily for its three major dealerships and 300 hire purchase outlets; it was also by the early 1960s producing 150 three-wheeled cars per week; it had also entered the sports car market with the Reliant Sabre.

There was a new group of three companies, first Reliant then Hodgkinson Bennes of Manchester, a company which manufactured automatic stokers for coal fired boilers, and Bond cars of Preston, the only other manufacturers of three-wheel cars in Britain. The new company was called the Reliant Motor Group. It made Hodge the second biggest British owned vehicle manufacturer. Another fire caused great problems in the business but Hodge's generosity in paying the laid off workers one-half to two-thirds their wage, created enormous goodwill. Many countries wanted the franchise to assemble Reliance car, and Tankey's first car the Anadol was designed and developed by Reliant.

The 1967 Budget produced a wonderful concession for Hodge the easing of hire purchase restrictions on three-wheeled cars. Under his management the work forces at Reliant had increases from 300 to 2500, Hodge owned it for fifteen years but was eventually sold off as things began to get harder.

In the years of rationalization the South Wales Cinemas Ltd. was also pruned from the Hodge Group. Howells the department store in Cardiff and all its accessories had become rather relevantly on Hodge's part one of his targets around 1961.

It was losing money and had a £2.5 million overdraft. Lloyds again came to the rescue and the completion of the deal made Hodge the overdraft king of Wales. The first year saw a turn round from a heavy loss to a profit of £75,000 thanks to a huge change in management and accounting procedures.

Hodge himself regularly briefed the staff and encouraged them mightily. Eventually he sold the store to House of Frazer despite his keenness to keep it in Welsh hands, but the sale was almost forced on him by Standard Chartered Bank who could see no place for a shop in the Hodge Group.

In 1960 a new company was formed - Julian S. Hodge & Co. as a type of merchant bank, an idea Hodge had been toying with for some time. Its operations were more of an American investment bank, new issues mergers and capital reconstructions. In addition to setting up this concern, he couldn't but help set up another merchant bank, Gwent and West Industrial Development Ltd. The nature of this company was to help and nurture minority businesses. It was generally disliked by the London establishment for its Cardiff base and its hire purchase foundation.

On Tuesday May 9th 1961, as a result of the conviction of the advantages of public companies, Hodge proceeded with the flotation of Gwent and West of England Enterprises. It gave the Hodge family holding of 3,187,532 shares a value in excess of £4.5 million. He had become a multi-millionaire. His additional funds gave him access to even more potential for borrowing. He established the Hodge Group, which was the old Hodge Insurance Company with the Gwent & West as one of its main five subsidiaries.

After some liaison with Edward du Cann who had launched the first of his six unit trusts in 1963, which were based in Cardiff, Welsh Dragon was the first of his trusts; the starting offer was of £5 million units. There was strong buying from the Welsh at home and abroad. By 1966 the Trust showed a 15% growth in capital.

His most interesting trust was High Income, which sold a record £10.5 million units within two weeks of its launch. Its yield settled at 7.5%, it was based on high-risk shares. Hodge rather lost interest after the initial burst of enthusiasm and sold out to First Finsbury Trust in March 1970 with a paper profit of £1.5 million. Hodge's headquarters in the early years was 31 Windsor Place, which was at one time the registered office for 200 companies. The morale of the staff in this complex network of offices was excellent. Hodge's office door was always ajar; he was almost always there first in the mornings.

He eventually moved lock stock and barrel to a fourteen storey building in the Newport Road designed by F.H. Skinner a Welsh trained architect. It was eventually built at the extremely low cost of £1 million. The new building was called the Julian S. Hodge Building, and was occupied at the end of 1966. The chairman's office was the top one-third of the building so he did not see as much of his employees.

The 1960s were a trying time for the Hodge Group including the early discovery that the new computer systems were incompatible. Hodge was not generally a risk taker but was often open to rather grand ideas and also to rather direct personalities.

Julian was always regarded with some suspicion, as he was very much an outsider in the city. However his connection with James Callaghan, who was an M.P. in Cardiff and a senior member of the government had him invited along to various I.M.F. companies where among others he established a connection with W.G. Pullen, chairman of the Chartered Bank, who was interested in Hire

Purchase and soon took a 22% stake in Anglo Auto Finance. As 1973 progressed Hodge became more jittery about the banking sector, and decided to sell to Standard Chartered, the assets of the Hodge group totalled £275 million and the purchase price was £45 million; Hodge was to join the Standard Chartered's board, and the board and management of the group was to stay the same. Hodge got out just before the secondary banking collapse. What timing! It is likely that because of the strict rules Hodge imposed on his business, it would have survived.

In 1978 the licences which many Hodge companies needed to carry on their business came up for renewal most of them passed without a problem. But both Julian S. Hodge & Co. and Hodge Finance Ltd. were issued with a warning from the Office of Fair Trading that it was minded to refuse their licence. This was a great blow to Hodge and to Standard Chartered. Hodge was so infuriated he applied to the O.F.T. for a licence in his own name which was issued immediately.

Hodge's date of retirement fixed as October 1978 was coming up and Sir Idwal Pugh former ombudsman and permanent secretary was recruited to take his place as chairman. Standard Chartered were not so generous towards Hodge, the name of his building was changed and the name of the Group to Chartered Trust to identify it more clearly with the parent group.

One of the great questions that always troubled and invigorated the great man was the absence of a home grown Welsh bank. Although the Lloyds had obviously started their bank a long time ago, Williams and Glyn sounded as if they had Welsh connections and the Bevans were one of the controlling families of Barclays.

The National Bank of Wales had gone bankrupt in 1907. The last of the notes of the private banks in the U.K. were withdrawn from circulation in 1921, although eight Scottish and six Irish banks still issued their own.

The idea of a Bank of Wales was not new. In 1968 John Ellis, a London Welshman who was chairman of Industrial Leasing & Finance Ltd. had by memorandum proposed to the Board of Trade the formation of a Bank to be known as the Bank of Wales. Julian meanwhile had his own plans, when he was supported by James Callaghan who had recently been Chancellor of the Exchequer and George Thomas the Minister of State for Wales. George and Julian had much in common, a deep faith and lifelong devotion to their mothers. In June 1968 the Welsh Council set up a Finance Panel to look in to the establishment of a Welsh bank. One of the propositions was that there was a shortage of rich capital in Wales which was an obstacle to economic growth. Some on the panel concluded that there was not so much a shortage of finance in Wales but a lack of demand for it. The panel however did eventually come to the conclusion that there was a shortage of rich capital in Wales, which was partly due to a gap in financial services. In a speech not long afterwards to the Wales Branch of the Institute of Directors, he said, *'Wales now needs an investment bank that will give greater investment structures to the development of indigenous Welsh industry... A Bank of Wales would be a profit making concern having as its main aims the providing of short medium and long term advances to small and medium Welsh industry. A large proportion of people employed in Wales especially in the manufacturing industry are controlled from other counties, this cannot be good for the principality.'*

There are fewer indigenous small firms as compared with other regions. This seems to emphasize the fact that there is not sufficient financial facility in Wales to get small businesses under way.

Hodge's view of a Welsh bank would be as a symbol of regional development in order to help indigenous industry and quicken the pace of diversification. Second it should attract foreign investment, third it would be a focal point of the Welsh economy.

Scotland owes much of its great industrial resurgence to the fact that it has the advantage of at least five note issuing banks who have attracted American and other capital from overseas, to revitalize and expand its industries. Scotland also has its great life assurance companies, its investment trusts and other financial institutions, Wales enjoys but little of these and it is that vacuum we should try to fill. In the ten years to 1968 the number of jobs in the service industries in Wales had grown from 76,000 to 126,000 but at the end of the decade only 16,000 of them were in banking, insurance and finance companies with 50,000 in Scotland. In proportion to the size of its population the figure in Wales should have been 28,000.

Hodge had been a lavish benefactor to Labour Party funds and his connections with the two arch Labour party members Jim Callaghan and George Thomas gave much speculation to possible corruption, but there appeared no truth in this as speculation of both sides of the political divide gave rise to problems for both the financier and the politicians.

Julian announced his plans for the Bank of Wales in 1969 but it took ages, thanks to problems caused by the Bank of England to resolve its name. It was finally called the Commercial Bank of Wales. It was incorporated as a £100 private company on 9 February 1971. Twenty months later on its public share offer its capital had been raised to £5m of which First Chicago had a million.

Julian Hodge's personal holding was 3,100,000 which was by far the largest. After a public meeting, which raised £18m from 14,000 applicants, the Banks opened for business from its H.Q. in St. Mary's Street. The building had been bought from the Co-operative Wholesale Society three years earlier and had been renamed Hodge House.

A large number of clients of the Hodge merchant bank turned to the Commercial Bank of Wales rather than the clearing banks. The Bank set out to market itself and spent endless time pursuing this goal. Its primary assets were its close knowledge of businesses in the Principality and some unconditional ways of helping them. An example of this was a company which had landed a substantial Middle East order, but needed to fulfil it. The Bank in order to try and get around the problem purchased the products before they were made and sold them back just before delivery.

After the secondary banking crisis in the late 1970s new rules were drawn to give full banking status to banking institutions. Unfortunately the Commercial Bank of Wales was denied this. Julian and many people in Wales felt insulted and disillusioned by the City's direct wager and its remoteness from Wales.

The bank meanwhile in 1981 was exceeding its previous year's turnover of £310.

The Jane Hodge Foundation

Julian Hodge was not a man who loved money for its own sake but for what he could do with it; he was thrifty like so many multi-millionaires but he always wanted to do useful and patriotic things with it.

He lived in a substantial Edwardian House in Lisvane called Ty Gwyn, which he lived in until 1933. Since then he lived in an extensive bungalow in the grounds of Ty Gwyn. He did some entertaining but made it a rule he would never go out the evening before a board meeting. From 1976 onwards he got rid of a large number of directorships keeping only thirty on. For offshore reasons he bought a house in Jersey and had also a cottage in Tenby.

Hodge was never one for laying people off and in many ways was very enlightened when dealing with his workforce, often employing people who could have been unemployable in any other circumstances. He certainly however was not a softie; he expected his employees to work hard. His workforce, including the senior managers, seemed to enjoy working for him; he tried to involve as many people as possible in the organisation.

Jane Hodge, his mother died before he reached his greatest heights as a businessman but he wanted desperately to remember her in some concrete way. Of all seven children who had all had disparate and interesting qualities she was extremely proud. Hodge set up the Jane Hodge Foundation on 15th October 1962, Julian's fifty-eighth birthday. It was launched with a gift of £2.5 million. By 1980 the Foundation and Sir Julian Hodge Charitable Trust between them owned more than 80% of the equity of the Carlyle Trust, the Hodge family's holding company. The Foundation had almost grown to £20m. Its aims were the encouragement of medical and surgical studies especially in the field of cancer, the advancement of education and religion. The Foundation has been concerned primarily with recognised charities. The charities that have been most successful with the Foundation are those that encourage self-help, even a request for 400 Italian - English dictionaries from a Catholic missionary station in India was met.

Hodge was determined that the Foundation should not be seen as a mere handout facility. He was always reluctant to be solely responsible for too many projects. After the ceremony he built a new home on the site of the former Lord Ninian Home in which Jane Hodge died. Julian was formally awarded a Papal Knighthood in the Order of St. Gregory by the Archbishop of Cardiff in the Home's chapel. He was also awarded an Honorary L.L.D. from the University of Wales after endowing a number of chairs at the university including a banking chair at U.W.I.S.T. Also instituted at U.W.I.S.T. was the annual Jane Hodge Memorial Lecture. One of the first speeches was given by Leslie O'Brian Governor of the Bank of England the first given by the Governor in the 276 years of the Bank's history.

Many more illustrious lectures followed, an occasion which became one of the highlights of the Welsh year. Hodge lives on still, and his impact on Welsh life has been enormous and is best summed up by George Thomas' speech.

'Everyone in public life has to take knocks from time to time; it is part of the price we pay for being in the public eye. But I believe that Sir Julian has had more than his share of unfair bickering and the time has come to put the record straight. His generosity to good causes cannot be measured. His life is based on a simple, truthful Christian faith. His faith is his life and all of us who know him know this to be true. Thus his genius is matched by massive integrity. Thousands of people in Wales are in his debt (a comment that drew unintentional laughter). Not only was he the architect of the Bank of Wales, which has been the means of keeping thousands of people in employment today, but also he has sustained every charitable cause that is worth the name that comes to his attention, many of which would have collapsed without his aid. I want to thank you, Sir, for what you have done, for what you are doing, but above all to thank you for what you are, a Christian gentleman who seeks to put his truth into practice, I am proud to call you a friend.'

Bibliography:

'Julian Hodge A Biography' by Timothy O'Sullivan, published by Routledge and Kegan Paul Ltd 1981 London & Boston
Various newspaper articles

Chapter Fifteen
Laura Ashley
1925-1985

Laura Ashley from the start was committed to Wales. She loved her grandmother's house in Dowlais and she never really looked back, building up her business in the Carno district of mid-Wales, giving much work to that low income area and a little like another of our entrepreneurs William Morris, she inspired a whole movement of new textile design and pattern which coincided with the revolutions of the 1960s. She epitomised this time of rebirth with her loose and free garments harking back to the days of Edwardian romanticism.

Laura had a genius for colour and pattern and brought joy and happiness not only to many parts of Wales but to many parts of the world.

Laura was born in Wales. Her grandmother's house, a colliery workers cottage in Merthyr Tydfil left an indelible impression on her. It was situated above the smog-filled valley at Station Terrace on Dowlais Top. Enoch Davies, Laura's grandfather bought 31 Station Terrace, having come from a large farming family in Pembrokeshire. Enoch himself did not become a miner but a policeman. Granny was a Welsh-speaking Beynon, whose great belief was in family values rather than radicalism. There was a veritable extended family in Station Road to where three of Granny Margaret's sisters also moved. Although Enoch Davies was a Conservative, theirs was Labour country where Keir Hardie

Laura Ashley.

got elected as the first Labour M.P. to Parliament. Lewis Stanley Mountney was a young man who had suffered in the First World War and was a cousin of the Davies's, who eventually married their daughter Bessie. Bessie started off married life living with his parents in a house in Camden Road, near Holloway. Stan was a clerk in the Civil Service but when Bessie became pregnant she fled back to Wales. The child a girl arrived on 7th September 1925 attended by that well-known and well-loved Dr. Cresswell and his midwife assistant Nurse Harris. She was called Laura, a name not in the family but that her parents had taken a liking to. Her father in particular was thrilled with a daughter and the baby was taken back from Dowlais to Holloway. They soon moved to the newly developing district of Beddington Park near Croydon in Surrey. It had a lovely garden not big but with a group of apple trees and lavender bushes. Two boys and a sister soon arrived in the household and Laura used to creep off to seek the quietude and relaxation of her Auntie Elsie who lived nearby. She even had her own bedroom in Auntie Elsie's house. It was Aunt Elsie introduced Laura to books, which she came to love especially romantic novels. She went to the local primary school where she observed and disliked the rather dank dark environment, which held all sorts of fears like spiders. She spent many happy holidays in Wales. It was a world that had remained unchanged for many years, the women would work unencumbered by the worries that beset Laura's own mother. The way of life was dictated by family, chapel and a sense of cleanliness. Laura was a spiritual child and such ideas as that of the Devil existed very really in her mind. Wales was the best part of her life, that old Victorian Wales. At the beginning of the war, the great evacuation took place; at least Laura went to a place where she was known and welcome in, Dowlais. It was so difficult in many parts of Wales to find an appropriate school as so many English children flooded in to the comparative safety of Wales. At fourteen she was sent to a sort of secretarial college in Aberdare, so in many ways her formal schooling was over. Laura was disappointed and rather disillusioned by her new existence in Wales so jumped at the opportunity to return to Wallington to keep house for her father. She had not found the golden age of her youth in Wales, but still harked back to it as an ideal. Also harking back in her imagination to the genteel and comfortable times of the Victorians; the images were Jane Austen rather than Dickens. Once she returned to London she carried on her secretarial training at Pitman's College in Croydon. She loved looking after her father who was devoted to her; she was marvellously ingenious at getting by in wartime, especially on the domestic front. She was a rather solitary girl, given to much reflection and this was often done in the study of other people, which led to the great sensitivity she later practised as a business owner and manager. In 1941 she joined the newly formed Girl's Training Corps. She had dark hair and brown eyes with a neat petite face and delicate skin.

In 1943 she was accepted for training in the W.R.N.S. but during her last year at Wallington in the local youth club she met Bernard Ashley, the leader of a gang of friends who had joined. Bernard's father owned two small grocer shops one in North London and one in Catford, which provided dairy produce and game for John Sainsbury. Bernard's father, Albert had joined up in 1914 and was involved in some of the bloodiest battles in the war, surviving against all odds. Bernard was brought up above the shop by a very ambitious mother and a gentle father. He went to Whitgift Middle School and although not good at passing exams excelled on the sports field, and was particularly intrigued by all things mechanical. He was a person of enormous energy and enthusiasm, certainly a leader with a full zest for living. Laura and Bernard met at the youth club and there at an Air Cadets dance they began to go out. They were only eighteen, she was accepted by his gang of friends and in many ways she preferred male company to female. She treated Bernard like a boy, he later said; he was eleven months older than her. Bernard in 1943 was accepted to a commission in the First Ghurkha Rifles and Laura went off to the Mill Hill Training Depot for new Wren recruits. She spent much time learning and sending out messages in code. Then she was sent to Southsea and worked on secret Naval business at a country mansion still corresponding with Bernard who was in India.

She was inevitably inextricably involved with communications at the time of the Normandy landings, Operation Overlord. She then became one of the first W.R.E.N.S. to enter Normandy after the landings, sustained by her religious faith. Laura moved back from France to Chatham, her father not allowing her to go to Germany. She was demobbed in August 1946. Bernard came back to England and they took up where they had left off; he was soon also demobbed and like thousands of other young soldiers had few proper qualifications so he became a clerk with a paint company. He soon became bored and eventually found a job with a small family run investment company in the City where he stayed for four years and learned a lot about money. They were finally married 1948, and moved into furnished rooms in Cheam but had soon moved into a rather elegant flat in Drayton

Bernard Ashley.

Gardens, Chelsea, very different from the suburbia they had been used to. Laura had a profound influence on Bernard; she managed him and his impetuosity, calmed him and soothed him. After Drayton Gardens they moved to a flat in St. George's Square, Pimlico. She resigned her job in the City to get something more amenable to domestic life and was offered a secretarial job in the handicrafts department of the National Federation of Women's Institutes in Victoria. Bernard never liked to be bored; he was always for excitement in life, and he thought at the time his destiny lay in writing but the rejection slips came in fast and furiously. He loved jazz, which gave him some of the excitement he longed for. She still had a great affection for the Women's Institute, which she retained into later life. Laura became very impressed by worked fabrics after she attended an exhibition of traditional handiwork organised by the Women's Institute at the Victoria and Albert Museum. She loved the embroidery, hand printed fabrics, patchwork and quilts; this heightened her interest and she sought to print her own fabrics that could be placed in patchworks; this became a project for her time when she found herself pregnant in 1953. She discovered mainly from books the necessity of a silk screen. Bernard's interest in engineering came to the fore and soon they had built their first textile painting screen stencil.

Neither of them could draw properly so the first designs were very basic. Bernard had learned almost all he needed to know about developing and printing. There was no time for social life; it was full steam ahead with this new enthusiasm. They visited Italy on holiday and quickly noted the fashion the Italians had of wearing simple sweater scarves, these were convenient to create with their screen limited to the table's width.

Laura had to resort to large shapes full of bright colours because of the unsophisticated nature of the printing arrangements. A week after production had begun Bernard sold six tablemats with a two colour African print to a handicraft shop in Ludgate Circus for a pound. They could only afford to order one roll of cotton and silk fabric at a time.

Laura meanwhile was awaiting the birth of her first baby and was rushing around at the same time promoting the business. She went to John Lewis's in Oxford Street and hesitantly approached the buyer in the boutique who thought her scarves delightful and offered to take two-dozen on a sale or return basis. Laura was cock-a-hoop and even more so when the buyer having sold all those ordered seventy-two more. Twenty-four hours later the order was repeated. Bernard decided to quit his job in the City to concentrate on the business. The best of the scarves sold at John Lewis and Peter Jones and were priced at three shillings each. Laura gave birth on 1st October 1953 to Laura Jane and returned home to find their flat converted into a factory. Between April 1953 and Christmas sales came to £1,500. By early 1954 Laura was pregnant again, Bernard found and rented a large basement in Cambridge Street, where he was able to construct a small factory. On 19th March they launched the Ashley Mountney Company with capital of £500. They were to be manufacturers and dealers of fibrous fabrics. Bernard in May to September was back in his grandfather's factory trying to build the necessary efficient machinery for production. Colours were varied and increased including the blues and browns, which the firm was to become famous for. He built the vitally important continuous printer, which led to increased continuous efficiency and expansion; they were printing 300 metres per week. In November 1954 David was born. Staff, often friends were employed and a graphics graduate from Camberwell Art College was employed on a full-time basis. Bernard did much of the designing at this time, creating quite loud brash patterns in contrast to the dullness all around in the fifties.

The climate was highly receptive to new ideas and forms. Bernard's skill at sales was essential for success at the time, he was always striving for improvement, and he never considered the possibility of failure. They had trouble with the police and neighbours with the fumes that came out of the basement factory but Bernard always had the last word and business carried on as usual.

They then started printing tea towels with Victorian themes, which were a great success. All extra cash was ploughed back into the business. Laura herself went out and researched the Victorian themes often from booksellers on the Charing Cross Road.

At about this time Laura spotted an advertisement in one of the newspapers for tenants for a country cottage on an estate on the Kent-Surrey border. She thought this would be ideal as a quieter place to live but near enough to London for Bernard to commute. It was here to which they moved and the idyllic environment gave rise to the many ideas she was beginning to have about designs. Although it was potentially a lonely existence Laura had a circle of friends who regularly came to stay. She roamed the fields and hedgerows fascinated by the plants and wild flowers, she kept goats in the orchard, collected fuel from the woods; it was all very much back to nature. Laura was very involved with the local church and taught at the Sunday school. There was a veritable lack of money but they managed. Within a year of moving she was again pregnant. The children ran wild in this natural environment and they experienced a wonderful freedom encouraged by their mother.

Back in London, *House and Garden* magazine had given the venture some publicity. Business mounted up and Laura and Bernard decided to rent a showroom in old Burlington Street. One buyer from San Francisco ordered the whole collection of Victorian tea towels on a continuous basis. They began to print cotton drill converting it into oven gloves and aprons.

Their second son Nick was born on 15th January 1957 and a new factory building was set up in an old coach house at Brasted four miles from their home; their old premises had been outgrown. Local women outworkers were employed, as were two school leavers. Laura was full of sympathy and caring for her workers, yet another example of such a trend among many of our entrepreneurs.

Their tea towels were beginning to sell all over the world even in *Macys* in New York. They were almost all black and white. Unfortunately in 1958 a flood on the River Derwent almost put them out of business.

They rebuilt after the flood on surer foundations and with the insurance proceeds were able to open a bigger office and showroom in London. It was often the simplest patterns that did best. They invented a Basic Dress partially for maternity wear, which went a bomb, and sold with a sun hat for only twenty-nine shillings and sixpence. They experimented with floral prints and these proved very successful. Many of the products were now signed with Laura's name. Sales from 1955 to 1960 grew from 2,000 to 8,000 per annum. Many of their friends felt they lived in near poverty but sheer persistence and determination got them through. However they never failed to pay an employee. Bernard was becoming increasingly frustrated especially with the banks and the taxmen. Laura could not take the tension any more and at the age of thirty-five and with three children she walked out. After a brief flirtation with Eastbourne she headed to Wales. It was as if instinct had taken her back there. She camped with her children on the banks of the Mawddach Estuary near Dolgellau. After three weeks and Laura knew he would, Bernard arrived. After six weeks she found a lovely small house in Machynlleth called Gwalia House. There were sixteen chapels and sixteen pubs in a town of 2,000 people.

They paid £1,500 for the house, the last of the insurance money. She started a shop in which Laura also sold Welsh flannel and walking sticks. The house became a gathering place for customers and friends and was known for its friendliness; it also became a place the Ashleys could test out their products. Young girls from the farms came to work for Laura; she was a perfectionist and sometimes the hours were hard but she was a much-loved employer who got the most out of her girls. Laura never stopped; she was the original all singing all dancing businesswoman and mum.

For a long time no factory premises were available in Machynlleth, but then the Chief Officer of the Mid Wales Industrial Development Corporation found a building for them, a disused social club at Tybrith. Bernard dismantled the factory in Kent and moved it lock stock and barrel still smarting from being turned down by so many banks for their planned expansion.

Bernard struck up a very positive relationship with the local M.P. for Montgomery Emlyn Hooson. The Ashleys were most sensitive to all things Welsh and were thoroughly appreciated, and welcomed for this. Laura employed young mothers and they all had a half-day on a Friday to give them a break before the chores of the weekend. Wages were considered excellent and lunch was paid for in the pub by the Ashleys. Within two years the factory had become profitable. Laura became aware that the full-length dress was a seller. She had a following of students from Aberystwyth, locals and tourists and she very quickly picked up the vibrations of what they wanted.

The Swinging Sixties were upon us, especially Flower Power. Although in some ways this was a brand new culture rejecting past conventions, there was too a retrospective about it. There was a romanticism about these years and an escapism. Laura although sensitive and egalitarian believed profoundly in the family.

Bernard in particular was still restless and the announcement Laura was  pregnant sent them out looking for a new house, which they found up in the hills, it was called Clagau and was an eighteenth-century farmhouse with eighty acres of land. Their years there were some of their happiest, although Laura's insistence that the children should be happy at school led to their moving schools an enormous number of times. Emma Mary, the Ashleys' youngest child was born at Machynlleth Hospital.

By the mid-sixties Ashley Mountney products were selling all over the world. Laura realised that in many ways they needed an outlet of their own, too many impediments were put in their way by the large stores. Bernard was however wary believing the company's skills lay with the dyers and printers.

The Ashley miracle was founded on the wholehearted commitment and loyalty of a Welsh community. It was essentially in Laura's eyes a Welsh enterprise. On 23rd February 1967 Carno Station was bought as the site for a new factory, at the same time after an enormous search Bernard was able to borrow £14,000 from the Industrial and Commercial Finance Corporation Ltd.

It was very much a gut feeling rather than market research, which led her to experiment with long dresses. She was convinced her own taste would be that of other people. Each machinist concentrated on a whole garment thus getting away from the boredom of a conveyor belt process.

The basic long dress took only fourteen concentrated minutes to make. All mail order went through the Carno sub-post office until eventually things got so chaotic that an extension had to be built. The company had the usual problem of being unable to afford the sophisticated machinery needed to expand but unable to generate the profits to buy the machinery without first having it to make a more sophisticated garment and earn the resulting increased profit.

It was about this time they decided to buy a London shop. Posters were placed on the Underground and their little shop was given as the stockist. This had a terrific effect on sales with girls queuing around the block, the *Observer* and *Express* wrote favourably about the patterns and sales rose to over £3,000 per week. Moira was quick to spot demand and the ability to make dresses quickly was a godsend. Meirion was at the end of a phone and Moira was quick to instruct him on orders although not colouring; he was the expert on dyes etc. The colours at the time were unique and they moved away from bright and ostentatious colours to darker mushroom brown and sage green that became so popular. The means of delivery was now a Ford Transit van, which often travelled all night to Pelham to deliver, the drivers reporting for work the next day. Despite the trouble unions caused in the sixties Laura Ashley was never unionised and the workers ate in the same canteen as the Ashleys and their children went to the same schools which all helped.

Laura was primarily concerned with prints, ideas for which were often found in old books, perhaps less so with style which was fairly interchangeable and well sorted out. She formed an extensive library of prints and had heraldic prints of lions and swans, plant prints of things like thistles and many flowers. Her new designer, hired from the  Royal College of Art, Jacqui Smale was sent to places like the Victoria and Albert Museum to do her research. Laura had to approve everything and it was preferable that the ideas came from her. At about this time in 1969 Laura and Bernard felt they needed a London base and bought a lovely nineteenth-century house in Raultons Square.

The seventies was really Laura Ashley's time, this was when she made her most impact. It was understood by so many that clothes were part of their personality and her fashions expressed best what they thought about themselves, pretty but not ostentatious. Laura had great fashion publicity from a fashion press who felt she was totally in touch with the times and mood. New outlets were needed to cope with demand of her products.

The policy continued with the maximum amount of stock being placed in minimal decoration.

In 1971 the firm had to move out of Pelham Street and moved to 71 Lower Sloane Road. A new shop also opened in Bath, which, being close to the American Museum and the Museum of Costume, intrigued Laura and gave her many new ideas.

An agency was set up in Australia and Canada.

The clothes were cheap but varied, often plain cotton but also using such materials as lace, velvet and silk.

Laura saw her clothes going primarily to working women; she intended to sell them a whole wardrobe from nightdress to wedding dress. The Laura Ashley dress was made out of natural fibres and with its cheap price appealed to many shapes and sizes of women; therefore it had a sort of universal appeal. She, like William Morris, had a strict sense of ethics and through her commitment to producing working clothes, which were at the same time artistic and beautiful, encouraged women to be their own person and do their own thing.

By 1973 there were eleven shops including Geneva, Paris and Amsterdam. In Paris in particular the company took off.

At this time Laura began to realise even the remnants from the factory were popular for patchwork and although they did not sell for much they appealed to Laura's sense of thrift.

At about this time Lynda Kee-Scott was employed as a graduate from the Royal College of Art. She confirmed the remarkable perception Laura had for designs and patterns. Lynda never found Laura's fairly stringent control suffocating but appreciated her guidance. Laura had her own ideas and rarely deviated from them even when her shop manager gave her contrary opinions. She, for instance, was adamant that her garments should be made of 100% natural fibres. Laura was not closed to advice and influence especially from the more qualified staff she now employed.

The home furnishing branch was in particular vogue in Paris; they introduced a cheaper form of fabric and paper to a French middle class market where formerly people had to have very expensive interior designers.

Laura was full of paternalism or should we say maternalism towards her staff. Like many of our other entrepreneurs she really cared and they appreciated this and were probably much more diligent as a result of it. In the mid-seventies Laura travelled extensively especially in Europe and found a plethora of interesting ideas and patterns which she faxed back to headquarters at Rhydoldog. Her ideas and hunches were inevitably right and this reinforced her faith in her own judgement. Control tended to be autocratic with her and Bernard dictating the fashions. She was always keen that staff should wear the Laura Ashley label. By 1975 the company had a turnover of £5 million pounds and employed 1,000 men and women, forty shops and three factories.

Bernard was still restless and with their shared love of France, he decided to splash out and buy a large house in France, departing from Wales. By 1978 the company had seventy shops worldwide and their existence was one of constant travelling. They moved out of Britain in the spring of 1978.

A new shop on Union Street, San Francisco was bought and converted and it was successful. Laura soon afterward had a highly successful trip to New York, where her products were sold in *Bloomingdales* and *Macys*. She was greeted with acclaim by the press who saw her as the founder of the Laura Ashley Empire and a role model for other women.

The company took the plunge and opened its own store on Madison Avenue at 69th Street. People poured in, Laura became a celebrity and almost quite enjoyed it. Her homespun philosophy went down very well in America. She was certainly not a feminist and believed profoundly that women tended towards domesticity. More shops were opened on the Eastern seaboard of America and Sarah Callander; an English rose was hired as Director of Publicity in America. Also, the fact that Lady Diana Spencer was photographed and known to buy Laura Ashley clothes helped enormously; even after the Royal Wedding she continued to shop there. One of the great promoters of Laura Ashley clothes was the British Ambassador's wife Mary Henderson. Laura Ashley almost became part of the American psyche; she was invited by the Governor to take over a small factory in Kentucky; it was rural with close links with the community, which made it similar to Wales. It also got around import tax. Shops were opening thick and fast in America and by the end of 1980 there were thirteen stores in the U.S.

In 1979 their position had been consolidated as self-made millionaires and it was the company's twenty-fifth anniversary. There were great celebrations culminating in a Ball for 700 people in the leisure centre at Deeside, Queensferry when they returned to North Wales.

Laura was always encouraging her young staff and enthused over their commitment to the firm.

Laura's philanthropy was shown in her attitude towards the Cambrian Wool Factory in Mid-Wales, which employed many disabled people. Her company heavily subsidised the many purchases she made there and provided much needed money for the enterprise. It was typical of her fondness for all things Welsh and her encouragement of these.

In her other attitudes towards her designs, she was never very interested in professional models flaunting her clothes on the catwalk. She didn't believe in sexual provocation, in fact heartily disapproved of it, an attitude deeply imbued by her Welsh valley upbringing.

By 1981 the company was launching so many new products that twice yearly catalogues appeared in five languages. The whole idea of the catalogue was not only to advertise the designs but also to promote an atmosphere of peace and tranquillity about them, which Laura believed every home should have. Soap and fragrances were added to the image of the complete Laura Ashley woman.

The re-design of the fabrics and appearance of her French chateau deepened Laura's interest in interior design, and she was continually being asked to decorate beautiful houses in Britain and America. Her designs were often taken from the pattern books of Victorian designers and architects. Laura was always having to choose between the exotic of the very rich and their country houses and Mr. Average in her choice of products and this dilemma was partially resolved by a very upmarket 'Decorator Collection' catalogue which catered for the rich. She spent much time concentrating on this and it gave her irrepressible creative energy.

Laura's designs harked back to Edwardian and Victorian times. She seemed to strike a chord with all those thousands of people who had bought Edwardian terraced and semi detached houses.

It was at this time that the company began to prepare to go public. Laura under the company description was to be deputy-chairman. She was not at all convinced that the company should go on growing. One of the qualities that kept her going even through the dark days was her spirituality.

Laura meanwhile was exhausted; all the moving around with Bernard made her resign her job as Design Director, which she handed over to her son Rich. She felt that she could no longer do the job properly.

Jane's baby was born in August and Laura set out to spend her 60th birthday with her daughter in England, a final visit to Carno took place. Laura despite her love of the high life on her sixtieth birthday had a quiet night in and she had begun to sleep badly so Bernard was not surprised to hear her wandering around that night. He woke up to hear a noise like a door slamming. Then rushed out of the bedroom only to find the corridor in darkness and his wife lying at the bottom of the stairs in a pool of blood. She was rushed to hospital, Bernard was told that there was very little hope for her as she was taken from Warwick Hospital to Walsgrove Hospital in Coventry. She survived on a life-support machine for ten days and finally died on 17th September. The cause of death was given as 'diffuse cerebral

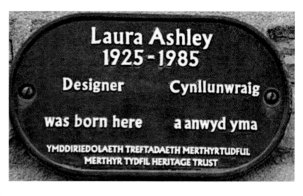

injury, trauma to the head', injuries consistent with the deceased having fallen heavily downstairs. It was shown that the nature of the staircase was such it was very easy for a person to lose their footing. The most likely cause of the fall was that Laura not wanting to disturb the rest of the household, kept the lights off and taking a wrong turning went falling down the stairs in the pitch dark she hated.

The funeral took place at Carno Parish Church; the church was packed and hundreds waited outside. Lord Hoosen gave the funeral address and pointed out her wonderful sense of the romantic and simple kindness and gentleness.

Two months after her death the firm went public.

Bibliography:
'Laura Ashley A life by Design' Anne Sebba Weidenfield and Nicholson London 1990
Many articles of the time

Chapter Sixteen
Tyrone O'Sullivan
and the workers of Tower Colliery
1945-

Tyrone O'Sullivan.

Coal, for long was the life-blood of South Wales, this is the story of its demise and partial rebirth.

Tower Colliery was situated at the head of the Cynon Valley near Aberdare. This was one of the areas where coal-mining began in earnest in South Wales, initially to provide for the needs of the iron-industry. The colliery, originally called the Goitre colliery, was re-named after a mediaeval-style tower built by the iron-master, William Crawshay after the workers' insurrection that broke out round Merthyr Tydfil and Aberdare in 1831. A depression in the iron-industry had produced a knock on effect in the coal-industry. Workers were laid off and a large crowd gathered in the centre of Merthyr, met by a detachment of 93rd Highlanders, brought from their new barracks in Brecon to restore order. In the riot that broke out twenty-four workers were killed and sixteen soldiers were injured. One of the rioters, Richard Lewis, known as Dic Penderyn was accused of injuring a soldier and was sentenced to death. He was hanged on 13th August, 1831. The insurrection led to the flying of the red flag on Hirwaun Common, near the Goitre colliery, when a white flag was dipped in calves' blood, the first use of the famous symbol of workers solidarity.

The events of 1831 showed that Welsh-workers were prepared to organise; this was in many ways, the start of worker combinations when the first stirrings of the unions began to be felt. As time progressed and coal became a much-exported commodity and the coalfields grew, so did the bargaining power of the unions. Friendly societies were formed, which supported those in need. Robert Owen is talked about elsewhere in this book and he greatly influenced the co-operative movement that spread throughout the country in the 1860s. The dividend that was paid out was most useful as a regular payment to many families. A whole culture developed on the basis of local organisations supported by the miners, many of whom had been independent craftsmen from all parts of the country before being forced to come to the valleys to look for work. In October 1898, the South Wales Miners' Federation was formed out of several smaller district unions to fight for the interests of the mine-workers. The period leading up to the First World War was full of battles over wages, and the war focused the minds of the miners when the government taking control of the mines was continually demanding that they produce more, often for the same amount of pay.

The end of the war promised good times that never materialised. Many of the old mine-owners resumed control and, in 1921, the miners were locked out by the pit-owners after the latter tried to introduce wage cuts. The miners suffered ignominious defeat and were forced to take a 50% wage cut. In the 1920s, a recession took place in the coal-industry, adding to the miners' woes. In 1925, after the mine owners threatened to cut wages, the miners supported by the T.U.C. went on strike. The General Strike went on for nine days, involving workers from many key industries. A state of Emergency was declared by the government, but the T.U.C. soon capitulated, leaving the miners to struggle on for six months before they too capitulated. During this strike, three hundred and ninety-five cases of intimidation were heard at the Courts in Swansea, and long prison sentences were the norm.

After the Second World War the mines were nationalised by the new Labour government and on 15th July 1946 the National Coal Board was set up. In the main, the miners were delighted at their new situation, believing they were working for the public good rather than for the private profit of the mine-owners. In 1947, there were approximately one hundred thousand miners working in South Wales, most of them giving support to the National Union of Miners, which had been formed in 1945 through an amalgamation of the old regional unions, including the South Wales Federation. Production was fairly steady in the 1950s, but the 1960s saw a rapid decline and as large number of pits closed in South Wales, as well as in the rest of the British Isles.

This very rapid overview of the South Wales mining industry provides some background to the life of our entrepreneur, Tyrone O'Sullivan. He was born in 1945. In his autobiography, *Tower of Strength*, he tells us of his childhood in what he remembers as a caring, and in some ways a care-free environment. His father was a mine official, but had at one time worked as a coal slasher in the pit. He was secretary of the officials. union, N.A.C.O.D.S. (the National Association of Colliery Deputies and Shotfirers). He encouraged his son to play rugby and tennis, and to sing and grow vegetables; he also loved popular opera. But one hard day, when Tyrone was attending Aberdare College as a mining apprentice, he was called out of class to be told that his father had been killed in a mining accident. Tyrone, at the age of seventeen, had to become the man of the house. His mother, whose health had not been good in the best of times, was never able to come to terms with the tragedy.

On the 14th October 1967, Tyrone married his childhood sweetheart Elaine, who was a year younger than he was. They waited for seven years before they had their first child, Taryn. Four years later they had a second daughter, Czarina.

Tyrone became branch secretary of the N.U.M. in 1969. He was proud that the Tower workers were at the forefront of all the great miners' battles that ran from an unofficial stoppage held in 1969 through the spectacular victories of 1972 and 1974 to the final defeat of 1992. The battles of 1972 and 1974 were over wages and established the miners as among the best paid workers in the British Isles. It was a point of principle on the part of the then miners' leader, Joe Gormley, to concentrate on wages and not to interfere with overall management decisions on the size of the industry. The policy in the 1960s had been to accept a high degree of wage restraint in the hope of keeping pits open. In his autobiography, *Battered Cherub*, Gormley explains why he thought this policy was wrong:

'I became quite a disciple of John L. Lewis, who was President of the American miners for forty years. His theory was that it wasn't his job to decide the size of the industry, but it was his job to fight like hell for the best wages and conditions for those who worked in it. I said at the time: 'There's a good deal of sense in what he says, because the fact is we're not able to decide the size of our industry. It's being decided by pressures from outside...' *I took the argument to the N.E.C. Bill Paynter was the Secretary, and I told him:* 'We must all be out of our sweet minds. Here we are, accepting pence or shillings for our members, simply because we're afraid of pit closures. But we're not stopping any pit closures. We've not even been able to defer many pit closures. Most of them have happened exactly as Alf Robens has planned them.'

Robens, formerly a Labour M.P., had been appointed under Harold Macmillan as chairman of the National Coal Board in 1961. At that time there 698 pits employing 583,000 workers throughout Great Britain but by the time he left in 1971 there only 291 pits employing 283,000 miners. The period had seen a huge reduction in the use of coal both industrially and domestically. By the 1970s the main remaining industrial use was the generation of electricity but even this was under challenge from oil, nuclear energy and the possibility of importing cheaper coal from other countries. The huge increase in the price of oil in 1972, however, gave the miners a considerable, if temporary, advantage.

The 1970s marked the high point of trade union power in Britain, culminating in the 1978-79 'winter of discontent', which brought down the Labour government and replaced it with the government of Margaret Thatcher. Even so, despite Thatcher's own deep commitment to the ideology of the free market economy, it was some time before the new government felt able to seriously confront union power. In 1981, while Gormley was still President, the government backed down over a proposal to close twenty-three pits. The following year, however, Gormley was replaced as President by Arthur Scargill. The great strike of 1984-85, held under his leadership, was the catalyst which saw the final breaking of trade union power in the British Isles.

The main issue was now not wages but pit closures. It began in Yorkshire in March 1984 as a spontaneous protest against the closure of five pits in Yorkshire, Durham, Kent and in Scotland. The logic of the miners' position was that no pits should be closed so long as there was coal in the ground. Purely economic considerations did not count. It was not an argument likely to appeal to other sections of the working class many of them also facing redundancy often on terms much less generous than those offered to the miners. For many of the miners, including those in South Wales, the issue was the preservation of tight knit communities but this fierce sense of community loyalty was unknown to many sections of the wider working class. Paradoxically the strike, presented as revolutionary and radical, was actually very conservative, aiming to conserve a way of life which to the radical free marketeers of the Thatcher government looked to be completely obsolete. It was a strike in favour of local, even 'parochial' interests that could only succeed by mobilising a nationwide movement. It did not receive the backing it needed either from the T.U.C. or the Labour Party or even from other individual unions. The enormous sympathy it did attract had more to do with a generalised opposition to the government, and disgust at some of the methods the government was using, than with any real understanding of, or identification with, the endangered way of life of the miners.

Tower Colliery was not itself in any immediate danger of closure. It was profitable and had substantial reserves of coal, but it was still very solidly behind the strike, with Tower miners present on picket lines throughout the country. After the failure of the strike, when Arthur Scargill was widely accused of leading the miners to disaster, Tyrone O'Sullivan was one of the main organisers of the campaign to secure his re-election as President of the Union.

Tower survived the wave of closures that followed the defeat of 1985 but after Labour's fourth consecutive defeat in the 1992 election it seemed clear there was no longer an effective Labour and Trade Union movement in the country. A major assault began on what was left of the mining industry under Michael Heseltine as Secretary of State for Trade and Industry. The miners were deeply demoralised, feeling quite unable to resist. The mood of the time is expressed powerfully in the well-known film *Brassed Off*, set in an imaginary Yorkshire mining town. By April 1994, Tower was the only deep shaft mine left in South Wales but the management wished to close it as well, possibly in the hopes of taking it over themselves and making a quick profit through exploiting its short-term potential as an open cast mine. The Tower miners led by Tyrone took their case publicly  around the country declaring the viability of Tower. Despite the threats and attempted bribes, they voted to fight on. On Thursday 14th April 1994, Ann Clwyd, the M.P. for the Cynon Valley, was smuggled down the pit. The sit-in lasted twenty-seven hours and gave the fight tremendous publicity. The management seemingly backed down but quickly came back with a proposal that involved reduced wages and an impossible production target. Despite a recommendation by the union that the fight should continue, the men had been put into an impossible position and could take no more. They voted to close the pit by 70% to 30%.

It was at this point that O'Sullivan and a small group of friends and associates had the idea which led to their unlikely inclusion in this book on Welsh entrepreneurs. If the mine was to be privatised - sold to anyone the government thought might have the competence to run it - why should the miners themselves not put in a bid? If the workforce supported it, a substantial sum could be raised out of their redundancy money and there was no lack among them of detailed knowledge of how the industry worked. The problem would lie in other skills, in particular management and marketing which they believed had been badly handled by the Coal Board and its successor, British Coal - perhaps deliberately with a view to running the pit down.

A meeting was held with 178 people present who each agreed straightaway to put £2,000 into the venture. O'Sullivan recalls that the money was mostly collected by his friend Glyn Roberts, *'put in a brown paper bag, taken home and put under his bed until he could get to a bank to open up a separate account for our wonderful new venture.'*

A team was put together under the name T.E.B.O. (Tower Employee Buyout) and they soon secured the enthusiastic support of Philip Weekes, ex-chairman of the National Coal Board, South Wales area. The project was surrounded by a great deal of good will, including, to O'Sullivan's immense surprise, from the then Secretary of State, John Redwood, known as one of Margaret Thatcher's most ideologically driven supporters. Redwood himself has said: *'I was the only person who saw nothing strange in the alliance. I had always believed in workers participation and employee ownership... I was delighted for them when they took possession of their mine, improved conditions and wages, and set about demonstrating that there were 13 years of profitable workings left...'*

As financial adviser, they employed Price Waterhouse, the firm used the 1984-85 strike to sequestrate N.U.M. funds. Price Waterhouse agreed to work without any down payment on condition that the workers would pay them

150% of whatever their final bill would be. *'After three months'*, O'Sullivan comments, *'we owed them so much money that they wanted the pit back more than me.'* A business plan was put together despite the refusal of the previous managers to have anything to do with them. They managed to secure the services of Tony Shott, an ex-surveyor from Tower, and of Cliff Jones, *'an experienced colliery manager who had been involved in many pit closures'* and *'was keen to join to try to put something back in to the industry after all the pits he had helped shut down.'* They secured a £2 million pounds loan from Barclays Bank on condition they could match it from money they had raised themselves. As a result they had to go back to the workers to ask for a further £6,000 each, bringing the total of each man's contribution to £8,000. And then there was the job of securing customers to buy the coal which they hoped to produce, knowing that their expenses in the first year would be some £8 million.

The achievement was enormous and it is generally agreed on all sides that it was a success. The Tower colliery website claims that by December 1995 (after the first year of working - the formation of the new company coincided with the final privatisation of the coal industry in December 1994) they had made pre-tax profits of over £4 million. Through their operations they improved wages, introduced a contributory pension scheme, 38 days holiday a year, a profit related pay scheme, a sick pay scheme. Profits were ploughed back into local community projects. They boasted that they were *'the only worker owned coal mine in Europe.'* In total they mined over 7 million tonnes (£300 million worth) of coal, finally closing because the pit really was exhausted.

I interviewed O'Sullivan around 2005, while the mine was still open. He stated that Tower was not run as a co-operative, but as a company with the miners as shareholders. Decisions were made on a majority vote and six directors were elected each year on a rotating basis. There were approximately three-hundred and ten shareholders and another hundred people employed as contractors. Much of the coal went to the South Wales power station at Aberthaw; some of the anthracite went to people's homes and some to public buildings. Clean coal technology probably added about another 10% to the cost of burning the coal.

He claimed that there were still two-hundred and fifty million tons of coal in South Wales. More mines could be opened and Tower planned two more in the relatively near future. There were about twenty-five years of reserves left in the coalfields, which would give time to formulate some new and efficient alternative technologies, not just nuclear. There would be a lot of turmoil in the world as we tried to solve our energy problems.

Tyrone was keen to see Wales to stand on its own feet and make a profit on its earnings. More subsidies were given to coal in Germany than in Wales, though the situation was improving. He did not object to opencast so long as it was used wisely. It seemed wrong to ask people to move from the valleys; they should be encouraged to start jobs there. The Rhondda was a particularly difficult valley to open up but the Cynon was not so bad with a good road network which was enormously helpful to Tower. Many people had started up small companies in the area but the small entrepreneurs quickly sold on their companies once they grow successful.

He was particularly keen to encourage apprenticeships in Wales, which should last for about three years. New technical colleges should be built. O'Sullivan felt that when people are made redundant, they should be given governmental seed corn money to start up enterprises. However, some people he was sure were born to be entrepreneurs. It is in their blood and no amount of formal teaching could give them this skill. But he was still a socialist, and believed in sharing wealth and that all should contribute to creating a profit. Now not so sure about Europe and the European Union, although he thought that from Tower's point of view, a single currency would be a good thing. The Assembly he approved of, as it was so much nearer to lobby. He still believed in the whole paraphernalia of Miners Institutes, Eisteddfodau and theatre that had done so much for the confidence of local youngsters and he believed the spirit of the valleys could be revitalised. A particular organization that had helped was Community First; it had started the work of rebuilding the valleys.

This sense of the future is also found in his book, published in 2001, which declares: *'We want to be here for as long as possible. There is plenty of coal; in fact there is plenty of coal in Britain. If we have extracted ten per cent of the total coal reserves in the country then that's about it... It is the word 'Future' that has to remain at the heart of this book and at the heart of Tower.'*

But after thirteen years Tower Colliery did finally close. To quote the account in the Sunday Independent, 3rd February 2008:

'And so, in the club on Friday, emotion and pride were shoulder to shoulder, just as the miners and their families had been throughout the traumatic 1984 strike, a hard-fought struggle to keep intact the pit and the community around it, the triumph of the buy-out and the 13 fulfilling years that followed - and, yes, the day of the march away after all the coal that could be mined was brought to the surface. 'We didn't leave an ounce down there,' Tyrone O'Sullivan declared.'

So, unlike the pits which closed in the 1980s and 1990s, Tower closed in glory, but it closed nonetheless. The Tower miners had prolonged deep shaft mining in Wales into the twenty-first century but in the end they could not prevent it going the way of the Welsh iron and steel industries. Nor were they able to prove that things could have been otherwise if a different policy had been pursued.

There is another, equally tragic, aspect to the story. Tower colliery proved that a pit - and, by extension other industrial enterprises - could be run successfully by a management responsible to the workforce, in this case workers who were also shareholders. The workers, after all, are the people with the most vital interest in the success of the enterprise. Yet it was only at the very last moment, the very last breath, of the coal industry in Wales, that this experiment was tried. And though O'Sullivan says *'This is the way forward and I hope the rest of Britain can learn from us'*, the example has not been followed anywhere else.

In January 1977, at the height of the power of the organised working class in Britain, the Labour government published proposals which would have enabled the workforce in all the major British industries to gain a controlling say in the management of their enterprises. These proposals, set out in the Report of the Committee of Inquiry on Industrial Democracy under the chairmanship of Lord Bullock, were rejected by almost all sections of the Labour and Trade Union movement, left and right. In particular, despite the keen advocacy of Jack Dunn, N.U.M. area secretary in Kent, they were opposed by the N.U.M. This was one point on which Gormley (the 'right wing' but stunningly successful miner's leader) and Arthur Scargill (the 'left wing' but stunningly unsuccessful miners leader) were in agreement. To quote Scargill at the time (speaking as President of the Yorkshire miners):

'It is impossible to have workers control within a capitalist society. Capitalism by its very nature, produces contradictions which cannot be resolved until and unless we change the system of society. We have to change the system, otherwise workers control cannot be obtained.

What we can have within our society is class collaboration and compromise with the mixed economy...

Participation will only perpetuate capitalism. The N.U.M. should not be misled into supporting the theory of workers control within our existing society.

It cannot work and it is against the basic constitution of our Union and the wider labour movement. Our constitution calls not for collaboration with capitalism, but for a change of society...

Those in our Union who support the concept of workers control are supporting measures which will hold back the development of the working class in its advance towards a socialist Britain.'

Scargill reaffirmed this position in 1992 when, addressing the N.U.M. National conference, he said: *'Britain's miners have attempted 'buy-outs' or co-operatives before with disastrous results... the co-operatives failed to recognize that they were operating in a hostile capitalist environment.'*

It is therefore surprising to learn from O'Sullivan's account that he was actually in Scargill's house when the news came through that Michael Heseltine had announced at the Conservative conference that the T.E.B.O. team had become the preferred bidders for the Tower Colliery, *'I told Arthur the fantastic news and he congratulated me and we shook hands...'* Not a word about class collaboration or holding back the working class in its advance towards a socialist Britain.

Tyrone O'Sullivan, one of Arthur Scargill's greatest supporters, had proved that he was wrong, but too late to save the mining industry in South Wales.

Bibliography:

Len Arthur, Tom Keenoy, Russell Smith, Peter Anthony: The employment relationship, trade unions and employee ownership: the five year experience of Tower Colliery, n.d. (c2001), available on the internet at http://www.uwic.ac.uk/ubs/research/wirc/buira.pdf.

Joe Gormley: *'Battered Cherub, The autobiography of Joe Gormley'*, London, Hamilton, 1982

Tyrone O'Sullivan, with John Eve and Anne Edworthy: *'Tower of Strength'*, Edinburgh and London, Mainstream Publishing, 2001

Report of the Committee of Inquiry on Industrial Democracy, London, HMSO, 1977

'The Miners Debate Workers Control', Ernest Bevin Society, 1984

Waddington, D. Parry, D. and Critcher, C. (1998) *'Keeping the Red Flag Flying? A comparative study of two worker takeovers in the British deep coalmining industry, 1992-1997'* in Work, Employment and Society, Vol. 12, No 2, 1998, p. 317 et seq. and Warwick Organizational Behaviour Staff (ed): Organizational Studies: Critical Perspectives on Business and Management, Routledge, 2001, p.2013 et seq

Chapter Seventeen
The New Entrepreneurs

The first person I interviewed was Sir Roger Jones, who had up until recently, been Chairman of the Welsh Development Agency, so had a bird's-eye view of the Welsh Economy. He started out at an early age organising his own log delivering business at home in Carrog, North Wales, but says he was accused of exploitation by some of the parents of his friends - he said this with very much tongue in cheek. Roger left school and went on to the Cardiff School of Pharmacy and, thereafter, to do a Post-Graduate qualification in Finance and Economics at Bradford. He was thrilled to combine the two sets of skills, and went off to work for the Welcome Foundation in the Middle East and Africa. Later he had responsibility for its development in the Communist countries, bringing off some spectacular deals in Hungary in particular. He was eventually disillusioned at the Foundation, feeling that the commercial side was losing to Research and Development. In his forties, he decided to set up his own company and, as luck would have it, he grasped the new found opportunities to speed up the R. and D. development time for new drugs for the

Sir Roger Jones.

N.H.S. in particular. His company Penn Pharmaceutical was established at High Wycombe and thence moved to Tredegar in 1986, and was subject to a successful management buyout in 1999.

In terms of the Welsh economy, which he had plenty of time to study as Chairman of the W.D.A., he feels we need to pull talented youngsters back to Wales. He says much of Welsh indigenous wealth is tied up in agriculture and some of this needs to be released. The Scots have a much firmer base of financial institutions derived from their initial independence, and have much less capital proportionally tied up in agricultural land. Roger was more optimistic about self-government before Devolution, which he feels has rather let us down and has merely rubber-stamped much of what Westminster has passed. It is now no use relying on inward investment but on indigenous and technological industry, much of which can come out of our best universities. Sustainability is a buzzword these days and it is important, but huge projects are not manageable sustainably. Tourism needs to be more upmarket, concentrating on sports like sailing, golf, fishing and shooting. Again we are not spending enough on our huge potential links with North America. There is still a lot to be done. Here we leave Sir Roger and move onto the Thomas brothers, Peter and Stan.

In 1957, the two brothers were in Cyfarthfa Grammar School in Merthyr. Peter, the youngest of the two went onto the famous public school at Shrewsbury. Their grandmother made faggots and people went to the house to buy them. A shop was then acquired, where again faggots were sold. Premises were bought at the bottom end of Plymouth Road, Merthyr in the 1950s. The bakery was behind the house and they made pies and pasties. Stan Thomas senior, the father, was the prime mover in the business at this stage and the vans were travelling ever further. Kunzle was bought into and part of the old gasworks taken over, from where pies were delivered all over the valleys. The firm was sold and they started their own firm at Bryn Glas Industrial Estate, Bedwas selling pies to local fish and chip shops under the name 'Peter's Savoury Products'. In 1976, the business moved to a new factory at Bedwas House Industrial Estate. From there, the brothers started to expand their business out of South Wales into London. Twelve years later, Peter's Savoury Products was sold to Grand Met for a reported seventy-five million pounds and from then, property has become their major asset. Stanley started T.B.I. with developer Paul Bailey in the early 1990s, and the firm became fully-listed on the Stock Exchange in 1994. Its move into airports came the year after when it bought Cardiff International, Belfast International and Orlando Sanford International. Stockholm followed quickly and Luton was bought in 2001. Stan now lives in Jersey and was named two-hundred and second in the *Sunday Times* Rich List. Peter has become very involved with the setting up of regional rugby in Wales, and is Chairman of Cardiff Blues. Both have put a lot back into Wales and are two of our most successful entrepreneurs.

Richard Griffiths comes from Llanfrynach in Breconshire, the same village where David Morgan, who started the famous store in Cardiff lived. I first met him in the village cricket side where I was very impressed by his determination, competitive edge and honesty. Richard was also a keen, successful and tough rugby player. He could not wait to leave Brecon High School at sixteen to build up the family farming business, which he did by buying and selling animals. Then he borrowed money to speculate on land. After meeting a greyhound trainer in a local pub, and hearing how his stockbroker clients were apt to bet ten-thousand pounds on a dog in one night, he realised that the way to make money was dealing in stocks and shares. He got up at the crack of dawn every day to buy the financial papers to try to teach himself about markets and stocks and shares. His father Gwyn was a tremendous influence on him. In 1973, he invested all the year's profits from the farm at the time of the secondary banking crisis. He used to find his way in to question directors on their companies' prospects. At the age of thirty-three, in the 1990s, on the eve of a global downturn, he sold his shares. He then set out to start an investment bank, having first succeeded himself in making a lot of money. The bank was called 'Evolution', because one either evolved or died. By reversing into the shell of another company, he got Evolution a listing on the Alternative Investment Market. What he wanted was the float cash and tax losses. In July 2002, Evolution expanded by acquiring Beeson Gregory, which had a stake in an intellectual property subsidiary. Ideas in research seemed to be the future. Now having left the Chairmanship of Evolution, he is out there trying to spot new companies and investments. Richard, despite not having a university education, has succeeded where many more have failed thanks to his tenacity and sharpness honed on the moors above Brecon. He has also looked after his own by buying the local pub and making it welcoming to all.

Terry Mathews was born in Newport, Gwent, on June 6th 1943. He went to school in Newbridge, collected a H.Sc. in mechanical and electrical engineering in London and a B.Sc. in electronics at Swansea University. Then he started work at sixteen in B.T.'s research labs in Dollis Hill, North London and he holidayed in Ottowa, which became a permanent stay. Terry set up Mitel in 1972, making integrated circuits and inventing private switchboards, he then set up with four-thousand dollars of borrowed money and went on to make one point five billion dollars in revenues. He sold his 51% stake in it in 1985 to B.T., then founded Newbridge Networks and fifteen years later on he sold it to the French group

Terry Matthews.

Alcatel for four point four billion pounds. In his career, he has started up around forty companies and he has lost only two, against the odds success. Terry has invested a hundred million dollars in five years, and the companies not floated are now worth over a billion dollars. He sees the potential unleashed by Broadband and digital subscriber lines, digital cable modems etc. as opportunity and sees recent development as only the tip of the iceberg. Celtic Manor, the golfing and hotel resort he has built on the site of the nursing home where he was born is his pride and joy. It has four hundred rooms, a Convention Centre and golf course, to which he has attracted the Ryder Cup.

Another entrepreneur was Dewi Parry who realised his dogs were reluctant to eat many of the proprietary brands on sale locally. He developed a formula for what is now known as Pero Original which his own dogs liked and he answered a call to create nutritious dog food for the local farmers and working dogs in his part of Wales. Pero Original was so successful that it now caters for dogs of all different types, ages and sizes totalling 13 products and also includes organic cat foods. It is distributed to independent stores and supermarkets and garden centres.

In the world of publishing, Y Lolfa was created in the mid 1960s as primarily a back up for their new active Welsh Language Society and also at the same time producing its own slightly scurrilous brand of popular and political books. In 1977 quite amusingly the company took over the old court room and police station in Aberystwyth. It published a lot of books in Welsh but also started to produce Anglo-Welsh books and has embraced the digital revolution and has four-colour and perfector presses. It supports home-grown artists and designers and its founder Robart Gruffudd has always adopted a relaxed approach and has abided by Schumachers 'Small is beautiful' principle.

Another press is Gwasg Carreg Gwalch which was established in Llanrwst, Dyffryn Conwy in 1980 by Myrddin ap Dafydd whose family owned the local bookshop. It has modern factory premises and takes its name from a rock on the western slopes of the valley where local Glyndwr followers hid. Originally a Welsh language publisher, it now also publishes in other languages publishing books that celebrate all the facets of Wales. It promotes the cultural tourism of Wales.

Another publisher who has a very high profile and although he was not born in Wales was brought up in Swansea and then went to Shrewsbury School, from there to Oxford with a short spell in the Welsh Guards for National Service was Michael Heseltine. In 1957 he bumped into a friend Clive Labovitch who had started a new guide book on Oxford for freshers. Part of it was a directory of opportunities for graduates. Michael spotted that this directory should be aimed at final year students at every university in the country. The same year a separate edition of opportunities for graduates was published with 169 pages of adverts by firms for graduates. Two companion publications were added, a directory of opportunities for school leavers and a directory of opportunities for qualified men. The company was called Cornmarket and also at the same time a property development company was started. This launched Michael Heseltine on the way to his Haymarket Publishing empire.

Michael Heseltine.

Elizabeth Daniel has set up the very successful firm Brecon Beacons Holiday Cottages. She started with a remote farmhouse which belonged to an old friend Donald Jones. No-one had any experience whatsoever of holiday cottages and letting, so Elizabeth just put an advertisement in the *Sunday Times* saying *'Remote shepherds cottage £100 per week'* and the phone started ringing. On a Saturday, still with babies in tow, Elizabeth went up to the cottage to do the changeover and to take the rubbish away. The cottage *'The Rhiwiau'* became very successful and another friend asked Elizabeth to take on another cottage in the village. Then George Melly and Jeremy Sandford, both friends, asked if Elizabeth could help do up and then let their houses when they were away. At this stage, her own little *'Mountain View'* cottage became vacant and so this was also set up as a holiday cottage. With the two quite high-profile owners the word spread quickly and she was approached by more and more people with properties they did not want to sell in the area and wanted access for themselves at certain times of the year. Typical owners were teachers who lived in for their work and came back over the holidays, a vicar, and people in the army wanting a place to retire to. Also cottages on farms waiting for a family member to move in. Some long-term tenants treated their homes badly and owners were keener to have short term holiday lets. In late 1988 Elizabeth took on her first member of staff. Juliet came to work part-time to help deal with the messages, telephone calls and letters that used to pile up and keep a check on the charts with the cottage names on, all on the back of the kitchen door. In 1987 Elizabeth had met Anthony David and eventually they looked for a house big enough for all their children. Then in 1989 they moved to Brynoyre, Elizabeth swapped her cottages and Anthony added the other half of the money by selling his cottage. This was a house she had always loved and felt she would live in one day. It was an organic small-holding where Major Sweeney had run the Tibetan Farm School in the 1980s. So Brynoyre became a rather chaotic, large, untidy family house, full of children and animals with the office in the back of the house along with the washing machine, central heating boiler and wellington boots. One day when the washing machine had flooded the office, Elizabeth realised she could no longer go on working in such conditions and so Anthony and Juliet's

Elizabeth Daniel.

husband set about clearing an old barn and stable for the business to move into. There was no running water, just a tap in the yard for filling the kettle and trips over to the house for the loo. Gradually the office was turned into something comfortable and efficiently home-grown. In 1997 to her surprise she won her first award, The Best Small Business in Wales and S.W. England for the Post Office and Parcel Force. The judging procedure was very thorough, looking through accounts, client bases and relationship with the Wales Tourist Board. This led to the company being noticed and in 1998, Liz was in the final four women for the Welsh Woman of the Year. In 2004 Brecon Beacons Holiday Cottages website was voted best website by the *Daily Telegraph* Sage Business awards. This was a very prestigious award. Putting this into perspective, Laithwaites Wines won the Best Marketing Award so Liz was in good company. By 1998 the company had grown steadily with 150 properties with owners who had come to Elizabeth by word of mouth recognition. With the profit from the business and a small grant from Powys County Council, Elizabeth developed a brand new office in the old stable block. In 2001 with about 200 properties on the books the business was completely devastated by the so badly handled foot and mouth epidemic. Elizabeth sadly had to shed experienced and trained members of staff which she found very difficult as the bookings just fell away and then had to be cancelled. Half the properties on the books were on farms and had to be closed down immediately and the other half unless they were in fairly urban environments were very reluctant to accept bookings. This really was a truly dreadful period as the company had always worked so closely with the farming community. Financially it was devastating for the company and Elizabeth was strongly advised to become a limited company as the possibility of losing the house came all too close. The company had to refund approximately £95,000 to cancelled visitors. It was a double blow to the local economy as all the moneys that would usually be spent in the local pubs, shops and tourist attractions went elsewhere. The farmers wives, many of whom were dependent on this extra money for such things as school trips, cinema trips and holidays and activities were really suffering. The business managed to survive through small grants from the Wales Tourist Board, a small grant from Powys County Council and mostly just by the fact that Elizabeths family home had just been sold and she was able to shore up the business for the next few years. In early 2009, Elizabeth feels very proud of the business and her achievement. She has 300 properties in her portfolio and an excellent and very professional award winning brochure, specialising in aerial photography, an award-winning website and a new booking system. She employs eight full and part-time members of staff all of whom live locally and have an intimate knowledge of the area and the properties. They all have a speciality bringing an expertise to the business, whether it be languages, accountancy, IT skills, people skills or design.

Simon Nixon would probably describe himself as a Welsh entrepreneur; he came from an R.A.F. family but was educated at the St. Richard Gwyn School, Flint. He left his accounting course in at Nottingham University and took up a job selling pensions and life insurance. Again he found this tedious but began to specialise in mortgages. He realised there was very little way for brokers to compare all the various mortgage deals available, and set up a magazine publishing best buy tables. Within two years it was earning him £10,000 a month. With Duncan Cameron, the brother of his then girl-friend, he formed IT company Mortgage 2000 which allowed brokers to check listings on a daily basis by computer. In 2000 he launched Moneysupermarket.com where customers could compare mortgage deals and the firm charged a commission every time a financial product was bought. In 2006 the group made pre-tax profits of £11.7 million. The Company has been floated at a difficult time and seems to have succeeded in its float. One of the problems has been buying out his co- founder but all that now seems to have been settled.

Simon Nixon.

David Emanuel was brought up in Bridgend. He excelled in music and became head choir boy at his local church, sang in the County Youth Choir, played violin in the County Youth Orchestra and taught himself to play the cello. However, he chose to study design at Cardiff School of Art and Design (1972-1975). He went on to study fashion Design at Harrow School of Art, London, where he met Elizabeth Weiner, whom he married in 1976. They studied design together at the Royal College of Art, the only married couple the College has accepted. Aged 25, David in partnership with his wife launched their own fashion house, they concentrated on couture and became favourite

David Emanuel

designers of Lady Diana Spencer and were chosen to design her wedding dress. The Emanuels have dressed some of the world's most beautiful women, Shakira Caine; Joan Collins; Catherine Zeta Jones; Madonna; Jane Seymour among others. Following his divorce from Elizabeth in 1990, David established the 'David Emanuel Couture' label offering his clients a personal service from his private suite in Knightsbridge. He is a Welsh speaker and has hosted the BBC2 programme on the National Eisteddfod of Wales.

These are all modern successful entrepreneurs and show if you are determined enough and have that sense of timing and know your business inside out, you can succeed and it is no disadvantage being a Welshman or woman or coming form the valleys. There has been a tendency in the past in Wales not to want people to stand out and succeed; but despite this many have, and are role models for our youngsters.

Sir Christopher Evans, although he has had some political difficulties, is one of Wales' current leading entrepreneurs. At one point, he was director of seventeen companies. It is now four, and he is Chairman of Merlin Biosciences. He has been a workaholic since leaving school, firstly founding Enzymatix, after discovering a previously unknown enzyme. He also set up Toad Innovations, which specialized in car security and also neuroscience, Cerebus. Sir Christopher was trying to act as chief executive of a number of companies and realised it as too much so set up one company to act as an umbrella for his life science companies. The businesses he founded have achieved combined value of one point six billion euros and employ two-thousand people.

Sir Christopher Evans.

Paul Russell and his younger brother Marcus are two more entrepreneurs. They both went to Rassau Primary School, then to Ebbw Vale Grammar before gaining degrees in Universities in London. Paul was worldwide marketing partner with Anderson Consulting and made a huge contribution to the campaign to raise Ebbw Vale Rugby Club status. He is now Chairman of Glamorgan Cricket Club and presided over the huge success of staging Wales first Test match. His brother Marcus steered Oasis to world fame in the pop world and helped him with Ebbw Vale Rugby Club.

The tale of Rachel's Dairy can be summed up by the efforts of three women and is described lucidly in Teleri Bevans book *'They Dare to Make a Difference'*. Bessie Brown came to Aberystwyth from Scotland over 100 years ago and built up her holding. Her daughter Diana took up the torch for organic farming becoming a knowledgeable and forthright ambassador for the soil association.

She was also a pedigree livestock breeder and farmer of distinction. Her daughter Rachel established a hugely successful business from local natural produce from quality Welsh organic farms.

The Institute of Welsh Affairs has just published a very useful booklet entitled *'Roaring Dragons'* which talks about successful companies in Wales. They are drawn from a variety of sectors of the economy. Some are recent; some, like North Wales builder Watkin Jones, are over a hundred years old. Some are owned by the family, others such as Wynnstay, the Powys Agricultural Supplies Group, have gone onto the London Markets. Nearly all have made it their business to trade beyond Wales' borders. They have made sure that structures for growth are in place and that they invest in people and in plant. There has been some public sector help for some of these companies but in many cases this has not been significant. Its construction can be seen in new sports stadia, bridges and office blocks on the banks of the Thames. It is also helping to bring water to some of the poorest and driest regions on the planet. Biotrace from Bridgend is the manufacturer of products to test for contamination and to clarify the cleanliness of products for manufacturers around the world.

Ifor Williams Trailers from Corwen reaches a wide range of users all over the world and is determined to stay ahead of the game through clever design. Leekes of Pontyclun has remained and cashed in on out-of-town locations as a retailer, and has added golf, hotel and other leisure activities to its business. Stephen and George, Printers from Merthyr Tydfil has survived for a hundred years by heavily investing in plant and training. Wynnstay from Llansantffraid-ym-Mechain is a quoted company that has been a major force in bringing together the agricultural supplies sector acquiring companies in Wales and England. It also has a position in retailing through its own chain of outlets in the countryside. Watkin Jones from Bangor is one of Wales' oldest construction companies. It has shed some less profitable activities and is winning big orders from outside Wales, including big names in retailing and leisure. Opco from Cardiff, another construction company has become a force for regeneration especially in South Wales. It has become involved in many projects including an outdoor display centre at Cardiff Castle. Thomas Carroll is Wales' biggest independent commercial insurance company, it has been pioneering in its adoption of new technology and techniques. It applies a local personal service while expanding nationally at the same time. Maelor Pharmaceutical Company from Ruabon is now focusing on certain product areas where it has key technologies and pushing these on world markets. Patchwork, the traditional Food Company from Llangollen has established itself worldwide as a supplier of quality products such as pate to restaurants and retail outlets and has become a very successful Welsh company. Much more can be found about these companies in the Institute of Welsh Affairs booklet, *'Roaring Dragons'* and these are just some of Wales' successes.

Admiral Insurance have generated a huge amount of money and Cardiff has benefited from them enormously. In North Wales a company called Windpower Wales has been set up which is firmly grounded in the communities of North Wales to help meet the challenge of global warming. Also, Brecon Beacons Natural Waters which was started as a cottage industry based in Tally in Carmarthenshire and has become Brecon Carreg becoming the leading Welsh bottled water brand. Many of these companies are finding the current down turn a struggle but we hope their strength and depth will keep them and the Welsh economy going. Many Welsh entrepreneurs don't want to progress into huge enterprises that they lose control of and they're not that motivated by ever increasing profits and revenues for themselves. They love the places they work in and are keen for their work force to have a good quality of life. Rural Wales in particular can be a great place to work and for a company to settle in.

Bibliography
'Roaring Dragons' by the Institute of Welsh Affairs
Various interviews and websites